THE HERMENEUTICS OF
POSTMODERNITY

Studies in Phenomenology and Existential Philosophy

GENERAL EDITOR
JAMES M. EDIE

THE HERMENEUTICS OF POSTMODERNITY

Figures and Themes

G. B. MADISON

INDIANA UNIVERSITY PRESS
Bloomington and Indianapolis

First Midland Book Edition 1990

© 1988 by G. B. Madison

All rights reserved

Manufactured in the United States of America

Library of Congress Cataloging-in-Publication Data

Madison, Gary Brent.
The hermeneutics of postmodernity.

(Studies in phenomenology and existential
philosophy).
Bibliography: p.
Includes index.
1. Hermeneutics.   2. Phenomenology.   I. Title.
II. Series.
BD241.M25 1988   121'.68   87-46089
ISBN 0-253-32190-5
ISBN 0-253-20617-0 (pbk.)

3 4 5 6 94 93 92

*To Paul Ricoeur and Hans-Georg Gadamer,
from whom I learned what is vital,
and to my graduate students over the
years, from whom I have continued to
learn what counts.*

Contents

Prologue: Toward a
Poststructuralist Phenomenology

Here, at the beginning, I will not, as is so often done nowadays, in this uncertain time, dwell on the problems of beginning, of prefacing a book. I would like simply, in the few pages of this prologue, to speak in my own name, that of the "I" who is the author of a prologue which seeks to set the stage for what is to come after, to the present reader of this book (at whatever time in the future he or she might be reading what I am writing "now"). It seems to me that every author has the right, at least from time to time, to address the reader directly, without having to sort out all the layered levels of imbricated authors (or narrators) and implied readers. If an author cannot speak directly to the reader in a prologue (when the author is writing it), where else could an author do so, and when? Where, if not in a prologue, outside of the book proper, can an author say what he or she means and say what he or she is going to do? So I shall tell you here, Dear Reader (to speak like Montaigne), directly, something about what is to follow and will reveal to you (in a somewhat indirect fashion) some of the circumstances presiding over the origin of this (these) text(s).

What you, Dear Reader, are about to embark upon is a smorgasbord of ideas. Not just any old smorgasbord, however. Most certainly not one of those which advertise themselves to the unwary customer as offering 250 different specialties "from around the world." No, the smorgasbord offered up here for your delectation is a coherent and consistent one, including only a few select items, like an all-Chinese or all-Swedish one. All the dishes have been prepared in the same mental kitchen, with the same, or complementary, spices and seasonings, and prepared with the same, or complementary, cooking techniques. However, just as some people are not attracted to spicy foods, so some people won't care for what is served up to them here. If, though, you believe that it is high time that philosophy abandoned the stock, fatty concoctions it has traditionally served up in its metaphysical soup kitchens (as William James referred to them), then you should definitely appreciate what is here offered for your *dégustation*.

This book, I say, is like a smorgasbord—in that it is not like a formal, six-course dinner; there is no special order in which the dishes need be consumed. The essays may be read in whatever order the reader pleases, according to his or her reading pleasure, for this is not a book in the traditional metaphysical sense of the term: It is not a systematic monograph embodying an imperious logic to which the reader must submit. Being without a fixed beginning, middle, and end, this book is not only about postmodernism, it is also postmodern; it is devoid of metaphysical closure.

This is not to say that it is devoid of meaning, or that its meaning is undecidable. Unlike a lot of postmodernist narratives, it most definitely does have a story to tell—and there is a plot to it. This, though, is a plot without a dénouement, since the story does not have an end, being, as it is, the story of our times, whose outcome or *sens* (meaning/direction) is as yet undecided. The story is one which is increasingly encountered in a number of different versions, depending on who it is who is doing the telling. It is the story of postmodernism, which is to say, of the end of modernism—even more, of the end of metaphysics (the "metaphysics of presence"), the end (according to some) of philosophy itself.

I owe it to the reader to say what I mean by postmodernism/the-end-of-modernism. Although in essay 4, "Merleau-Ponty and Postmodernity," I make a distinction between "postmodern" and "postmodernist" (or "postmodernistic") thinkers, and although the distinction is an important one in the context of that particular story, it can no doubt be glossed over here.[1] Just what is postmodernism? There seems to be no canonical answer to this question. As one writer pertinently observes: "Every student of modern culture is evidently required to state a position on modernism and postmodernism, even though it is not clear what these words denote. They mean, it appears, whatever we want them to mean."[2]

While "modernism" does indeed mean different things to different people, to architects and to literary theorists, for instance, its meaning for philosophers can be pinned down fairly neatly. "Modernism" denotes what the traditional term "modern philosophy" denotes: that movement of thought which originates with Descartes and which has perpetuated itself up to and into the twentieth century. The term has definite connotations as well. It connotes all the concerns which were constitutive of modern philosophy. These concerns were, basically, of a dual nature; epistemological and foundationalist. What above all characterizes that form of the logocentric metaphysics of presence known as modern philosophy is that it seeks to realize philosophy's traditional goal of achieving a basic, fundamental knowledge (*epistemē*, *Wissenschaft*) of what is (*ta onta*) by turning inward, into the knowing subject himself (conceived of either psychologistically or transcendentally), where it seeks to discover grounds which will allow for certainty in our "knowledge" of what, henceforth, is called "the external world." As I say below in essay 11, the methodological conviction of the modern philosopher is that he may come to know truly that reality which is only indirectly present (re-presented) to him by the senses if only he can order his own "ideas" (*cogitationes*) in accordance with the unquestionable laws of logic (*vide*, for instance, Leibniz's *ars combinatoria*). If only he can string his ideas together in the right way, the result supposedly will be that they will form a true "representation" or likeness of "objective" reality. *Representationalism* has been the name of the game from Descartes up to our twentieth-century positivists and analysts. As Heidegger observed in his essay "The Age of the World Picture," the two ontological characteristics of modernity are the world's becoming a *picture* or representation and, simultaneously, man's becoming a representing *subject* in the midst of mere objects. Or, in Merleau-Ponty's phraseology, man becomes a *kosmotheoros*, a pure Spectator, at the same time that the world becomes *le Grand Objet*.

The two great theoretical by-products of modern, epistemologically centered philosophy which places all the emphasis on method (as opposed to insight [*noesis*], as in the case of the ancient metaphysics of presence), are the notions of subjectivity and a fully objective, determinate world—the essential business of the "knowing subject" ("man") being that of forming true "representations" of so-called objective reality. The end of modernism means, accordingly, the end of epistemologically centered philosophy (as Richard Rorty has remarked). It means the end of what modernism understood by "the subject," and it means as well the end of the "objective world" (a world which is fully what it is in itself and which simply waits around for a cognizing subject to come along and form a "mental representation" of it).

What are we left with after the demise of the epistemological subject and the objective world—after the demise of the very ideas of "knowledge" and "truth" (the "true representation of objective reality")? The attempt to spell out the consequences of the end of modernism, of metaphysics in general (modernism being the "metaphysics of representation")—Nietzsche's "death of God"—is what postmodernism is all about.

On this subject, a number of stories could be told, and in fact are told. The distinctive mark of the story that I shall be telling—not in the form of one grand, interconnected narrative, to be sure, but in many different, partial, overlapping versions—is that it is not the same as all the others. It is different, above all, from the kind of story that would likely be told by poststructuralists of various assorted stripes and colors. For these, postmodernism would have its origins in the various backlashes against phenomenology (the quintessence, according to them, of the metaphysics of presence or of "humanism") that started to make their appearance after the death of Merleau-Ponty. In their rush to bury their philosophical progenitor and to liquidate his intellectual estate, these writers turned a conscientiously blind eye to the decisive contribution that Merleau-Ponty had made toward dissolving the epistemological-metaphysical project. What is important for us to keep in mind, with our conscientiously clearer hindsight, is that Merleau-Ponty himself was simply radicalizing a beginning that had already been made.

Whereas in the English-speaking world the beginning of the end of modernism has only begun to be made with the emergence of what is now known as "postanalytic philosophy," the beginning of the end of modernism began much earlier on the Continent. One thinks naturally of Nietzsche's devastatingly deconstructive critique of the entire metaphysical-Platonic tradition ("Philosophy," in Rorty's sense of the term). Nietzsche is indeed the great "prophet of extremity,"[3] but, as is generally the case with prophets, his message at the time fell on ears which were mainly deaf. Were one seeking to elaborate a grand narrative, Nietzsche's place in this *récit* would have to be dictated not by chronology but by his effective history (as Gadamer would say), the history of his influence. Nietzsche makes his effective entry into the history of postmodernism only with Heidegger's problematic reading of him and with the cult erected in his honor by the French post–Merleau-Pontyian Nietzscheans.

The real beginning of postmodernism in the (academic) philosophical world must be looked for elsewhere. James's Pragmatism was a genuine beginning. But it was a beginning without a follow-up and without an effective history (James's radical critique of epistemological philosophy having been thoroughly ignored by the metaphysical positivism and analyticism which later occupied central stage in America). The beginning, both genuine and real, of postmodern philosophy occurs with the promotion of phenomenology by Edmund Husserl. (The year 1900 witnessed both the death of Nietzsche and the birth of phenomenology in the form of Husserl's *Logical Investigations*.) Any detailed history of postmodern thought would have to begin here, with a detailed sorting out of what is new and what is old in Husserl's creative reappropriation of the Tradition. A key text to reexamine in this regard would be *The Idea of Phenomenology*. In attempting in this work to overcome decisively what Alexandre Lowit, in his remarkable preface to the French translation of the text, calls "la situation phénoménale du clivage"—in other words, the subject-object split which is at the origin of modern philosophy—Husserl effectively deconstructed both the "epistemological subject" and the "objective world."

Like many a pivotal thinker, Husserl is an ambiguous figure, and thus the beginning he inaugurated is ambiguous also—as is only fitting, since in human affairs there is never any such thing as an absolute beginning anyway. Husserl's express, intended goal was metaphysical through and through: His lifelong ambition was to bring to fulfillment the innermost yearnings of the Platonic-metaphysical traditon by finally putting, by means of phenomenology, philosophy into a position to become what it had always sought to be: a *strenge Wissenschaft*. The irony (for us who come afterward and thus find ourselves in a position to understand) is that in seeking to realize the inner teleology of metaphysics Husserl at the same time realized its *telos*, brought it to its end. From one point of view, it makes perfectly good sense to say, as Derrida in fact does, that " . . . in criticizing classical metaphysics, phenomenology accomplishes the most profound project of metaphysics."[4] However, it would make even better sense, hermeneutically speaking, to say, instead, that in seeking to accomplish the most profound project of classical metaphysics, Husserl's phenomenology actually results in its most devastating critique.

Viewed in this way, the beginning of philosophical postmodernism coincides with the end of modernism and is inseparable from it, as inseparable as Saussure's *signifiant* and *signifié*. This is something that one of Husserl's own assistants and philosophical heirs, Ludwig Landgrebe, saw quite clearly and said in 1962. With unrivaled hermeneutical perspicuity, Landgrebe wrote (I quote *in extenso*):

. . . the history of the origin of the text before us [Husserl's *Ideas*] is the history of a shipwreck. If it was simply a question of the shipwreck of a new attempt to introduce phenomenology, however, one must view the undertaking of publishing such a text as highly questionable. But this shipwreck—and this could be clear to neither Husserl himself nor to those who heard the lectures at that time—is more than an author's accidental misfortune. It is not the sign of a failing systematic creativity; it is rather the case that in no other of his writings is Husserl's radicalism concerning the continually new "presuppositionless" beginning and the questioning of all that had so far been achieved so visibly confirmed. In no other work has Husserl exposed himself to the "force of the absolute" (Hegel) to such an extent, so that this basic feature of his thought is manifested here to a unique degree, a thought which does not aim at a will to mastery through system, but one which advances toward the "affair" (*Sache*) with restless abandon. A retrospective glance from the historical distance we have now achieved permits us to understand that there occurs within this text a departure from those traditions which are determinative for modern thought and a breaking into a new basis for reflection. It is a reluctant departure insofar as Husserl had wished to complete and fulfill this tradition without knowing to what extent his attempt served to break up this tradition. It is therefore a moving document of an unprecedented struggle to express a content with the terminology of the tradition of modern thought that already forsakes this tradition and its alternatives and perspectives.

The risk of publishing this problematic text is thereby splendidly justified. Not only because it is the key for understanding the development of Husserl's phenomenology; for the problems that emerge here first make it possible to situate correctly Husserl's later work within the course of this development and to relate it properly to his earlier work, so that within this context it is comprehensible why in the later *Crisis* Husserl found himself forced to strike out on a new path (whose novelty is once again partially obscured by the self-interpretation he gave it); but because, in addition to its significance for the interpretation of phenomenology itself, here, before the eyes of the reader, occurs the shipwreck of transcendental subjectivism, as both a nonhistorical *apriorism* and as the consummation of modern rationalism. Today, primarily as a result of Heidegger's work, the "end of metaphysics" is spoken of as with a certain obviousness. We shall first properly understand the sense of such language if we follow closely how, in this work, metaphysics takes its departure behind Husserl's back. One can state quite frankly that this work *is* the end of metaphysics in the sense that after it any further advance along the concepts and paths of thought from which metaphysics seeks forcefully to extract the most extreme possibilities is no longer possible. To be sure, neither Husserl nor those who were his students at that time were explicitly aware of this, and it will still require a long and intensive struggle of interpretation and continuing thoughtful deliberation until we have experienced everything that here comes to an end. From this, new light will also be cast upon Heidegger's relation to phenomenology. Heidegger knew the thoughts affecting Husserl at this time from his first stay at Freiburg and from his many conversations with Husserl, and had therefore also experienced the shipwreck of this attempt through his own observations and had drawn the proper consequences in attempting, from that point on, to take leave of the language of metaphysics which Husserl himself still employed.[5]

A number of the essays included in this volume consider, accordingly, Husserl's contributions to the development of a postmodern, postmetaphysical hermeneutical philosophy. If I differ with certain poststructuralists—and, above all, with their epigones—on where to locate the beginning of philosophical postmodernism, I differ with them also, necessarily, on the *meaning* of subsequent developments and on the *direction* in which these developments point—or, should I say, on the direction in which they should point us. There can be no doubt that many of the deconstructions of modernism— "objectivism," in Richard Bernstein's sense[6]—point only in the direction of relativism and, even more, of nihilism, the kind of nihilism which Nietzsche prophesied and which he and his philosophical heirs have sought—vainly—to conjure away by means of a joyful affirmation of the pointlessness of our effective history. This is a direction that I find neither desirable nor inevitable. Thus, as I said above, the multivalent story I wish to tell in this book has a definite plot to it. There is, as I also said, no dénouement, since the full story remains to be told and will be told only when, through our continued rereading of the texts of our tradition, we will have made the history of postmodernity become what it then will be.

The story I shall be telling has for its express purpose to point us—in our collective endeavors to overcome definitively modernism and the logocentric metaphysics of presence—in a certain direction. If I locate the beginning of philosophical postmodernism in Husserl, it is because it seems to me that the enterprise that he instituted—phenomenology—points us in the right direction, beyond both objectivism and relativism. The history of the phenomenological movement is the history of the progressive attempt to eradicate the traces still present within it of the very resilient metaphysics of presence, to exorcise the metaphysical ghosts that continue to haunt our discourse, the house of being, as Heidegger called it. "Existential phenomenology" was the name, at one point, for this endeavor; "phenomenological hermeneutics" is the current one. Merleau-Ponty's radicalization of the phenomenological critique of the Tradition was one of the most significant of them all. We have yet to appreciate fully all that here genuinely begins (and ends)—a task not made easier by the obstinate silence that most of the post–Merleau-Pontyians in France have maintained in his regard. But the (often only insinuated) criticisms that these writers have made of what they consider to be "phenomenology" are of great hermeneutical worth. Deconstruction in particular has—to a large extent with unacknowledged borrowing from Merleau-Ponty himself—exposed in a ruthless fashion the unacknowledged metaphysical inheritances off of which we still to some extent tend to live. What remains in the history still to be told—and, in the telling, to be made—is the story of *poststructuralist phenomenology*,[7] a phenomenology which will have made profitable use of the many pertinent criticisms that poststructuralism has addressed not only to the Tradition but also to phenomenology itself. This is the conclusion the essays gathered together in this book collectively aim at—but which, it goes without saying, is still outstanding. If the author does not get around actually to writing it, he hopes that his readers will.

One afternoon, back in the early 1970s when poststructuralism itself was only beginning, after a lengthy conversation in the rue Michelange, Emmanuel Lévinas presented a copy of one of his books to me and inscribed it thus: "Pour Monsieur Madison, / qui fait sans doute la philosophie d'après-demain / En vive sympathie / E. L." If not me, then, I sympathetically hope, you, Dear Reader. One simply can no longer do philosophy as it was done yesterday, nor can we be satisfied with what is going on today, which resembles a kind of Rimbaudian *dérèglement systématique de tous les sens* (where *sens* would be best [freely] translated as "meanings" rather than as "senses"). Nor can we be satisfied with what tomorrow will bring, since it will likely be more of the same, pushed to its absurd limits—a problematic time for philosophy which will not know how, or even if, it differs in any significant way from "literature," i.e., as Roland Barthes would have it, a language which says nothing other than itself, which is dense and opaque, which expresses neither "facts" nor "thoughts" nor "truth." No, we must look forward to the day after tomorrow when we may finally attain to a poststructuralist phenomenology and we will have witnessed, after the end of metaphysics, the end of "the end of philosophy."

The essays to follow are all original texts. By that I do not mean that what they say is completely *inédit*, that they say something never before said. A genuine "original thought" is, as we now know, a metaphysical fiction. A whole host of other texts speak in these texts, and there is little, if anything, that they say which has not already been said in one form or another, to one degree or another. But this cannot be grounds for criticism.

Long before people had become conscientiously aware of the diacritical nature of meaning and the *bricolage* nature of writing, of the fact that, as Italo Calvino puts it, "writing is purely and simply a process of combination among given elements,"[8] Pascal remarked: "Different arrangements of words make different meanings, and different arrangements of meanings produce different effects."[9] Accordingly, when his critics accused him of a lack of originality he replied:

> Let no one say that I have said nothing new; the arrangement of the material is new. In playing tennis both players use the same ball, but one plays it better.
>   I would just as soon be told that I have used old words. As if the same thoughts did not form a different argument by being differently arranged, just as the same words make different thoughts when arranged differently![10]

These essays are original, not in that they say something completely new,[11] but in that the arrangement of their material is new; they were all specific responses to the original contexts which called them forth in the first place. They are not simply set pieces, but were deliberately addressed to their specific audiences, listeners or readers, as the case may be. No attempt has been made here to obscure this fact, to make what was, for instance, meant to be a spoken text into a merely written text. As a member of the rhetorical countertradition who believes in the difference between the two genres, who believes that one shouldn't present *written* texts to audiences which can only *hear* (one can, of course, always afterward read a paper which was read), I have, while retouching some of the pieces somewhat for their appearance in this volume, made no attempt to make them out to be anything other than what they were when they first saw the light of day.

These pieces are therefore context-specific, as the reader will readily notice. In editing this volume I have deliberately avoided the metaphysical conceit of affecting an atemporal mode of discourse, pretending to a temporally and culturally invariant truth- and relevancy-status for what I have to say. Any such pretension is incompatible with the historicity of human understanding that postmodernism has so much emphasized. And yet, it would be my hope that there is something in these pieces that transcends their immediate context and that they will have something to say to all those who, wherever and whoever they be, are struggling to think the death of metaphysics and what this means for the furture of philosophy.

I will not comment here on the various essays, but I should say a word about the first of them, "A Critique of Hirsch's *Validity*." The oldest of the lot by far, dating from the early 1970s, it was written before Gadamer's *Truth and Method* made its appearance in English and began to exercise fully its effectivity on philosophy in North America. It was composed before there was any talk (reaching me, at least) of philosophical postmodernism. The interest it can have for readers today stems precisely from that fact. This essay quite nicely sets the stage for the ones which follow it. Written in reply to E. D. Hirsch's critique of Gadamerian hermeneutics, this critique of Hirsch's own modernist, objectivistic hermeneutics points, by means of this critique, to the need to work out a decisive alternative to the traditional epistemological paradigm, to articulate alternatives to the traditional metaphysical conceptions of truth and reality. The essays which follow it attempt, in small steps, to do just that.

The philosophical interest of this essay lies, therefore, in the fact that it is not simply a reply to one particular individual but is—through this—a reply to modernistic thinking in general; Hirsch is, indeed, a superb, made-to-measure exemplification of modern objectivism. This critique of modernism in the person of Hirsch serves, as it should, to situate properly phenomenological hermeneutics in the overall spectrum of human understanding; as a thoroughgoing critique of objectivism, phenomenological hermeneutics is fully a form of postmodern thinking. As subsequent essays will show, however, phenomenological hermeneutics differs from other forms of postmodernism in that it does not seek merely to deconstruct the traditional, metaphysical notions of "knowledge" and "truth"; it seeks to provide *alternatives* to them.

With the publication of these texts in book form, they are set free to drift where they will and to enter into other, newer contexts. Their proper addressee is, as Ricoeur would say, anyone who knows how to read. Or as Calvino says: " . . . the spirit in which one reads is decisive: it is up to the reader to see to it that literature exerts its critical force, and this can occur independently of the author's intentions."[12]

Notes

1. I argue there that while Merleau-Ponty is a postmodern philosopher, he is not (like various poststructuralists) a "postmodernist." A subtle distinction, to be sure, but a most important one, as the context makes clear. Much the same argumentative tactic

is followed, this time in regard to Gadamer, in essay 7, "Beyond Seriousness and Frivolity."

2. Denis Donoghue, "The Promiscuous Cool of Postmodernism," *New York Times Book Review*, June 22, 1986, p. 1.

3. To use the favored expression of Allan Megill, who greatly deplores all the various postmodern developments, disparagingly grouping them under the heading "aestheticism." See his *Prophets of Extremity* (Berkeley: University of California Press, 1985).

4. Jacques Derrida, *Writing and Difference*, trans. A. Bass (Chicago: University of Chicago Press, 1978), p. 166.

5. Ludwig Landgrebe, "Husserl's Departure from Cartesianism," in *The Phenomenology of Husserl*, ed. R. O. Elveton (Chicago: Quadrangle Books, 1970), pp. 260–61. For a discussion of the relation between Husserl's phenomenology and the "existentialism" of his successors, see my study, "Phenomenology and Existentialism: Husserl and the End of Idealism" in *Husserl: Expositions and Appraisals*, ed. F. Elliston and P. McCormick (Notre Dame, Ind.: University of Notre Dame Press, 1977).

6. See Richard Bernstein, *Beyond Objectivism and Relativism* (Philadelphia: University of Pennsylvania Press, 1983).

7. I owe this expression to David Wood of the University of Warwick in England, who used it once in the course of a conversation at McMaster and who gave me permission to use it myself. In accordance with my conviction that all texts (contexts) are inter(con)textual, I do so freely.

8. I. Calvino, *The Uses of Literature*, trans. P. Creagh (San Diego: Harcourt Brace Jovanovich, 1986), p. 17.

9. Pascal, *Pensées*, trans. A. J. Krailsheimer (Harmondsworth, Eng.: Penguin Books, 1966), 784 (Lafuma), 23 (Brunschvicg).

10. Ibid., 696 (Lafuma), 22 (Brunschvicg).

11. In many cases, what the author says, he believed was "new" at the time (not knowing any better); much to his chagrin, he found afterward that what he had said had already been said (or almost) in publications that he had never taken the time to read. This only serves to confirm him in his belief in something like a *Zeitgeist*, or a *logique des choses*—which Merleau-Ponty, for one, was always fascinated with and sought to understand.

12. *The Uses of Literature*, p. 26.

THE HERMENEUTICS OF
POSTMODERNITY

Part One

Figures

ONE

A Critique of Hirsch's *Validity*

The subject of hermeneutics, or interpretation, has in recent years come to command increasing attention in North American philosophical circles. The subject is not, of course, a new one in philosophy; a sizable literature on the topic already exists, although many of the key works still remain to be translated. We will no doubt soon possess an English translation of one of the more important of these: H.-G. Gadamer's *Wahrheit und Methode*.[1] In the meantime, the most notable publication in English remains E. D. Hirsch's *Validity in Interpretation*.[2] Hirsch's brand of hermeneutics, taking its inspiration from the work of Emile Betti,[3] represents, however, but one side of the hermeneutical debate, one which is outrightly antagonistic to another main current, that represented by Gadamer, who situates himself in the line of Heidegger. Hirsch's book can itself be viewed as an attack on Gadamer's position.[4] It puts forward and attempts to defend a thoroughgoing realism in matters of interpretation. Hirsch denounces the absence of a realist doctrine in Gadamer or in what for the sake of convenience I shall simply call the phenomenological current in hermeneutics. Hirsch accuses the latter of giving rise to skepticism, relativism, subjectivism, and historicism.

Such an accusation is in my opinion totally unfounded. Moreover, I believe that Hirsch's own realist position calls for a critical appraisal. The critical observations that I shall accordingly attempt to set out in this essay center on Hirsch's key notion of validity and, more basically, on what this notion implies, the further notions of absolute or objective meaning and truth. Since I cannot hope to do justice here to the many issues Hirsch raises, I shall concentrate on a few questions which are basic to a general theory of interpretation. I believe, and hope to show, that the notion of "meaning" in Hirsch has, in the last analysis, little or no meaning.

1

The goal Hirsch sets himself is that of establishing the bases of a *science* of interpretation. This is why, as he points out, he has (in a Popperian fashion) nothing to say about the art of making guesses as to a text's meaning, since this is necessarily an intuitive, imaginative, subjective, and unmethodological process for which no precise rules can be devised. It is not the divinatory but rather the successive, critical moment of interpretation, wherein one arbitrates between various possible interpretations in an attempt to arrive at the most *valid* one, that a science, as opposed to a mere art, can be established.

Now it is precisely this focus of Hirsch's analysis on the notion of validation which makes for the strength of some of his arguments but which, at the same time, accounts for the many weaknesses to be found in his book. For the fact of the matter is that at no point does Hirsch ever ask if interpretation can or could be a science; he merely argues that *if* interpretation is to be a science, *then* it must be of such and such a sort. This is obviously an unpardonable *petitio principii* for a work which claims to deal with "general hermeneutical theory" and to determine its "general principles" (p. viii). Because Hirsch gratuitously assumes at the outset that hermeneutics can be a science, his analyses lack the necessary critical grounding. This also accounts for the principal difference between Hirsch and his archrival, Gadamer, for, whatever the deficiencies of Gadamer, it is at least the case that, unlike Hirsch, he has attempted a *fundamental* analysis of what is necessarily involved in all acts of understanding and interpretation. It is this fundamental type of analysis that is totally lacking in the rigorous yet superficial analyses of Hirsch. Although Hirsch proposes to defend the objectivity of meaning, at no time does he attempt to clarify in what sense knowledge can properly lay claim to objectivity and what the very meaning of objectivity is. The possibility of interpretation's being a science is not, however, the only presupposition in Hirsch; the very notion of what science or scientific knowledge is is naively presupposed.

Hirsch wants to make of interpretation a science and a respectable business. "What is at stake is," he says, " . . . the right of interpretation (and implicitly all humanistic disciplines) to claim as its object genuine knowledge" (p. 205). To seek after genuine knowledge is a most laudable endeavor. Unfortunately, however, Hirsch uncritically takes over the doctrinaire positivistic position which dogmatically equates genuine knowledge with scientific knowledge, in the physicalistic sense. It is not surprising, therefore, that when it comes to the long-standing question of the relation between the humanities and the natural sciences (*Geisteswissenschaften* and *Naturwissenschaften*), Hirsch takes the direct, but simplistic, approach of denying that there is or should be any significant difference between the two at all. He writes: " . . . the much-advertised cleavage between thinking in the sciences and the humanities does not exist. The hypothetico-deductive process is fundamental in both of them, as it is in all thinking that aspires to knowledge" (p. 264).

This identification of all rigorous knowledge with scientific knowledge—the identification of rigor with exactitude—leads Hirsch to conceive of the work of the textual interpreter after the model of the laboratory researcher in experimental science. He thinks of "literary study as a corporate enterprise and a progressive discipline" (p. 209). The logic of interpretation is none other than the classical logic of physical science, that of first of all marshaling all the evidence and then constructing hypotheses and claims which will explain the phenomena. What Hirsch calls for in interpretation is nothing other than the experimental method:

> Conflicting interpretations can be subjected to scrutiny in the light of the relevant evidence, and objective conclusions can be reached. . . . Devising subsidiary interpretive hypotheses capable of sponsoring probability decisions is not in principle different from devising experiments that can sponsor decisions between hypotheses in the natural sciences. (P. 206)

"In principle," therefore, as Hirsch says, hermeneutics is no different from any other branch of genuine knowledge, i.e., any other science. Like all the other sciences, it does no more than draw "probability judgments": "An interpretive hypothesis is ultimately a probability judgment that is supported by evidence" (p. 180). There is obviously much to criticize here, even if criticism be thought of only in the narrow sense as the pointing out of unanalyzed presuppositions. There are, however, further complications stemming from this identification of interpretation with natural science that should be noted.

Indeed, when one has assigned oneself the goal of setting up a new science, one must also look about for two additional things: a specific *object* and a particular *method*. A science is not a science, obviously, unless it is a science of *something*. Hirsch thus needs an object for his science of interpretation, and he accordingly devises one which will suit his needs. Like the scientist of former times who thought that he was looking for Laws present in Nature itself, waiting only to be reproduced in scientific, human language, Hirsch, *qua* scientific interpreter, seeks to discover and lay bare an equally "objective" entity existing independently of the inquirer. Hirsch calls this entity "the author's meaning." "The root problem of interpretation," he says, "is always the same—to guess what the author meant" (p. 207). And as Hirsch goes on to describe it, "the author's meaning" assumes all the characteristics of a self-subsistent, transphenomenal existence, not unlike a Platonic Form or a Scientific Law (as these were formerly understood). In order to defend the objectivity of interpretive knowledge, Hirsch insists on the strictly objective character of the author's meaning, i.e., on its complete independence from the consciousness of the interpreter: "If a theorist wants to save the ideal of validity he has to save the author as well . . . " (p. 6). Because Hirsch implicitly and uncritically takes objective knowledge to be a form of knowledge that *corresponds* to and *reflects* a fixed, independent entity, he claims that the author's meaning leads this kind of objective existence and can, accordingly, serve as a stable point of reference by which to assess the rightness or validity of interpretations.

> If his [the interpreter's] claim to validity is to hold, he must be willing to measure his interpretation against a genuinely discriminating norm, and the only compelling normative principle that has ever been brought forward is the old-fashioned ideal of rightly understanding what the author meant. (P. 26)

"What an author meant" becomes for Hirsch an *absolute object*, a super-historical essence, a determinate, selfsame object accessible to anyone and everyone alike provided only that they approach it scientifically. Such an object is properly noumenal; it is timeless, unchanging, determinate, stable, self-identical, and so on, and so on. Witness the following statements:

> When, therefore, I say that a verbal meaning is determinate I mean that it is an entity which is self-identical. Furthermore, I also mean that it is an entity which always remains the same from one moment to the next—that it is changeless. (P. 46)

> Validity requires a norm—a meaning that is stable and determinate. . . . (P. 126)

> . . . the author's meaning, as represented by his text, is unchanging and reproducible. (P. 216)

The list of such statements could be extended considerably, but the ones quoted suffice to reveal some interesting points. They show, for instance, that Hirsch is arbitrarily constructing his object—the author's meaning—to conform to a prior idea as to what validity is: the faithful reproduction or representation of a thing-in-itself. In other words, since validity is conceived of as deriving from the coincidence of an interpretive hypothesis with a definite, unvarying object, then the object of interpretation, textual meaning, must possess the characteristics of this invariant object. But what, above all, is striking in these quotations is the author's uncritical acceptance of the traditional notion of *substance*. Hirsch endows meaning with all the properties of the classical notion of substantial reality (*res*), which is to say that he reifies it.

Such, then, is the object of scientific interpretation. However, once a would-be scientist has devised his object, it remains for him to find an appropriate method for dealing with it. Hirsch remains consistent with himself and proposes a method of interpretation that is fully in accord with its supposed object. If the object of interpretation is an absolute object, i.e., exists in and of itself (*in et per se*—the traditional definition of substance), then the only just method is one that leads us outside ourselves in such a way that we may coincide with the object itself. What is needed is a method that will enable the interpreter to conform or approximate to the object which, as something existing in itself, serves as the standard of the truth or falsity of all statements about it. Hirsch, after Betti, calls this method *re-cognition*. "All valid interpretation of every sort," he writes, "is founded on the re-cognition of what an author meant" (p. 126). Since it is fully determinate in itself, meaning, for Hirsch, is something that needs only to be *rediscovered* and *copied*. Interpretation is nothing more than a matter of the psychological reconstruction of an author's intention; it is a matter of putting one's feet in the author's shoes (see p. 238) or, again, according to Hirsch's Cinderella analogy, a case of merely matching up the right person with the right shoe (p. 46).

Such, in outline, and presented with a view to its basic presuppositions, is the position Hirsch puts forward in his book. As should be evident, Hirsch is simply reiterating in his own way certain traditional concepts, those principally of *substance* and *truth* (as correspondence). An adequate response to Hirsch would have to proceed by way of a critique of these traditional categories. It is just such a critique that I shall attempt partially to sketch out in section 3 below. Before doing so, it would perhaps be useful to take a second look at the meaning of one author in particular to whom Hirsch appeals in an attempt to justify his realistic conception of the hermeneutical object. This author is Edmund Husserl, and what I wish to show is that Hirsch has himself insufficiently and incorrectly construed Husserl's meaning. It will also become apparent that a different (and more faithful) reading of Husserl suggests a conception of interpretation altogether different from the one espoused by Hirsch.

2

Hirsch looks to Husserl for philosophical justification of the idea that the object of consciousness (or interpretation) is something "objective." However, Hirsch does not look very far, for while it is true that a defense of the "objectivity of the object" can be found in Husserl, much more besides can be found there as well. Hirsch seems only to have read Husserl's early work, *Logical Investigations* (this, at any rate, is the only work he alludes to). What interests Hirsch here is the notion of intentionality. According to this key phenomenological notion, it is the essence of consciousness always to be directed to an object, an object which, as Sartre would say, it—consciousness—itself is not; all consciousness is consciousness of something. That is, in all conscious states one can and must distinguish between an *act* of consciousness and an *object* of consciousness that this act intends. The object of which one is conscious cannot, therefore, be reduced to and be identified with the acts by means of which one intends it. According to this notion, many different conscious acts can therefore intend one and the same object, and, even more, different conscious subjects can intend one and the same object. The rainbow that I see is the same as seen by the person standing next to me. From a phenomenological point of view, Hirsch is thus quite correct in saying that textual meaning (as an object of consciousness) is not and cannot be identified with the subjective mental acts of the interpreter. He says:

> The general term for all intentional objects is meaning. Verbal meaning is simply
> a special kind of intentional object, and like any other one, it remains self-identical
> over against the many different acts which "intend" it. (P. 218)

It is, however, at this point that Hirsch leaps to a premature conclusion. Because the object of consciousness cannot be identified with acts of consciousness, Hirsch assumes that it must therefore exist fully in its own right as something permanent, self-identical, unchanging, and reproducible. If it were not autonomous in its own right, how else, Hirsch reasons, could it be intended by the same consciousness at different times or by different consciousnesses at the same or different times? While the main gist of Husserl's antipsychologistic argument in *Logical Investigations* was to deny the identity of meaning with subjective acts, Hirsch is above all concerned to affirm the complete independence of the object. This leads him naturally into his version of Platonic realism as regards meanings alluded to in section 1 above.

Like Hirsch, the early Husserl was concerned above all with refuting psychologism and historicism; to this end he insisted on the irreducibility of the object to the subjective acts which intend it. Husserl's position in *Logical Investigations* is, however, ambiguous. In certain ways he seems to be defending implicitly a modified version of Platonic realism. It is not without reason that some commentators refer to this as Husserl's realistic period. However, as is well known, Husserl was not content to remain at the level of the early *Logical Investigations* and went on in later works (as well as in the revised, second edition of *Logical Investigations*, the sixth Investigation especially) to defend a position which to many seemed to represent an abrupt about-face.

Having hit upon the notion of the phenomenological reduction, Husserl was led to the notion of constitution. His thinking underwent a "transcendental turn," and the meaning-object that in *Logical Investigations* he had interpreted antipsychologistically, he traced back to and linked up with, in his later works, certain constitutive acts on the part of consciousness itself. This is the reason why Husserl referred to his later thought as "transcendental idealism." The object of consciousness, as Husserl went on to maintain, is an ideal (nonreal, *irreal*) object having neither meaning nor being apart from consciousness. "The objective world . . . this world, with all its objects, I said, derives its whole sense and its existential status, which it has for me, from me myself, *from me as the transcendental Ego*, the Ego who comes to the fore only with the transcendental-phenomenological epoche."[5]

Husserl's transcendental turn disconcerted many of his early disciples. What they saw appeared incomprehensible to them; Husserl seemed purely and simply to be changing positions and abandoning realism in favor of idealism. He seemed to have undergone a "conversion" to idealism. However, such a view is, in my opinion, impossible to justify if we keep in mind the general drift of Husserl's thought, if we understand rightly his *Problematik*. Gaston Berger, a first-rate interpreter of Husserl, rejected the idea of a "conversion" in his thought, seeing instead a "progressive deepening of an investigation which does not wander from its axis"; " . . . it is only a question," he said, "of the normal progress of a thought which is not idling in place."[6]

Indeed, Husserl, the "perpetual beginner," the constant searcher after an ever more radical intelligibilty, could not but see that the bare notion of intentionality calls for a deeper analysis. It is not sufficient—necessary though it be at first—to insist merely on the objectivity of the object. It is above all necessary to account for this objectivity. "What it means, that objectivity is,"

Husserl wrote, "and manifests itself cognitively as so being, must precisely become evident purely from consciousness itself, and thereby it must become completely understandable."[7] The notion of intentionalty is, therefore, not the final solution Hirsch takes it to be. Intentionality is a *fact* of conscious life, and, as such, just like life itself, it calls for further analysis if it is to become intelligible, if, precisely, we are to understand what it *means* that consciousness is intentional. Husserl's originality does not consist in having discovered intentionality—this was not *his* discovery—but in his attempt to clarify this notion. Accordingly, after first having saved objectivity from psychologism, Husserl went on to ask what the meaning of objectivity is. And what he came to see is that the objectivity of the object is entirely *relative* to the subjectivity of the (transcendental) subject.

Intentionality is indeed a two-way street. If all consciousness is consciousness of an object, if there can be no act which does not intend some object, conversely, there can be no object apart from an actual or possible consciousness which intends it. To say that consciousness is intentional does not just mean, as Hirsch sees it, that consciousness transcends itself toward its object. This much would indeed justify philosophical realism, and phenomenology is—from *one* point of view—a realistic philosophy. But to say that consciousness is intentional means *also*—but Hirsch stops short here—that the object is always given with consciousness and in fact has no meaning, no significant being, apart from consciousness. This is assuredly an "idealistic" conclusion, but the idealism in question is a very special sort of idealism—a transcendental idealism—for in no way does it deny the reality or objectivity of the object. Rather, it clarifies it by linking it up with the structures of pure, transcendental consciousness. Reality is nothing other than that of which consciousness is conscious. This is to say that it is the *correlate* of consciousness and that the meaning of reality is to be sought for in consciousness alone.

Let us see what in this context the real object is for the mature Husserl. This will provide us with the means for conceiving of the hermeneutical object quite differently from the way Hirsch does; it will, in short, provide us with a countermodel for a theory of interpretation. In the fourth part of *Ideas*, entitled "Reason and Reality," Husserl takes up the question of the relation of consciousness to the object (reality). This widening-out of the preceding noetico-noematic analyses is a source of perplexity for many of his readers. The question of what the object is seems to have been dealt with already in the preceding section of the book. Is not the object of consciousness nothing other than the noema, which itself is ideally immanent to consciousness? Has not Husserl bracketed the "real" object and substituted for it the intentional object (noema)? Paul Ricoeur, translator and commentator of *Ideas*, remarks: "This rebound of the description poses the most extreme difficulties of interpretation."[8] These difficulties can be alleviated if we realize that what Husserl is attempting to do in this fourth part of *Ideas* is, precisely, to give an immanent account not only of the conscious object but also of reality itself. For this reason, the question of what the real object is, the object itself apart from consciousness, cannot be simply bracketed and ignored; reality itself must be clarified phenomenologically, i.e., *explicated in terms of consciousness.*

Having already, in his description of the intentional structure of consciousness, distinguished between the intentional act and intentional object, Husserl now says that both the act (noesis) and the intentional object (noema—the "content" of consciousness) are themselves related to and intend an object, the "real" object: "Every intentional experience has a noema and therein a meaning through which it is related to the object."[9] This is the object *simpliciter*, what in ordinary language is called the real object outside consciousness. The intentional object is merely the object *qua* intended, the object as it appears; it is not itself identical with the object *simpliciter*, which is what gives rise to a multiplicity of determinations or meanings (noemas or intentional objects). What, then, is the object itself? "What properly does the 'claim' of consciousness to really 'relate' to something objective, to be 'valid' (*triftig*) mean?"[10] As this question makes evident, the problem Husserl is dealing with is essentially none other than the one which so absorbs Hirsch: the *validity* of consciousness or interpretation. What is it that legitimates, that validates conscious meanings? For Husserl this is the question: What is the status of the object? What is the relation between consciousness and reality? What is Reality?

The essence of Husserl's answer can be given succinctly, even though a fully faithful and adequate presentation of his thought on this matter would necessitate a considerable amount of careful interpretation. Husserl writes: " 'Object' as we everywhere understand it is a title for eidetic connexions of consciousness."[11] And again: " . . . [the] 'real object' . . . acts . . . as an indication of fully determined systems of conscious formations teleologically unified."[12] In essence, Husserl is saying here that the transcendence of the real object is itself something constituted in consciousness. The "object" or "reality" is nothing other than that which corresponds to an "infinite ideal manifold of noetic experiences."[13] Thus the difference between the intentional object and the object *simpliciter* is that while the former is the correlate of only one type of intending, the latter is that which corresponds to an ideally indefinite number of intentional acts. As such, it is, therefore, not something "outside" consciousness and unrelated to it.

> Neither a world nor any other existent of any conceivable sort comes "from outdoors" into my ego, my life of consciousness. Everything outside is what it is in this inside. . . . [14]

> *There is no conceivable place where the life of consciousness is broken through or could be broken through,* and we might come upon a transcendency that possibly had any sense other than that of an intentional unity making its appearance in the subjectivity itself of consciousness.[15]

Reality is inseparable from consciousness; it is consciousness which "in itself legitimates this reality."[16] Interpreting Husserl, Ricoeur writes: "The true being of the thing remains an Idea in the Kantian sense, i.e., the regulating principle of an open series of appearances which are continuously concordant."[17] And in an interpretation that Husserl himself countersigned, Eugen Fink stated:

> Here "relation to the object" only has the sense of referring an actual noema (i.e., the correlate of an isolated transcendental act) to the manifold of act-correlates which, through the synthetic cohesion of constant fulfillment, first forms the unity of the object as an ideal pole.[18]

The relation between the noematic object and the object *simpliciter*, between consciousness and reality, is itself constituted by consciousness. Reality is nothing other than the ideal object of all possible conscious acts, and in this sense it is immanent to and inseparable from consciousness. It is the immanent teleological goal or ideal pole of all conscious acts.

With this conception of objectivity, Husserl has succeeded in overcoming the subject-object dichotomy, the traditional dilemma which is still at the very heart of Hirsch's analyses. Husserl has succeeded in making sense of reality by showing what, in concrete terms of experience, it means to speak of reality. The real object is not some mysterious *Ding-an-sich* outside consciousness to which we approximate without ever knowing if, in fact, we have coincided with it; it is, rather, nothing other than the immanent, ideal unity of an indefinite number of experiences. The object, reality, or the world, is for Husserl nothing other, and nothing more, than a "pole of unity"[19] *within* experience and *of* experience:

> . . . this world, I say, has and, by essential necessity, retains the sense only of a *presumptive existence*. The real world exists, only on the continually delineated presumption that experience will go on continually in the same constitutional style.[20]

Now what I wish to suggest is that the hermeneutical object is best understood when it is conceived in the way in which Husserl conceives of the "object" and "reality." On this analogy, various interpretive "hypotheses" would correspond to the different noemas, the different ways in which an object may be intended. These interpretive meanings are themselves related to and intend the hermeneutical object *simpliciter*, i.e., the meaning of the text. When, then, is the meaning of the text? Obviously, it is not in this case something subsisting apart from the interpretive, reading consciousness, "out there" in some mysterious, transcendent realm of self-subsistent, reified meanings. It exists only in the interpretive consciousness as the meaning which is there for this consciousness. This is not to say that the meaning of a text, e.g., a text of Heraclitus, is purely and simply what I decide to say it is. This is not to open the door to arbitrariness, subjectivism, relativism, historicism, and so on, and so on. The meaning of the text is no more identical with any given interpretation than the object *simpliciter* is reducible to any given noema or intentional object. But the meaning of the text, like the object, is not, of course, something totally other than its various determinations, either. It is precisely the *ideal* (nonreal) *telos* of interpretation, its immanent teleological goal. This is the only meaning that the meaning of the text can be said to have. The objectivity of the text cannot be divorced from the subjectivity of the interpreter; in fact, the only conceivable criterion for textual meaning *is* the interpreter (the whole interpretive tradition). Apart from interpretive consciousness, it is impossible to speak of the meaning of a text.

This is not a subjectivistic position, for consciousness here is not understood subjectivistically, i.e., as the consciousness of myself or of any other empirically existing human being. One could say of the text what Peirce says of Reality: "reality is independent, not necessarily of thought in general, but only of what you or I or any finite number of men may think about it."[21] The opposite of the naive realism we find in Hirsch is indeed a kind of subjective idealism. But we need be impaled on one of the horns of the realism-idealism dilemma only if, like Hirsch, we persist in operating with concepts expressive of the modern subject-object dichotomy. We will fear subjectivity and overreact by investing our hopes in an uncontaminated—and illusory—realism only so long as we have not fully elucidated the sense of reality itself. Had Hirsch been less selective in his reading of Husserl, he would perhaps have come across the following admonition regarding subjectivity:

> For children in philosophy, this may be the dark corner of solipsism and, perhaps, of psychologism, of relativism. The true philosopher, instead of running away, will prefer to fill the dark corner with light.[22]

3

Our counterreading of Husserl has furnished us with a countermodel for the hermeneutical object and, by implication, for interpretation in general. An adequate presentation and defense of this new model would require as fully developed a treatise as Hirsch's own. Therefore, I shall take a different line, a negative approach, so to speak. If Hirsch's position can be seen to be unsatisfactory, then the need for a different approach to basic hermeneutical theory will be appreciated. There are three areas where Hirsch's position necessarily results in especially undesirable consequences, those, namely, having to do with the questions of truth, time, and creativity. The remainder of this essay will consist of a number of observations in regard to these notions.

In general, it can be said that Hirsch's basic conceptual framework wherein the subject-object dichotomy dominates generates a number of false dichotomies and pseudo-alternatives which serve only to obscure the real issues. This is certainly the case in what has to do with the issue of truth and meaning. As we have seen, Hirsch wishes to make of interpretation a serious business, i.e., a science. Now to be a science a discipline must be able to lay claim to truth or validity as regards its statements. And validity is achieved when what we say about a thing actually corresponds to what the thing itself is: *veritas est adequatio intellectus ad rem.* Or as Hirsch puts it: "Validity implies the correspondence of an interpretation to a meaning which is represented by the text . . . " (p.10). Furthermore, if correspondence is to be achieved, then there must be something that can be corresponded to, i.e., there must be a fully determinate object if valid determinations of it are to be possible. In pursuing this line of reasoning Hirsch is led into absolutizing the hermeneutical object. Without a fixed object there can be no rigor in interpretation. Hirsch leads his reader in this way into one of the most pernicious of pseudo-alternatives: absolultism vs. relativism—either there is an absolute or else everything becomes utterly relative. Now sheer relativism is indeed an inadmissible position for any discipline seeking genuine knowledge, for it destroys the very notions of truth and validity. It is something we can accept no more than can Hirsch. However, what I wish to suggest is that on Hirsch's own grounds relativism is inevitable.

Hirsch's correspondence theory of truth actually renders truth inaccessible, which is to say, impossible. Hirsch himself admits that we can never *know* if, in fact, our interpretations are valid, i.e., faithfully reproduce the author's meaning: "I can never know another person's intended meaning with certainty because I cannot get inside his head to compare the meaning he intends with the meaning I understand, and only by such direct comparison could I be certain that his meaning and my own are identical" (p. 17). But in order nonetheless to save the abstract notion of truth as coincidence, Hirsch immediately adds: "It is a logical mistake to confuse the impossibility of certainty in understanding with the impossibility of understanding." But it is actually Hirsch who is the victim of a logical mistake and of fuzzy thinking. For while he maintains, on the one hand, that the hermeneutical object is the author's intended meaning and maintains as well that this is a fully determinate, self-subsistent, really existing entity, he denies, on the other hand, that we can ever *know* (or, to be more precise, know that we know) this meaning. Such a statement is devoid of any *concrete* logic. Actually, it might be more appropriate to say that what Hirsch offers us with one hand he takes away with the other. Of course, this is not a perversity of Hirsch alone; it is, as Montaigne observed, a characteristic of all metaphysical defenders of "absolute" truth and meaning. The fact of the matter is that the notions of absolute truth and meaning are *meaningless* notions, for the simple reason that they have no equivalent and play no actual role in our own experience; they have no experiential content. As Merleau-Ponty observed in a passage which is too pertinent and too eloquent not to quote at length:

> . . . if we wish to base the fact of rationality or communication on an absolute value or thought, either this absolute does not raise any difficulties and, when everything has been carefully considered, rationality and communication remain based on themselves, or else the absolute descends into them so to speak—in which case it overturns all human methods of verification and justification. Whether there is

or is not an absolute thought and an absolute evaluation in each practical problem, my own opinions, which remain capable of error no matter how rigorously I examine them, are still my only equipment for judging. It remains just as hard to reach agreement with myself and with others, and for all my belief that it is in principle always attainable, I have no other reason to affirm this principle than my experience of certain concordances, so that in the end whatever solidity there is in my belief in the absolute is nothing but my experience of agreement with myself and others. Recourse to an absolute foundation—when it is not useless—destroys the very thing it is supposed to support.[23]

To be sure, Hirsch does try to salvage the notion of absolute truth by saying that if I can never be absolutely certain of an interpretation, I can nonetheless be *probably* certain. Such is the way in which the notion of probability judgments come to play a decisive role in his thinking. It is, one might say, a kind of stopgap measure—but one which is doomed to failure as well. For if, as I have maintained, absolute truth and self-subsistent meanings are meaningless notions, then the notion of an approximation to such entities (probability) is equally meaningless.

Thus, if we are arguing against Hirsch's conception of understanding, this is not because we wish to deny the possibility of understanding, as Hirsch would have it, but because we wish to conceive of understanding anew— precisely in order to defend (in a meaningful way) the possibility of understanding and of truth. It is actually Hirsch's position which gives rise to relativism and skepticism, for an inaccessible, absolute-in-itself, which must necessarily be a source of continuous frustration when it is searched after, ends up by provoking a doubt as to its very existence or, at the least, a kind of resigned agnosticism. As Nietzsche well understood, nothing devalorizes human experience and truth more than the positing of an absolute value and truth. The only conception of understanding capable of justifying the possibility of understanding is, consequently, one which conceives of it in purely experiential terms, one, that is, which does not divorce the hermeneutical object from the interpretive experience but which, instead, gives an immanent account of it, the only meaningful kind of account possible. Such a conception is the phenomenological one, the one sketched out by Husserl.

Even though it denies the notion of the absolute object, Husserl's position does not for all that lead to subjectivism and relativism, for to give a purely experiential account of the object is not to "subjectivize" it. There is indeed something about a real object that induces one to posit for it a kind of extra-experiential existence. When falsely interpreted, however, this fact of experience can give rise to the philosophical absurdity of an absolute-in-itself. To avoid this kind of absurd realism and to conceptualize experience properly, we should perhaps speak rather of a transexperiential reality, for to speak of a real object at all is indeed to speak of a kind of transcendency. But we must never forget that this is a transcendence that we ourselves discover *within* our own experience. Therefore, we should say of the object not that it is a reality in itself but, rather, that it is a "transcendence within immanence." The concept of "transcendence within immanence," properly worked out, is, I maintain, the only viable alternative to an absurdly naive realism, as well as to an unacceptably subjectivistic idealism. It is just such a concept which can provide the basis for a satsifactory theory of interpretation. A totally extra-experiential reality is a meaningless notion, but it is not impossible that we should discover, *in* our experience, a transcendence which, though related to this experience, could never be reduced to it.

In opposition to Hirsch's highly abstract approach, we would perhaps be better off to ask not: What makes an interpretation true or valid? since this can easily induce us to take refuge in a copy theory of truth and will expose us to all the pitfalls latent in such a theory. Instead, we should ask: Why *in fact* do scholars working on a given text accept one interpretation over another? When the question is asked in this concrete way, we immediately see what the answer *cannot* be. We cannot say that they accept the interpretation because it is the true or most valid one, for obviously this is begging the question and tells us absolutely nothing. They cannot compare their interpretations with the truth and choose accordingly, for the "truth" is something they will possess only after or when they have opted for and agreed upon a given interpretation. It would make more sense, pragmatically, at least, to say that the true interpretation is true for no other reason than because it is accepted as so being. To say that an interpretation is true comes down to, and is no more than, saying that it is generally accepted by the community of interpreters. Any other notion of truth can (as is the case with metaphysical entities in general) have only a merely verbal significance.

The answer to the question: Why is one interpretation accepted over an-other? can only be: because it seems more fruitful, more promising. It seems to make more and better sense of the text than other interpretations; it opens up greater horizons of meaning. This amounts to saying, of course, that truth is essentially of a presumptive nature. All interpretation works under the prom-ise of truth. To speak of promise is to speak of the future. "Validity" does not, therefore, come from the past but from the future; validation is nothing other than the harmonious unfolding and reciprocal confirmation of successive ex-periences (interpretations). This is to say also that knowledge is not so different from faith. When we opt for a given interpretation, we do not do so because we *know* it to be true (even Hirsch admits to this) but because we *believe* it to be the best, the one which offers the most promise and is the most likely to make the text intelligible, comprehensible for us.

Just as we have seen Husserl say that the world's existence is an entirely presumptive existence, and just as for Husserl to say that the real world exists is to say only that we believe that experience will continue to unfold harmo-niously (Husserl's *Urdoxa*, what Merleau-Ponty called *la foi perceptive*), so also we should say that the reality of the hermeneutical object is entirely pre-sumptive. The meaning of the text is in no way separable from its meaning for us; what a text means is nothing other than the immanent goal of the interpretive

process. Its being is essentially futural. Deciding among possible textual interpretations is, as Hirsch himself would say, not all that different from deciding
among interpretive schemas of reality in science. But, I believe, a better grasp
of just what goes on in science is to be found in Thomas Kuhn rather than in
E. D. Hirsch (or, perhaps I should say, in Karl Popper, who furnishes Hirsch
with his canonical texts on scientific knowledge). In his book *The Structure of
Scientific Revolutions*, Kuhn, considering the question as to why scientists opt
for a given interpretive schema, or "paradigm," as he calls it, writes:

> . . . paradigm debates are not really about relative problem-solving ability, though
> for good reasons they are usually couched in those terms. Instead, the issue is
> which paradigm should in the future guide research on problems many of which
> neither competitor can yet claim to resolve completely. A decision between alter-
> nate ways of practicing science is called for, and in the circumstances that decision
> must be based less on past achievement than on future promise. The man who
> embraces a new paradigm at an early stage must often do so in defiance of the
> evidence provided by problem-solving. He must, that is, have faith that the new
> paradigm will succeed with the many large problems that confront it, knowing only
> that the older paradigm has failed with a few. A decision of that kind can only be
> made of faith.[24]

It is perhaps no coincidence that certain of Kuhn's remarks are applicable
in the matter of hermeneutics.[25] For one thing that Kuhn has in effect shown
is that science itself is to be understood as one way in which human beings
interpret the world. And what is of interest above all in Kuhn's exposition is
its overall implications regarding the nature of the scientific enterprise itself.
Our usual picture of science is that it is an "objective" representation and
description of nature. The history of science and of scientific revolutions has,
however, quite a different story to tell. It shows that science is, in actuality,
something quite different from this abstract idea of it. What science says of the
world is dependent not on the way things supposedly are in themselves but
on the fact that the scientist views the world by means of a particular paradigm
or model (interpretive schema). The way the scientist views the world determines what the world that he sees is. This is to say that when a scientific
revolution occurs, it is not merely the doctrinal content of science that changes;
it is the world itself that undergoes a transformation: "When paradigms change,
the world itself changes with them."[26] This is perfectly understandable when
we realize that what the world appears to be is entirely dependent on our way
of looking at it and of acting on it. The only answers the world gives are to
questions we have asked of it. And Nature answers the scientist's questions in
much the same way as the god whose oracle is at Delphi, neither affirming nor
denying, as Heraclitus said, but only indicating enigmatically. Indeed, as Heraclitus also remarked, Nature likes to hide, answering only those questions asked,
and then with all the ambiguity and sly reticence permitted by the question
itself. As the answers change and vary according to the questions asked, it is

immensely difficult ever to know if we have the answer we're really looking for (can we ever be sure we have asked the right question?). The lesson to be learned from this is that before we tempestuously set out in a Quixotic search for a pure and pristine "objectivity," we should first of all clarify our own subjectivity, for it is precisely this which determines what we shall find. This is why Husserl ended his Paris lectures with the following exhortation of Saint Augustine: *Noli foras ire, in te redi, in interiore homine habitat veritas.*

Scientific knowledge is, therefore, no passive copying of reality but is, rather, an active construction or constitution of it. In sum, science is but one way in which we creatively interpret reality, and no more than in any other mode of interpretation do we have access here to absolute reality and truth.

As I see it, the morale of Kuhn's historical-hermeneutical analyses is that we must change our traditional idea of what science is. Not only that, we must change our very conception of truth and reality. Kuhn himself seems actually to be hinting at as much when he remarks in passing about the need for "a viable alternative to the traditional epistemological paradigm."[27] Kuhn expresses dissatisfaction with the "epistemological viewpoint that has most often guided Western philosophy for three centuries,"[28] but, lacking a developed alternative, he cannot quite bring himself to relinquishing entirely that viewpoint. What is called for, we might say, is precisely a viable and well-worked-out alternative to the traditional metaphysical and epistemological viewpoint, the same one that we have seen at work in Hirsch. Philosophy, whose business is the articulation and elucidation of basic "paradigms," is itself in a state of crisis today, not unlike the periodic crises in science which Kuhn describes and which are more often than not the prelude to a revolution or change of paradigms. The traditional philosophical paradigms are proving more and more unsatisfactory to more and more people, but as yet there seems to be no general consensus as to what should replace them. Radical critiques of the traditional metaphysical and epistemological outlook have been formulated in this century by movements as diverse as phenomenology and pragmatism. The traditional concept of substance has come under heavy attack in more than one type of philosophy and by contemporary thinkers who otherwise have precious little in common. But if the tradition has been severely criticized, it has not, at least as regards philosophers in the aggregate, been overcome successfully. Philosophy in general still lacks a viable alternative to the traditional substance-oriented paradigm, to the traditional conceptual framework, or *Begrifflichkeit*, as Heidegger would say. However, a certain movement in a given direction does seem to be discernible. Philosophy in general seems to be moving away from a conception of reality as something static, immutable, self-identical, and timeless to one which views it as essentially historical and creative, as some would say, or as process, as others would say. It is understandable nonetheless that in the present crisis many thinkers will prefer to hold on to the traditional *Begrifflichkeit* when the only alternative they can see is one which abandons fixity in favor of chaotic flux, relativism, skepticism, the denial of truth altogether, with the nihilism which follows from this. Nietzsche is here paradigmatic

of the present malaise. While his critique of the tradition is absolutely devastating, the only alternative to the "will to truth" he denounces which seems
to follow or to be found in his thought is an abysmal nihilism—notwithstanding
his own proclaimed aversion to nihilism. If there is nothing better than a
Nietzsche, it is understandable that many will wish to deny and ignore his
criticisms, clutching even more desperately to a worn-out, bankrupt system.
A little light is preferable to the absence of all light; the will to truth is preferable
to the idolization of madness and irresponsible innocence.

Thus the task confronting philosophy is that of developing an alternative to
the traditional epistemological paradigm, as Kuhn would say. The subject-object
dichotomy arising from Cartesian subjectivism which has plagued all of modern
thought, which was incorporated into the conceptual framework of natural science, and which Hirsch is now attempting to impose upon the humanities—
it is this dichotomy that philosophy must overcome in a decisive way. Just as,
in science, the Newtonian epoch has come to an end, so also the more basic
and inclusive Cartesian epoch has reached its conclusion. However, like Zara-
thustra's townsmen who ignored the "death of God" (i.e., the end of
Platonism), many today seem oblivious to the fact that the bases of their traditional world are collapsing under their feet. Philosophy lacks the Einsteins
and Heisenbergs necessary to effectuate for it the needed conceptual revolution,
or, rather, it may already have had them; it may be that we have still to learn
from them the necessary lesson. Philosophical revolutions, it is true, occur in
more subtle ways than do scientific ones.

The basic defect with Hirsch is that his attempt to rethink hermeneutics in
the light of positivistic science has prevented him from seeing that it is the
traditional paradigm of scientific objectivity and the traditional notions of truth
and reality that are themselves in need of rethinking. It is not so much that
Hirsch is wrong as that he is misguided and has been misled into fighting a
rearguard action on behalf of a cause which has by now lost most if not all of
its vital force and "relevance." Hirsch's error in hermeneutics is of the same
order as that of the hard-line behaviorist in psychology; in both cases the attempt
to be ultrascientific and an irrational aversion to everything "subjective" has
led them into modeling their disciplines after a conception of physical science
which is by now plainly outdated. Hirsch's positivistic conception of science is
one which has been demolished by many recent theoreticians of science, by
Michael Polanyi, for instance, who writes:

> It goes without saying that no one—scientists included—looks at the universe this
> way, whatever lip-service is given to "objectivity." Nor should this surprise us.
> For, as human beings, we must inevitably see the universe from a centre lying
> within ourselves and speak about it in terms of a human language shaped by the
> exigencies of human intercourse. Any attempt rigorously to eliminate our human
> perspective from our picture of the world must lead to absurdity.[29]

It is precisely this kind of absurdity that we encounter in Hirsch's hermeneutical
realism.

Up to now I have dealt with the underlying notion of truth in Hirsch. In addition to this, there are two other key items which call for at least a minimal criticism: time and creativity. Hirsch's naive copy theory of truth leads him to conceive of meaning as something copyable, reproducible, i.e., as a self-subsisting, determinate entity. Such a way of conceiving of meaning makes it all but meaningless. Hirsch's uncritical scientism also results in a hypostatization of meaning as a *timeless* entity. He says, as we have seen:

> When, therefore, I say that a verbal meaning is determinate I mean that it is an entity which is self-identical. Furthermore I also mean that it is an entity which always remains the same from one moment to the next—that it is changeless. (P. 46)

Indeed, for Hirsch meaning must be changeless, subsisting outside the ebb and flow of history, if it is to be—as it must be if it is to be "objective"—always the same meaning which is "reproduced" in different interpretations. Once again it is Hirsch's fear of relativism which makes him overreact by investing meaning with of kind of petrified eternity. Hirsch argues for the timelessness of meaning since without this "there would be no permanent norm on which validating judgments could be made" (p. 21). He says even: "The significance of textual meaning has no foundation and no objectivity unless meaning itself is unchanging" (p. 214). Once again we are forced into the straitjacket of an uncompromising either-or: Either there is an absolute, time-less foundation to the phenomenal world (to interpretations) or else all is relative and vain.

This false and unacceptable alternative leads Hirsch to make a pseudo-distinction between "meaning" and "significance," i.e., between the meaning of the text in itself (which is unchanging) and its meaning or significance for us, for contemporary criticism (which is necessarily in constant change). It is not textual meaning that changes, merely our interpretations of it: "the his-toricity of interpretation is quite distinct from the timelessness of understand-ing" (p. 137). While the "meaning"-"significance" distinction might seem, on the face of it, rather ingenious, it is actually rather difficult, if not impossible, to see what experiential reality it corresponds to. If, as Hirsch himself admits, our interpretations are constantly changing, what is it that so much as enables us to form the idea of an unchanging meaning (understanding) beyond inter-pretation? Certainly not these interpretations themselves, since by definition they are characterized by "historicity." Since as a matter of fact the most we can do is to devise good *interpretations*, the actual consequence of Hirsch's position is to condemn us to an eternal errancy in the shadows of an inaccessible, timeless Understanding. Once again it is actually Hirsch who is destroying the possibility of any *real* understanding. His overvaluation of the hermeneutical object results—although obviously he does not see this—in a complete de-valuation of *human* understanding. One would have to possess the timeless mind of a Thomistic angel to grasp Hirsch's timeless meanings. Hirsch's notion of understanding certainly does not have any relation to the finite understanding of historical human beings.

Hirsch grants that the "cultural givens" of interpretation change in the course of time, but he asks: "does this imply that textual meaning itself changes?" (p. 213). This is, of course, merely a rhetorical question, since for Hirsch it is unthinkable that meaning itself should change; if it did, there would be no norms, just sheer chaos. Nevertheless, we must say that meaning *does* change; the history of human understanding is not for all that an utter chaos. One can always find in it a kind of inner logic. It must be said that with new interpretations the meaning of a text itself undergoes a development, just as the world itself changes, as Kuhn said, when scientific paradigms change. There can be no other meaning of a text than its (actual or potential) meaning for us, and this does change. To say that our understanding of textual meaning undergoes change is equivalent to saying that the meaning which is there for us also changes. When, in the course of interpretation, we draw more and more meanings out of a text—and often one of these newly formulated meanings will appear to contradict a previous one—when we actively discern more and more meaning in a text, it is the text itself which becomes more meaningful, more laden with meaning. To be sure, there is something about a text considered in its own right that justifies and solicits its own interpretation—not any text will permit any interpretation—but these interpretations are not mere copies of fully developed meanings existing already in the text; they are realizations of an ever richer meaning. Instead of drawing false dichotomies between textual meaning in itself and its meaning for us, between "understanding" and "interpretation," and others of this sort, we should recognize the existence of a dialectic between text and interpretation, an irreducible dialectic which is the proper locus of emergent meaning. Interpretation, it could be said, is a motivated creation.

Hirsch's distinction between "meaning" and "significance," between "interpretation" and "criticism," could possibly be retained if in each case the two terms are not taken as polar opposites. It is the task of what Hirsch calls "criticism" to make a textual meaning relevant to one's contemporaries by relating it to their own interests and preoccupations. And it is quite true that a meaning can be made relevant only if it has first of all been determined by interpretation. There is a difference between the discernment of meaning (interpretation) and the application of meaning (criticism). However, the meaning of a text as determined by interpretation is not for all that immutable and self-subsistent; it arises and exists only in and through acts of interpretation and is related essentially to them. While interpretation and criticism are two somewhat different kinds of activity and have two somewhat different kinds of roles to play, it is, nonetheless, impossible to separate them radically, in Hirsch's fashion.

In the last analysis, Hirsch's position leads to a thoroughgoing devalorization of history, a devalorization of the same order as we find in the usual scientific view of things. The history of his discipline is a matter of little or no interest to the ordinary practitioner of science. His knowledge of this history usually does not extend beyond what he has learned from text books. And in these, as Kuhn has shown, a very particular conception of history is present, one which looks upon it as a merely cumulative affair wherein what is old is quite simply superseded and displaced by the more developed current truth. History is here seen as proceeding in a linear fashion, with various truths being replaced by ever better and more comprehensive ones. When, through the practice of Hirsch's "experimental" method, a "valid" interpretation is arrived at, this automatically displaces all preceding interpretations which are therewith relegated to the garbage dump of history. Here the history of human understanding is no more than an enormous rubbish heap of invalidated interpretations.

Finally, what is perhaps the most disconcerting element in Hirsch's position is its implications for creativity. As a matter of fact, Hirsch (like Popper) has practically nothing to say on this score, and what little he does say is purely negative. This is not surprising, of course, since Hirsch is attempting to be "scientific" and in his haste to be so fails completely to see that science is itself, basically, a creative enterprise. There are no objective, in-itself truths which constrain scientists to formulate their revolutionary theories in the way they do. In cases such as these, the world achieves a greater intelligibility only because scientists have freely chosen to view it in a certain, original way. Freedom and creativity, however, have no place in Hirsch's "science" of interpretation; "when we construe another's meaning we are not free agents" (p. 142). Scientists, it is true, often like to say that they had no choice but to formulate the theories they did; it was, they may say, the "evidence" which forced them to their conclusions. The history of science shows this up for the myth it is. Not only does the "evidence" not automatically produce a given theory in the mind of the scientist, what the "evidence," the "facts of the matter" are depends on the way the scientist chooses to view the matter. Thus, far from maintaining that creativity and freedom should be banished from interpretation, we should recognize that interpretation is possible only because human understanding is creative.

The issue does not stop there, however. Just as Hirsch banishes creativity from interpretation, so also, I believe, he renders meaningless the notion of creativity in the composition of texts. For when we speak of inspired works, we mean, if anything at all, that the meaning of what the author wrote surpasses what he either *knew* or *willed*.[30] It is precisely this extra- or transintentional element in a work that makes it a classic, a living classic, as we so aptly say, a work which is capable of leading a life of its own beyond that of its author and which makes it something more than a lifeless object of merely historiographical and archival interest. A text itself is not a self-contained, determinate meaning but is, rather, the "promise" of meaning. Unlike the physical document which is its support, the meaning of a text is not a substantial *entity* (if it were, we would be faced with the absurd question: Where does this entity exist?). The meaning of a text is what the text gives us to understand; it is an invitation and a call to interpretation, and interpretation is the effective realization of a text's promise. What a text really means is, therefore, inseparable from the history of the interpretations that it engenders. The text, one might say in a way reminiscent of Rudolf Bultmann, is an event whose essence is eschatological. Or as Paul Ricoeur has said:

> . . . the text's career escapes the finite horizon lived by its author. What the text says now matters more than what the author meant to say, and every exegesis unfolds its procedures within the circumference of a meaning that has broken its moorings to the psychology of its author.[31]

Ricoeur has attempted to interpret action on the model of a text, but one could turn this analogy around and say of the text what Hannah Arendt says of action:

> Action reveals itself fully only to the storyteller, that is, to the backward glance of the historian, who indeed always knows better what it was all about than the participants. All accounts told by the actors themselves, though they may in rare cases give an entirely trustworthy statement of intentions, aims, and motives, become mere useful source material in the historian's hands and can never match his story in significance and truthfulness. What the storyteller narrates must necessarily be hidden from the actor himself, at least as long as he is in the act or caught in its consequences, because to him the meaningfulness of his act is not in the story that follows. Even though stories are the inevitable results of action, it is not the actor but the storyteller who perceives and "makes" the story.[32]

In the case of great, thought-provoking, "eminent" texts, we are in contact with an *overdetermination* of meaning, and it is precisely this *surplus of meaning* that actually calls for and engenders an open-ended process of creative interpretation, a process which ultimately confirms the text in its own meaning. However, as long as like Hirsch we persist in thinking according to the metaphysical category of substance, creativity will ever remain a vain word.

In conclusion, it could be said that the main value of Hirsch's book lies in its deficiencies, for it is precisely these which can force us to recognize the urgent need for a theory of human understanding capable of overcoming them.

Notes

This text, which was meant as a kind of Gadamerian response to the objectivistic hermeneutics of E. D. Hirsch, was composed in the early 1970s, before the publication in English of Gadamer's *Truth and Method*, and was subsequently published as "Eine Kritik an Hirschs Begriff der 'Richtigkeit' " in *Seminar: Die Hermeneutik und die Wissenschaften*, ed. H.-G. Gadamer and G. Boehm (Frankfurt: Suhrkamp Verlag, 1978). It appears here for the first time in its proper English version.

1. Tübingen: J. C. B. Mohr, 1960.

2. New Haven, Conn.: Yale University Press, 1967.

3. See E. Betti, *Die Hermeneutik als allgemeine Methodik der Geisteswissenschaften* (Tübingen: J. C. B. Mohr, 1962); *Teoria generale della interpretazione* (Milan: Dott. A. Giuffre, 1955); and *Zur Grundlegung einer allgemeine Auslegungslehre* (Tübingen: J. C. B. Mohr, 1954).

4. Hirsch's article "Gadamer's Theory of Interpretation," first published in *Review of Metaphysics* (March 1965), is included as an appendix in *Validity in Interpretation*.

5. E. Husserl, *Cartesian Meditations*, trans. D. Cairns (The Hague: Martinus Nijhoff, 1960), § 11.

6. G. Berger, *The Cogito in Husserl's Philosophy*, trans. K. McLaughlin (Evanston, Ill.: Northwestern University Press, 1972), p. 7.

7. E. Husserl, "Philosophy as a Rigorous Science," trans. Q. Lauer, in E. Husserl, *Phenomenology and the Crisis of Philosophy* (New York: Harper Torchbooks, 1965), p. 90.

8. E. Husserl, *Idées directrices pour une phénoménologie*, trans. P. Ricoeur (Paris: Gallimard, 1950), p. 431, n. 1.

9. E. Husserl, *Ideas*, trans. W. R. B. Gibson (New York: Collier Books, 1962), § 135

10. Ibid., § 128.

11. Ibid., § 145.

12. Ibid.

13. Ibid., § 135.

14. E. Husserl, *Formal and Transcendental Logic*, trans. D. Cairns (The Hague: Martinus Nijhoff, 1969), § 99.

15. Ibid., § 94.

16. *Ideas*, § 135.

17. *Idées directrices pour une phénoménologie*, p. 477, n. 1.

18. E. Fink, "The Phenomenological Philosophy of Edmund Husserl and Contemporary Criticism," in *The Phenomenology of Husserl*, ed. R. O. Elveton (Chicago: Quadrangle Books, 1970), p. 125.

19. *Formal and Transcendental Logic*, § 99.

20. Ibid.

21. C. Peirce, "How to Make Our Ideas Clear," in *The Collected Papers of Charles Sanders Peirce*, ed. C. Hartshorne and P. Weiss (Cambridge, Mass.: Harvard University Press, 1931–1935, 1958), vol. V, p. 408.

22. *Formal and Transcendental Logic*, § 95.

23. M. Merleau-Ponty, *Sense and Non-Sense*, trans. H. Dreyfus (Evanston, Ill.: Northwestern University Press, 1964), pp. 94–95.

24. T. Kuhn, *The Structure of Scientific Revolutions*, 2d ed. (Chicago: University of Chicago Press, 1970), pp. 157–58.

25. After the publication of his book, Kuhn was introduced to phenomenological hermeneutics and began to refer to his own work as "hermeneutical."

26. *The Structure of Scientific Revolutions*, p. 111.

27. Ibid., p. 121.

28. Ibid., p. 126.

29. M. Polanyi, *Personal Knowledge* (Chicago: University of Chicago Press, 1958), p. 3.

30. For Hirsch, in contrast, meaning "is what the author meant by his use of a particular sign sequence" (*Validity*, p. 8). "*A verbal meaning is a willed type*" (ibid., p.51). " . . . the consciously willed type which defines the meaning as a whole" (ibid., p. 54).

31. P. Ricoeur, "The Model of the Text: Meaningful Action Considered as a Text," *Social Research*, vol. 38, no. 3 (Fall 1971), p. 534. This article was subsequently reprinted in P. Ricoeur, *Hermeneutics and the Human Sciences*, ed. J. B. Thompson (Cambridge, England: Cambridge University Press, 1981); the passage cited occurs on p. 201 of this edition.

32. H. Arendt, *The Human Condition* (Chicago: University of Chicago Press, 1958), p. 192.

TWO

Method in Interpretation

> . . . it is the mark of an educated man to look for precision in each class of things just so far as the nature of the subject admits; it is evidently equally foolish to accept probable reasoning from a mathematician and to demand from a rhetorician scientific proofs.
>
> —Aristotle, *Nichomachean Ethics*

> Likely conjecture about useful things is far preferable to exact knowledge of the useless.
>
> —Isocrates, *Helen*

Interpretation theory, or hermeneutics, is a subject of much current debate. One reason for this is, no doubt, the wide variety of specialized topics which fall under its scope and in regard to which it promises to open productive avenues of approach—topics such as the relation between the natural sciences and the humanities, the methodological status of the social sciences, the nature of language and its role in human understanding, the structures of understanding itself, in its various modes, the relation between language and reality, and so on. Hermeneutical theory is a veritable crossroads where tendencies as diverse as phenomenology and linguistic analysis, semantics and the critique of ideologies, structuralism and conceptual analysis, Marxism and Freudianism come together. Hermeneutics is a subject as central to theology as it is to jurisprudence, as central to philosophy as it is to literary criticism.

Indeed, one of the major ongoing debates in hermeneutics is one in which one of the major protagonists is an American professor of English, and the other, a German philosopher. I refer to E. D. Hirsch and H.-G. Gadamer, respectively. Both Hirsch and Gadamer have their antecedents in the nineteenth-century hermeneutical tradition of Schleiermacher and Dilthey, and both appeal, to a greater or a lesser degree, to Husserlian phenomenology. Despite this, Hirsch and Gadamer represent two divergent and irreconcilable tendencies in contemporary hermeneutics. Hirsch's *Validity in Interpretation* is, in effect, a systematic attack on the version of hermeneutics worked out and defended by Gadamer in his major treatise, *Truth and Method.*[1] The principal difference between these two leading theorists is that whereas Gadamer seeks to defend what is proper to the humanities against encroachment by the ideal of "scientific" knowledge and to this end attacks the concept of "method," arguing that method, as it it is understood in the positive sciences, has no role whatsoever to play in the humanities, Hirsch, inspired by logical positivism, argues that there is or should be no significant difference between the empirical sciences and the humanities and that the hypothetical-deductive method as advocated by positivist-style philosophers of science is as applicable in the matter of literary textual interpretation as it is in the physical sciences.[2] The main thrust of Hirsch's criticism of Gadamer is that his position opens the door to arbitrariness and cannot therefore serve to make the métier of the interpreter a serious, respectable business.

This conflict is an extremely fundamental one, in that it involves two irreconcilably different theories of understanding and interpretation. It is a conflict between what could be called positivistic hermeneutics and phenomenological hermeneutics. While I do not believe that Hirsch's criticism of phenomenological hermeneutics is itself "valid" or that his version of hermeneutics can be defended and have myself taken a place in this ongoing debate by arguing against it elsewhere,[3] I do believe that Hirsch's criticism of the Gadamerian, phenomenological version of hermeneutics must be taken seriously. For only if it could be shown that phenomenological hermeneutics does *not* afford a license for arbitrariness and does in fact provide for methodological rigor in interpretation could phenomenological hermeneutics be positively argued for and defended.

The problem is that in arguing against the application of scientific method to interpretation, Gadamer has extremely little to say about what the methodological criteria of interpretation *should* be. I do not think that Hirsch is entirely without justification when he says that "Gadamer's most precise statements are those which declare what the norm is not" (*VI*, p. 251). In deliberately opposing truth to method and in saying that "a philosophical theory of hermeneutics is not a methodology" (*TM*, p. 466), Gadamer tends to give the impression that method has *no* place in interpretive understanding.[4] I do not feelthat this is the case, i.e., that there is no place for method in interpretation, and even a phenomenological thinker as close in so many ways to Gadamer as Paul Ricoeur has expressed reservations as to the satisfactoriness of Gadamer's stance.[5]

The point I wish to argue here is that while Gadamer does indeed tend to ignore the subject of what the criteria of interpretation should be, phenomenological hermeneutics, as represented by him, can provide for norms or criteria for assessing interpretations, and I wish to list of few of the more important of them. Before doing so, I should indicate why I think that the question of method is so important. There are, I think, two major reasons why an acceptable hermeneutical theory must provide for methodological criteria.

In the first place, while I agree with Gadamer that the scientific and Hirschian preoccupation with "objectivity" is itself a supreme instance of modern subjectivism, I feel that in his own reaction to subjectivism, which is influenced by Heidegger's rejection of "humanism," Gadamer does not accord enough importance to the notion of subjectivity, understood in a nonsubjectivistic sense. His key notion of "effective history" tends to privilege "what is said" over "the speaker" and tends to make of subjectivity a mere "expression" of the really active factor (the real "subject") in interpretive understanding: the Tradition itself.[6] In other words, Gadamer does not appear to make a sufficient distinction between what, in traditional terms, is referred to as the *ordo essendi* and the *ordo cognoscendi*. While, in order to counteract subjectivism, it is necessary to maintain that the Tradition, Being, or What-not has *ontological primacy* and that "in the last analysis" it is this which "expresses itself" or "comes to expression" in the understanding of the individual, it is nevertheless necessary to recognize that it is the subjectivity of the interpreter himself which has *methodological primacy*. This is necessary because only the individual, human, conscious, reflecting subject can be held *responsible* for what he or she says or does (Being, the Tradition, and so on, cannot be held accountable for what it "does"). To be responsible means to be able to respond, i.e., to be able to make an attempt at defending or justifiying one's own words and deeds, which is to say, at providing arguments for them. Now to argue is always to appeal to certain principles, the ensemble of which can be said to constitute a set of criteria. In short, correct method is necessary if interpretation is to be a responsible business.

In the second place, a viable hermeneutics must allow for method if it is to be in a position to grapple with what is after all the most urgent problem arising out of the actual work of interpretation. This problem is pinponted by Hirsch when he remarks: "Suppose, as it often happens, two readers disagree about the meaning of a text at exactly the same moment of time. What principle would they have for determining who is more nearly right?" (*VI*, p. 249). In other words, methodological criteria are needed in order to arbitrate what Ricoeur would call "the conflict of interpretations." How is one to decide which of two or more conflicting interpretations is the better, and to do so impartially, nonarbitrarily, if there are no general, recognized criteria one can appeal to? It does not suffice to say (as one sometimes gets the impression Gadamer is saying) that the criterion is "die Sache selbst."[7] This, at the very least, amounts to a *petitio principii*. It also does not enable one to come to grips with the problem of choosing between interpretations (anyone and everyone can claim that their interpretation is the meaning of the thing itself, and thus such a claim gets us nowhere). At its worst, it can provide a license for irresponsibility (why should one have to defend one's views in the forum of public opinion if they are sanctioned by the thing itself?).

A satisfactory philosophical theory of hermeneutics must therefore include, in addition to a basic theory of just what understanding is (of the sort provided by Gadamer)—and on the basis of this—an organon or set of criteria to be adhered to in the actual work of interpretation. Theory is always the theory of a certain praxis, which means that theory should be able to serve as a guide in certain concrete activities, in this case, interpreting texts. There is always a back-and-forth between theory and practice, in the sense that a theory can always be translated into a concrete procedure to be followed in practice, and also in the sense that the satisfactoriness (or lack thereof) of the practice is a measure of the truth (or falsity) of the theory. The question then is: What would be the appropriate methodological criteria for a phenomenological hermeneu-

tics? Or again: Is phenomenological *theory* such as to allow for *practical* criteria
to be derived from it?

To respond to this question, it is first necessary to indicate in general what
sort of method is compatible with a phenomenological hermeneutics, for it is
most certainly the case that method, as Hirsch understands it, the hypothetical-
deductive method of science, is not compatible with it. It seems to me that
there are two general ways of viewing method and that the second of these has
its place in a phenomenological hermeneneutics.

(1) METHOD IN AN ABSTRACT AND FORMAL SENSE. This is method in the modern
sense of the term. Method in this sense dispenses with personal, subjective
judgment (this indeed is one of its *raisons d'être*). One has only to learn the
method itself, in and for itself; it is an intellectual technique (like the "scientific
method"). Having done so, one has only to apply it to whatever subject matter
one chooses; the only criterion in applying the method is *correctness* of application (not *appropriateness* in choosing to apply it in the first place); one's
guide is the method itself, not the subject matter (such as human beings) to
which it is applied. This is assuredly a *rational* undertaking, where rationality
refers to what people like Habermas would call "instrumental rationality." The
purpose of method in this first sense is to make possible *exact* knowledge.

(2) METHOD IN A NORMATIVE SENSE. Method in this sense, far from supplanting
personal, subjective judgment or eliminating the need for it, is meant as an
aid to *good judgment* (I say "good," not "correct"). It is what ensures that
judgments or conclusions arrived at are not gratuitous or the result of subjective
whim. It therefore makes for *rational* judgments—not in the aforementioned
sense, but in the sense that one can give *reasons* (persuasive arguments) for
the judgments one makes: One can defend one's judgments or interpretations
by arguing that they embody or conform to certain generally accepted criteria,
norms, or principles. It therefore makes for *responsible* judgments. The norms
here in question could be compared to ethical norms. As moral theology teaches
us, such norms can never be simply "applied" to concrete situations where an
ethical decision is called for in such a way as automatically and unequivocally
to tell us what exactly we should do. They (much to the chagrin of medical
students and nurses, for example) do not tell us what decisions we must make
in a given case; they serve only as guiding principles in choosing among courses
of action. "Applying" them cannot, therefore, be a science but is always only
an art. Strictly speaking, they are more properly referred to as *principles* than
as *rules* (they are more like laws than like orders). Rationality here does not
consist merely in subsuming an individual under a general rule, requiring
nothing more than the recognition of the necessary and sufficient conditions
for application of the general rule. Rationality here demands interpretation, as
when a judge interprets the law in "applying" it. Unlike the methodological
norms Hirsch would like to see in place, these have no "capacity to enforce
practical decisions" (*VI*, p. 206). Thus the implication here is, again, that there
can be no *science* of interpretation, i.e., there can be no "ruthlessly critical

process of validation" (*VI*, p. 206). One cannot become a good interpreter simply by mastering a certain method. One therefore does not "test" interpretations, one *evaluates* them. The set of interpretive principles can be called a method, if by method we mean a system whose purpose it is to orient action. Method in this second sense can be defined as a rational discipline which formulates the norms for a certain procedure. Or, again, it is a norm-governed way of doing something (in distinction from arbitrary, whimsical behavior).

Understanding method in this second sense, we can ask: What are the methodological principles appropriate to, or derivable from, a phenomenological hermeneutics? I advance the following as some of the more likely candidates (wherever possible I have illustrated these "rules" with Gadamerian texts).

(a) COHERENCE. The interpretation of an author's work must be coherent in itself; it must present a unified picture and not contradict itself at points. (This rule holds true even if the work being interpreted has contradictions of its own; the interpreter must then attempt to make coherent sense of these contradictions.) —"The harmony of all the details with the whole is the criterion of correct understanding. The failure to achieve this harmony means that understanding has failed" (*TM*, p. 259).

(b) COMPREHENSIVENESS. Unlike (a), which concerns the interpretation as such, this concerns the relation of the interpretation to the work itself which is interpreted. In interpreting an author's thought, one must take account of his thought as a whole and not ignore works of his which bear on the issue. Whether or not a philosopher seeks to express, à la Hegel, a "system," the thought of any author worth interpreting—even an "unsystematic" one such as Kierkegaard—forms something like a "system," i.e., a unified whole. —" . . . the 'fore-conception of completion' . . . is obviously a formal condition of all understanding. It states that only what really constitutes a unity of meaning is intelligible. So when we read a text we always follow this complete presupposition of completion, and only when it proves inadequate, i.e., the text is not intelligible, do we start to doubt the transmitted text and seek to discover in what way it can be remedied" (*TM*, p. 261).

(c) PENETRATION. A good interpretation should be "penetrating" in that it brings out a guiding and underlying intention in the work, in this way making an author's various works or statements intelligible by seeing them as attempts to resolve a central problematic. (The need for this rule is especially apparent in the case of authors such as Heraclitus, of whom we possess only fragments).

(d) THOROUGHNESS. A good interpretation must attempt to answer or deal with all the questions it poses to the interpreted text, or which the text poses to one's understanding of it.

(e) APPROPRIATENESS. To be considered a valid interpretation of a text, the questions the interpretation deals with must be ones which the text itself raises; if one claims to be interpreting, one must not simply use the text as an occasion for dealing with questions of one's own having nothing to do with the questions the original author was concerned with.—"The real power of hermeneutical consciousness is our ability to see what is questionable" (*PH*, p. 13).

(f) CONTEXTUALITY. This principle is related to the preceding one. An author's work must not be read out of context, i.e., without due regard to its historical and cultural context. (Herein lies the usefulness for interpretation of philology, historiography, and other such disciplines.)

(g) AGREEMENT (1). An interpretation must agree with what the author actually says, that is, one must not, or normally not, say that the "real" meaning of what an author says is something quite other than what he actually does say and intends to say. (This is a principle rejected by reductive interpretations such as those of a Marxist or a Freudian variety, what Ricoeur calls the "hermeneutics of suspicion." It should be noted, however that to the degree that the suspension of this criterion enables us to see in the text things we might not otherwise have seen, and to the degree it can be buttressed by the other criteria, it is a worthwhile countertactic of reading.)

(h) AGREEMENT (2). A given interpretation should normally be in agreement with the traditional and accredited interpretations of an author. This principle must not be blindly adhered to, however, for often a good interpretation will be precisely one which breaks with traditional readings, in that it opens up new perspectives on the work. (In this case the interpretation must still take account of previous interpretations, by showing how they are deficient.) This is related to the following principle.

(i) SUGGESTIVENESS. A good understanding will be "suggestive" or fertile in that it raises questions that stimulate further research and interpretation. This is where originality finds its place in interpretation. —"It is imagination that is the decisive function of the scholar. Imagination naturally has a hermeneutical function and serves for what is questionable. It serves the ability to expose real, productive questions, something in which, generally speaking, only he who masters all the methods of his sciences succeeds" (*PH*, p. 12).

(j) POTENTIAL. The ultimate "validation" of an interpretation lies in the future. A given interpretation can be judged to be "true" if, in addition to meeting the above requirements, it (like a good metaphor or model) is capable of being extended and if in the process the implications it contains unfold themselves harmoniously (cf. in this regard what Husserl and Merleau-Ponty have to say about perception and its veracity). —"The only 'objectivity' here is the confirmation of a fore-meaning in its being worked out. The only thing that characterizes the arbitrariness of inappropriate fore-meanings is that they come to nothing in the working-out" (*TM*, p. 237).

In laying out these criteria I have not attempted, à la Hirsch or anyone else, to lay down new rules for interpretation; I have simply attempted to articulate, theoretically, the practice which is followed, I think, by most interpreters. I have simply attempted to raise to the level of theory a certain widespread practice. Nonetheless, I can anticipate a possible objection from Hirsch and others like him. The norms I have set out are so general, they will say, as to be practically useless when it comes to, as they say, sponsoring validity claims."[8] As I shall argue in a moment, this is not at all the case. I am afraid, however, that if they do not work, interpretation can never be a "serious business," for the kind of norms Hirsch advocates—ones which have "the capacity to enforce practical decisions" (*VI*, p. 203)—simply do not exist. Just as in science (as the postpositivists have come to realize) there can be no *experimentum crucis* which decisively verifies (or even falsifies) a theory, so there can be no "ruthlessly critical process of validation" (*VI*, p. 206) in interpretation. The notion that one can "test" interpretations and subject them "to scrutiny in the light of the relevant evidence" such that "objective conclusions can be reached" (*VI*, p. 206) is a purely utopian notion. There can be no *science* of interpretation. This, however, does not mean that interpretation cannot be a rigorous (if not an exact) discipline, an art in the proper sense of the term, and that one cannot rationally *evaluate* interpretations.

The problem with Hirsch is that he appears not to see that there is a difference—a most important one—between *demonstrative* or theoretical reasoning and *persuasive* or pratical reasoning, and that it is the rules of the latter, not of the former, which can and ought to serve as the method of interpretation. Hirsch is in a sense trying to base a methodology of rational behavior (textual interpretation, in this case) on a calculus of probabilities.[9] For the true humanist, however, this is unacceptable because it amounts to an uncritical acceptance of a scientific prejudice which is itself unacceptable, the prejudice, namely, that there are two and only two forms of knowledge which can lay claim to truth: absolutely certain, apodictic, fully demonstrated knowledge (of the sort found in mathematics) and, for the rest, knowledge based on the "objective" measurement of probability (conjectural or stochastic knowledge). The positivistic hermeneut fails to realize that besides this kind of decision theory there also exists what could be called a *logic of argumentation* which is something else altogether, something which is not at all concerned with the quantitative determination of probability.[10]

What are some of the principal traits of the theory of argumentation I am alluding to? What is the conception of rationality involved here?

Like demonstrative reasoning, persuasive reasoning is a method for arriving at what people like to call "the truth." What "the truth" means here is, however, *agreement* or *consensus* as to what shall be held to be true. Persuasive reasoning is a means for, as Peirce would say, the "fixation of belief," for, that is, coming to an agreement with an interlocutor as to the legitimacy of a *decision*. Persuasive or practical reasoning is what justifies or legitimates decisions.

In arguing persuasively for a given interpretation one adduces *reasons*, i.e., one appeals to certain commonly or widely accepted principles and maintains that interpretation 1, as opposed to interpretation 2, more faithfully embodies such principles. Perceiving this conformity is always a matter of *discretion*, which is to say that agreement is never coerced (as it is in deductive reasoning). Assent always remains a free choice, but it is not an arbitrary, or irrational, choice, since it is "reasons" which serve to motivate the choice (these reasons forming, as Cardinal Newman might say, the "grammar of assent").

This allusion to Newman and to the question of the rationality of religious faith is not accidental, since the theory of argumentation has played a key role in this area. The traditional theological problem of faith and reason arises out of the need to *argue* for religious belief. The typical question theologians have had to deal with is: Can choosing or opting to believe in Christianity be rationally justified, or does it amount merely to an irrational "leap of faith"? The position of Saint Augustine was that, although the truth of the Catholic faith cannot be demonstratively proven, nevertheless reasons can be given for faith after its acceptance and reasons can induce us to believe prior to our believing. In short, in practical reasoning reasons *influence* but do not *determine*; they *justify* one's decisions but do not *demonstrate* the truth or validity of them.[11]

It should be noted as well that the principles one appeals to in practical reasoning need not, like logical princples, be "universally" and "eternally" valid. They need not themselves be demonstratively proven or apodictically self-evident, such as to be binding on all men at all times and in all places. All that is required of them is that they be generally accepted by those with whom one is arguing (by one's audience, to speak in terms of rhetoric). Practical or persuasive reasoning both aims at agreement on a specific subject and presupposes a prior agreement on certain basic norms. Thus there does exist here a kind of universality, that is to say, a communality. Practical reasoning is as impossible in a normative vacuum as it is incompatible with the supposition of a determinate and eternal system of norms which would be universal in the sense of being always and everywhere the same for everyone. This is an important point, for it allows one, unlike Hirsch, to make sense of Gadamer's remark: "Being bound by a situation does not mean that the claim to correctness that every interpretation must make is dissolved into the subjective or the occasional" (*TM*, p. 359).

Practical reasoning, therefore, bases itself on recognized, commonly accepted norms and seeks, through argumentation, to legitimate new, concrete decisions. This is not a deductive procedure, nor are the norms in question simply "applied," for, and this is a most important point, the decisions one makes tend to have a retro-effect on the norms themselves. Like juridical decisions, decisions argumentatively arrived at modify in an ongoing way the norms themselves.[12] Canons simply express what, over the course of time, has become "canonical," i.e., accepted and authoritative. Canons are simply what have managed to impose themselves as normative and binding for a given, historical community of human beings. Thus temporality is as essential an element in argumentative reasoning as timelessness is in logical proof. Just as the norms or argument need not be "universally" valid, so they need not be "eternally" true (or, as Hirsch would say, "genuinely stable").

In answer to Hirsch (or his likes), I would say, therefore, that the principles I have listed above are adequate and sufficient for performing what Hirsch himself insists is the most important task in interpretation: arbitrating between conflicting interpretations. When phenomenological hermeneutics rejects the notion that there is *an* interpretation which is "correct in itself" and when it maintains that hermeneutical understanding is historical through and through, it is not providing a license for subjectivism, arbitrariness, or irrationality. One is still left with a perfectly good, intersubjectively valid basis for arguing for or against various interpretations. To argue, for instance, that interpretation 2 is more coherent, more comprehensive, and so on, than interpretation 1 is ample and sufficient reason for deciding to accept it and to take it as "true." In answer to Hirsch I would say, with Gadamer: "Thus there is a criterion here too. . . . this places hermeneutical work on a firm basis" (*TM*, p. 238).

It should be noted, moreover, that these norms are as pertinent to assessing the worth of already worked-out interpretations as they are to informing critically one's own understanding in working out an interpretation. The analogy with ethical norms holds valid here, too: Just as ethical norms enable us to assess rationally the value of accomplished deeds, so also they guide us when we ourselves are faced with the necessity of choosing or acting. For, as the great rhetorician Isocrates pointed out, "the same arguments which we use in persuading others when we speak in public, we employ also when we deliberate in our own thoughts."[13] Thus the model of practical reason does away with yet another of Hirsch's false antinomies, namely, his radical opposition between the forming of an interpretation and the assessment of it, between what he calls the "divinatory" moment in interpretation and the following, "critical" moment. Like other positivists, Hirsch says that arriving at an understanding is "unmethodical," is a mere "imaginative guess," whereas assessing interpretations involves a "high intellectual standard" and is a matter of "testing" (*VI*, p. x), and he contrasts "the whimsical lawlessness of guessing with the ultimately methodical character of testing" (*VI*, p. 204). This leads him to assert: "There can be no canons of *construction*, but only canons which help us to choose between alternative meanings that have already been constructed from the text" (*VI*, p. 204). There is, he says, no "method or model of correct interpretation" but only "a ruthlessly critical process of validation" (*VI*, p. 206). However, once we abandon the model of demonstrative reasoning as being inappropriate to hermeneutics and adopt in its stead that of persuasive or practical reasoning and view interpretation in the light of the theory of argumentation, it can be seen that arriving at an understanding is, in its own way, as methodical as the assessing of it. For a phenomenological hermeneutics, the working out of interpretations is not an altogether different process from that of evaluating or defending them; both involve methodical reasoning, although in neither case is method reducible to mere technique.

I have obviously gone beyond Gadamer in defending actively methodical reasoning in hermeneutics and in suggesting a number of specific criteria. What I wanted to show in so doing is that phenomenological hermeneutics can allow for method (the fact that I was able to illustrate a number of my "rules" with texts from Gadamer indicates that methodical norms are not ruled out by his hermeneutics) and that it can make of interpretation a serious business.[14] Now if it can do this while at the same time ridding us of the highly objectionable conceptual baggage that Hirsch has imported into the humanities from positivism, if, in short, it can make the humanities rigorous while preserving their integrity vis-à-vis the natural sciences, then this seems to me to be ample reason for accepting it as a more satisfactory methodology and theoretical basis for interpretation.

One of the central theses of phenomenological hermeneutics, derived from its theory of understanding, is that, like understanding, the object of understanding, textual meaning, has a temporal mode of being, which is to say that it is ever in the process of becoming and thus (like Merleau-Ponty's "Being") never fully *is*. It is not something fully determinate, unchanging, timeless, eternally the selfsame. I submit that this is the main reason why the model of interpretation should be sought in practical reason and not in theoretical reason, for the proper object of the former is what is contingent and changing while the proper object of the latter is what is timeless and immutable (the paramount instance of the latter being the objects of mathematics and the superlunary bodies). As Aristotle pointed out, ethics is concerned with things which "admit of much variety and fluctuation of opinion, so that they may be thought to exist only by convention and not by nature"; it is concerned with "things which are only for the most part true and with premises of the same kind to reach conclusions that are no better." And as he goes on to say, we must not, accordingly, expect from it scientific proofs, as when in mathematics we deal with things that exist of necessity.[15]

Moreover, unlike theoretical reason, whose purpose is to lead one to an insight into what simply is and which, in principle, exists as what it is independently of the knowing subject, practical reason is concerned with all those situations where one must make a choice, produce something, or decide on a course of action, the outcome of which is contingent in that it depends, precisely, on the subject oneself. This is another reason why practical reason should be taken as the model for interpretation, for interpretation is always a creative business; it is, as Gadamer says, "not a reproductive but always a productive activity."

The great advantage of taking practical reason as a model is that when one does so one is no longer plagued with the false antinomies which drive such people as Hirsch into an uncritical objectivism. At the same time, the "inner conflicts and inconsistencies" (VI, p. 247) Hirsch thinks he detects in Gadamer's theory disappear. It then becomes perfectly reasonable to maintain that, while the meaning of the text cannot be equated with "what the author meant," the interpreter cannot, for all that, simply project his or her own meaning onto the text. It becomes perfectly reasonable to say that while no interpretation can ever be shown to be the "correct" one, some interpretations are, nonetheless, clearly better than others. With practical reason as our model, it becomes perfectly reasonable to assert that while (to use Hirsch's words) there is no "genuinely stable norm," we can nevertheless make "a valid choice between two different interpretations" and are not "left with the consequence that a text means nothing in particular at all" (*VI*, p. 251).

In conclusion, therefore, I submit that while phenomenological hermeneutics cannot provide a *logic of validation* and a procedure for arriving at *"correct"* decisions in interpretation, it nevertheless does not afford a license for arbitrariness, for it can allow for a *logic of argumentation* in the light of which *rational* decisions can be made. Interpretation should be viewed as a mode of practical reasoning and of persuasive argumentation. The model for interpretation should therefore be looked for in the theory of argumentation and not in what is called the logic of (scientific) explanation. It is not to science but to *rhetoric or the theory of persuasive argumentation* that interpretation should look for its theoretical and methodological grounding. For what, throughout its long history, as long as that of science itself, to which it has always opposed an alternative conception of rationality, rhetoric has taught is that while in the realm of human affairs and action we can never be absolutely certain of anything, we can nevertheless have legitimate grounds for believing that some things are clearly better than others.

As I was able to illustrate a number of my "rules" with Gadamerian texts, so, to finish, let me appeal to Gadamer in defense of the central thesis I have here been arguing for:

> Where, indeed, but to rhetoric should the theoretical examination of interpretation turn? Rhetoric from oldest tradition has been the only advocate of a claim to truth that defends the probable, the *eikis* (verisimile), and that which is convincing to the ordinary reason, against the claim of science to accept as true only what can be demonstrated and tested! Convincing and persuading, without being able to prove—these are obviously as much the aim and measure of understanding and interpretation as they are the aim and measure of the art of oration and persuasion. And this whole wide realm of convincing "persuasions" and generally reigning views has not been gradually narrowed by the progress of science, however great it has been; rather, this realm extends to take in every new product of scientific endeavor, claiming it for itself and bringing it within its scope.
>
> The ubiquity of rhetoric, indeed, is unlimited. . . . one may go further, in view of the ubiquity of rhetoric, to defend the primordial claims of rhetoric over against modern science, remembering that all science that would wish to be of practical usefulness at all is dependent on it. (*PH*, p. 24)

Notes

This paper was originally presented to the Faculty of Philosophy of the University of Ottawa, February 8, 1980, and was subsequently read at the annual meeting of the Canadian Philosophical Association, Montreal, June 3–6, 1980.

1. E. D. Hirsch, *Validity in Interpretation* (New Haven, Conn.: Yale University Press, 1967) (henceforth cited as *VI*); H.-G. Gadamer, *Truth and Method* (New York: The Seabury Press, 1975) (henceforth cited as *TM*). A number of subsequent essays on hermeneutics has been published in Gadamer, *Philosophical Hermeneutics*, trans. D. Linge (Berkeley: University of California Press, 1976) (henceforth cited as *PH*).

2. "Conflicting interpretations can be subjected to scrutiny in the light of the relevant evidence, and objective conclusions can be reached. . . . Devising subsidiary interpretive hypotheses capable of sponsoring probability decisions is not in principle different from devising experiments which can sponsor decisions between hypotheses in the natural sciences" (*VI*, p. 206). " . . . the much-advertised cleavage between thinking in the sciences and the humanities does not exist. The hypothetico-deductive process is fundamental in both of them, as it is in all thinking that aspires to knowledge" (*VI*, p. 264).

Of Hirsch's position Paul Ricoeur has written: "Some, opposing to the work of Gadamer that of E. Betti, in whom they see the true heir of Dilthey, develop hermeneutics in the direction of a logic of proof; thus E. Hirsch . . . basing himself on the logic of probability of Keynes, Reichenback and K. Popper . . . develops a theory of 'validation' of the probable meaning, corresponding in hermeneutics to the theory of 'verification' in the empirical sciences. In this way, contact is reestablished between hermeneutics and logical positivism." *Main Trends in Philosophy* (New York: Holmes and Meyer, 1979), p. 269.

3. See my article, "Eine Kritik an Hirschs Begriff der 'Richtigkeit,' " in *Seminar: Die Hermeneutik und die Wissenschaften*, ed. H.-G. Gadamer and G. Boehm (Frankfurt: Suhrkamp Verlag, 1978), pp. 393–425 (reprinted in this volume as essay 1). Boehm is referring to this ongoing debate when he writes in the introduction (p. 8): "Die Debatte, die schon sehr früh zwischen E. Betti, E. Hirsch, später Thomas M. Seebohm u. a. auf der einen und Hans-Georg Gadamer auf der anderen Seite ausgetragen wurde, hatte die Forderung zum Inhalt, das Verhaltnis zwischen Wahrheit und Methode so zu gestalten, dass, in diesen Fall, der 'Objektivitätsanspruch der philologisch-historischen Methode' gewahrt Bleibt. Der bislang angedruckte Beitrag von G.B. Madison nimmt diese Einwände nochmals auf."

4. He does so when he says, for instance, that the work of hermeneutics "is not to develop a procedure of understanding, but to clarify the conditions in which understanding takes place. But these conditions are not of the nature of a 'procedure' or a method, which the interpreter must of himself bring to bear on the text . . . " (*TM*, p. 263). And: "Our enquiry started from our dissatisfaction with the modern concept of methodology" (*TM*, p. 421). Gadamer has all along insisted that his primary concern is not to lay down rules for interpretation but, more basically, to clarify the actual conditions under which understanding occurs. "My revival of the expression 'hermeneutics,' with its long tradition, has apparently led to some misunderstandings. I did not intend to produce an art or technique of understanding, in the manner of the earlier hermeneutics. I did not wish to elaborate a system of rules to describe, let alone direct, the methodical procedure of the human sciences. Nor was it my aim to investigate the theoretical foundation of work in these fields in order to put my findings to practical ends. . . . My real concern was and is philosophic: not what we do or what we ought to do, but what happens to us over and above our wanting and doing" (*TM*, p. xvi). He expressed the same point in a letter to Hirsch's predecessor, E. Betti: "Fundamentally I am *not proposing a method*, but I am describing *what is the case*. . . . I consider the only scientific thing is *to recognise what is*, instead of starting from what ought to be or could be. Hence I am trying to go beyond the concept of method held by modern science (which retains its limited justification) and to envisage in a fundamentally universal way what *always* happens" (*TM*, pp. 465–66).

5. According to Ricoeur, in Gadamer's work "those conclusions of Heideggerian philosophy that are not only anti-psychological but also anti-methodological are devel-

oped. There must be a choice between truth and method: whence the title *Wahrheit und Methode*. In this work, the author contrasts the power of truth which lies concealed in comprehension with any methodology, any technology which might be ascribed to the sciences of the mind. . . . This orientation of hermeneutics, firstly anti-psychological, secondly anti-methodological, ushered in a crisis within the hermeneutic movement; in correcting the 'psychologizing' tendency of Schleiermacher and Dilthey, ontological hermeneutics sacrificed the concern for validation which in the founder's world made up for the element of divination." *Main Trends in Philosophy*, pp. 268–69.

6. See the following texts: " . . . understanding is never subjective behavior toward a given 'object', but towards its effective history—the history of its influence; in other words, understanding belongs to the being of that which is understood" (*TM*, p. xix); "In fact history does not belong to us, but we belong to it" (*TM*, p. 245); "Understanding is not to be thought of so much as an action of one's subjectivity, but as the placing of oneself within a process of tradition, in which past and present are constantly fused. This is what must be expressed in hermeneutical theory, which is far too dominated by the idea of a process, a method" (*TM*, p. 258); "What we mean by truth here can best be determined again in terms of our concept of play. . . . It is worth recalling here what we said about the nature of play, namely that the attitude of the player should not be seen as an attitude of subjectivity, since it is, rather, the game itself that plays, in that it draws the players into itself and thus itself becomes the actual subjectum of the playing. What corresponds to this in the present case is neither play with language nor with the contents of the experience of the world or of tradition that speak to us, but by the play of language itself, which addresses us, proposes and withdraws, asks and fulfills itself in the answer" (*TM*, p. 446); "It is not really we ourselves who understand: it is always a past that allows us to say, 'I have understood' "(*PH*, p. 58).

The net impression one gets from texts such as these is that it is not, properly speaking, *we* who understand, that it is, rather, history or the tradition which *understands itself* in and through us. Thus it must, I think, be admitted that Gadamer is not simply undertaking what could be called a fundamental ontology of understanding which would be completely without prejudice to the question of correct understanding, i.e., method. The fact is that Gadamer incorporates into his hermeneutical theory a number of Heideggerian elements and that his concept of "effective history" parallels to a considerable extent Heidegger's notion of the "essential destiny of Being." For Heidegger, it is not man, the individual human subject, who thinks or speaks; it is, rather, language which speaks itself in man and Being which thinks itself in man, such that man's thoughts about Being are the thoughts *of* Being, thoughts belonging to Being, thoughts that Being has of itself, such that the history of human thought is actually the history of Being's self-manifestation (or self-concealment). When Gadamer speaks of "the 'language of things' " and writes "Is not language more the language of things than the language of man?" (*PH*, pp. 76–77), one is reminded of nothing so much as Heidegger's statement at the end of his *Letter on Humanism*: "Language is thus the language of Being, as the clouds are the clouds of the sky."

Gadamer has himself clearly remarked on his indebtedness to Heidegger: "The role that the mystery of language plays in Heidegger's later thought is sufficient indication that his concentration on the historicity of self-understanding banished not only the concept of consciousness from its central position, but also the concept of selfhood as such. For what is more unconscious and 'selfless' than that mysterious realm of language in which we stand and which allows what is to come to expression, so that being 'temporalizes itself'? But if this is valid for the mystery of language it is also valid for the concept of understanding. Understanding too cannot be grasped as a simple activity of the consciousness that understands, but is itself a mode of the event of being. To put it in purely formal terms, the primacy that language and understanding have in Heidegger's thought indicates the priority of the 'relation' over against its relational members—the I who understands and that which is understood. Nevertheless, it seems to me that it is possible to bring to expression within the hermeneutical consciousness itself Heidegger's statements concerning 'being' and the line of inquiry he developed out of the experience of the 'turn'. I have carried out this attempt in *Truth and Method*" (*PH*, p. 50).

It is one thing to say, as Gadamer does say, that (1) the "prejudices" that shape an individual's understanding are not "subjective" and "individualist" in that they are not freely adopted by him and are not under his conscious control but proceed from the communality that binds him to a tradition and that they constitute the historical reality of his being; it is quite another thing to say that (2) the historical consciousness of the individual is in fact the consciousness of history, where the "of" means: the consciousness that history has of itself. *If Gadamer has little to say about method, it is, I think, no accident but is due to the fact that under the influence of Heidegger (as well as of Hegel) he tends to confound assertion (1) with assertion (2).*

The issue at stake here, that, in effect, of the importance of "subjectivity," could be approached in another way, by a consideration of the phenomenological project. Phenomenology is the description of the various structures of experience as they present themselves to the conscious, reflecting subject. Phenomenology thus entails the *methodological primacy of consciousness*. This is not to say that phenomenology need necessarily be a "philosophy of consciousness" or that it tends toward subjective idealism. For in this case the method of approach is without prejudice to the object approached. Phenomenology can even allow that there is something like an *unconscious* (in the Freudian sense), but it would insist that if we are to know anything about this unconscious it can only be by means of consciousness. Husserl's error was to have "ontologized" this purely methodological primacy of consciousness. Because he was guided by the rationalist ideal of an absolute science and thus needed a *fundamentum inconcussum* on which to erect it, he was led to assert that consciousness is not only one mode or region of being (*Bewusst-sein*) but is itself absolute, is that outside of which there is nothing (*omnitudo realitatis*). Phenomenology need not, however, follow this path, which is indeed that of subjectivism (albeit of a nonpsychologistic, transcendental sort). For it could be perfectly well maintained—and on a strictly phenomenological basis (i.e., while granting methodological primacy to consciousness)—that being, not consciousness, has absolute priority, that being "transcends" irreducibly consciousness and is thus absolutely irreducible to it, that consciousness itself "belongs" (in the Heideggerian sense) to being. None of this is incompatible with holding to the methodological primacy of consciousness. In fact, it is precisely "by means of" consciousness that the ontological primacy of being is discovered and asserted (this was, precisely, the tactic of the later Merleau-Ponty). It could *even* be said that consciousness is the universal measure of all things (including being itself)—in the sense that it is the only means for sounding out the *unfathomable* depths of being.

Thus, in regard to hermeneutics, recognizing the ontological primacy of tradition and effective history does not necessarily mean that one must downplay the importance of method and subjectivity (although it does of course mean rejecting the modern, subjectivistic conception of method). Emphasis on method need not give rise to what could be called "methodologism," i.e., subjectivism. Indeed, if we are to let the thing itself speak (cf. Heidegger's "letting Being be") and not simply project onto it our own subjective fantasies and desires, then we need to *discipline* ourselves and must make a *consistent* (methodical) and *conscientious* (which means conscious) effort to *control* ourselves in our dealings with the thing. The name for this discipline is *method*.

7. For instance: "Certainly, there is here too for all understanding a criterion by which it is measured and a possible completion. It is the content of the tradition itself that is the sole criterion and expresses itself in language" (*TM*, p. 430).

8. Hirsch writes: "It may be set down as a general rule of interpretation that there are no interpretive rules which are at once general and practical. A truly general rule will fail . . . to guide us in a specific case, and a practical rule—that is, a specific and

concrete one—cannot be truly general: it may or may not lead to the valid conclusion. . . . Every practical rule of interpretation has an implicit 'unless' after it, which
means, of course, that it is not really a rule" (*VI*, pp. 202–203). Whence he concludes:
"The notion that a reliable methodology of interpretation can be built upon a set of
canons is thus a mirage."

9. See, for instance, *VI*, p. 236: " . . . no one can establish another's meaning with
certainty. The interpreter's goal is simply this—to show that a given reading is more
probable than others. In hermeneutics, verification is a process of establishing relative
probabilities."

10. Thus the reason why Hirsch thinks that there can be no methodological canons
of interpretation (see note 8 above) is because he confuses the rules of practical reasoning
with those of demonstrative reasoning. This is fully apparent in the following text, where
he equates "practical interpretive canons" with mere "preliminary probability judgments": " . . . since all practical interpretive canons are merely preliminary probability
judgments, two consequences follow with regard to their intelligent application. First,
the canon is more reliable the narrower its intended range of application. Second, since
any interpretive canon can be overturned by subsuming the text under a still narrower
class in which the canon fails to hold or holds by such a small majority that it becomes
doubtful, it follows that interpretive canons are often relatively useless baggage. When
they are general, they cannot compel decisions, and even when they are narrowly
practical, they can be overturned" (*VI*, p. 203).

Hirsch's trouble is that he wants to reduce methodology to technology and is looking
for practical rules which can *"compel"* decisions. He therefore fails to see that the rules
of practical reason have an altogether different function. They are not binding rules
capable of *compelling a choice* between different interpretations but are, instead, norms
enabling one to *argue for* a given interpretation and to *justify rationally* one's choice.

11. The history of Catholic thought in the Middle Ages is a veritable but much
underexploited mine of information for theorists of argumentation, for it was in fact an
immense workshop in which thinkers were continually attempting to arrive at a satisfactory solution to the problem of rationality in belief. What makes it so interesting is
that Catholic orthodoxy seemed to demand the impossible: The truths of revelation must
be rationally defensible but they must not be claimed to be rationally demonstrable or
discoverable by reason alone. The twin error to be avoided was irrationalism and gnos-
ticism. The problem faced by phenomenological hermeneutics today is strictly homolo-
gous: Interpretation must be shown to be a rational discipline, but it cannot be allowed
to be a science. If, then, it is not a science, but if it nevertheless is a rational discipline,
what kind of methodology is appropriate to it?

12. Herein, in the fact that decisions form precedents, lies the rationale for rule (h),
which prescribes that a given interpretation should (like a legal judgment) normally be
in agreement with traditional interpretations.

13. Isocrates, *Nicocles*, 8.

14. I should emphasize that I put forward these "rules" as suggestions only. It would
be the task of a general, philosophical hermeneutics to work out a proper organon of
methodological norms. The procedure to be followed in doing so would be twofold.
Similar to the twofold approach of Aristotle in the *Nichomachean Ethics*, one would,
on the one hand, attempt to derive practical norms from the general theory of understanding, seeking to determine what exactly it is one expects from any given interpretive
understanding, given the way, according to the theory, understanding actually does
work. In other words, by means of a kind of *transcendental (or phenomenological)
reflection* on human understanding one would ascertain what norms or criteria are
actually presupposed by any interpretation which seeks to be believed. On the other
hand, on would, by way of complement to this approach, ascertain the norms which are
in fact generally accepted by the overall community of interpreters.

15. Aristotle, *Nicomachean Ethics*, 1094 b 15–27 (Ross translation).

THREE

Husserl's Hermeneutical Contribution to the Explanation-Understanding Debate

The problem of the epistemological status of the social or human sciences is one which has been debated continuously for several decades now, especially since Wilhelm Dilthey's famous article of 1900, "The Development of Hermeneutics." It continues to give rise to a great deal of discussion and debate, as is evidenced by the forthcoming publication in English of K.-O. Apel's *Understanding and Explanation*.[1] As the title of Apel's book illustrates, the general effort of modern thought has been to reconcile somehow explanation and understanding, the *Naturwissenschaften* and the *Geisteswissenschaften*. The problem has generally been treated as a problem in the philosophy of science or the philosophy of knowledge, which is to say: epistemology.

Epistemology can be defined, in the words of Richard Rorty, "as the quest, initiated by Descartes, for those privileged items in the field of consciousness which are the touchstones of truth."[2] Epistemology is a foundational discipline, not itself a science in the narrow sense of the term, but the theory of science which secures for each and every science its legitimacy by establishing for it its foundation and method. Like Rorty, I believe that epistemology is a supreme expression and embodiment of the spirit of modern philosophy, that it is essentially a Cartesian-Kantian enterprise, and I believe as well that the categories of modern philosophy have outlived their usefulness.[3] Epistemology must give way to hermeneutics.[4] In this paper I would like to explore some of the consequences of approaching the problem of the social sciences from a hermeneutical point of view rather than an epistemological one. Such an undertaking amounts to nothing less than an attempt to discern some of the far-reaching consequences of Husserl's great archaeological-hermeneutical discovery: the *Lebenswelt*.

The *epistemological* problem of the status of the social sciences, that is, the problem of justifying the *Geisteswissenschaften* in the face of the *Naturwissenschaften* and of according to the former equal validity with the latter is one which we have inherited from Dilthey. We all know how Dilthey attempted to reconcile the two epistemic endeavors so as to secure for the *Geisteswis-*

senschaften a legitimate and respectable place in the academic pursuit of knowledge (science). Conceding, like Kant, to the *Naturwissenchaften* an exclusivity in the explanation of natural being, Dilthey sought to go beyond Kant by arguing that the *Geisteswissenschaften* must be accorded their own specific subject matter and their own equally specific method (whence his project *Critique of Historical Reason*). Basing himself on a *Lebensphilosophie*, Dilthey maintained that the proper object of the *Geisteswissenschaften* is what is specifically human, by which he meant the inner, psychic life of historical and social agents. This object dictates a specific method for the *Geisteswissenschaften*, which is that of *understanding* (*Verstehen*). To understand is not to explain causally but is, rather, to transport oneself into an alien or distant life experience, as this experience objectifies itself in documents, texts ("written monuments"), and other traces of inner life experiences and world views (*Weltanschauungen*). It is because I am a living being, a part of Life, that I can reconstructively understand other objectivations of Life. To understand is thus to *interpret*, and interpretation (*Deutung*) is the means whereby we can come to know in its own otherness what is humanly other, in effect to coincide imaginatively with it, to *relive* it. The goal of interpretation is to achieve a *reproduction (Nachbildung)* of alien life experiences. The *Geisteswissenschaften* become thereby respectable disciplines by being asssured their own unique epistemological status, as well as their own scientific objectivity. Dilthey viewed himself as doing for historical reason what Kant had done for pure reason; his task was to secure for the *Geisteswissenschaften* their epistemological "foundations." There can be a science of the subjective as distinct from the objective, but its method must be appropriately different: *Verstehen* as opposed to *Erklärung*.

Dilthey's solution to the problem of the social sciences (as I shall refer to it for the sake of brevity) is not of merely historical interest. It was in fact resurrected by Peter Winch in the 1950s and 1960s in the context of the well-known discussion in Anglo-Saxon, post-Wittgensteinian philosophy on "understanding other cultures."[5] In the wake of Dilthey, Winch drew a radical distinction between empathetic understanding and causal explanation and suggested that social science should limit itself to the former. He maintained that human or social relations are an "unsuitable subject for generalizations and theories of the scientific sort to be formulated about them."[6] He even went so far as to assert that "the concepts used by primitive peoples can *only* be interpreted in the context of the way of life of those peoples."[7]

Winch's solution to the problem of the relation between the *Naturwissenschaften* and the *Geisteswissenschaften* amounts therefore to a complete dichotomization between them. The Diltheyan-style attempt to make of Life a special and irreducible category and to set it up as the foundational justification for a special and irreducible sort of science is by that very fact, and by necessity, to oppose it to another distinct category, that of Nature, which generates another, opposed kind of science. Explanation and understanding are viewed as two different, and even antagonistic, modes of inquiry. To say that "the concepts used by primitive peoples can only be interpreted in the context of the way of life of those peoples" is to say that there is in fact no place at all for explanation in social science. The task of the latter is simply that of empathetically projecting oneself into an alien "form of life," as Wittgenstein would say. When one has empathetically described in this way a particular "language game," there is nothing more to be done.[8] A notable consequence of this way of resolving the issue is that it leads directly into cultural relativism and the idea of incommensurable paradigms. Reason itself is thereby fragmented.

Moreover, it is hard to see what this way of epistemologically sorting out the *Naturwissenschaften* and the *Geisteswissenschaften* has to contribute to resolving or arbitrating what Ricoeur would call "the conflict of interpretations." In particular, it is hard to see how it can effectively counteract the persistent "naturalistic" tendencies in the social sciences, the attempt, that is, to *explain* "consciousness" or human life forms in purely natural, causal terms. It does not suffice simply to decree that "explanation" has no place in the social sciences. If a science of man is at all possible, it must surely attempt to explain as much as it can.[9] The overriding hermeneutical question, which is not faced here at all, is that of determining the status of "explanation" itself and its place in the all-inclusive phenomenon of human understanding—and self-understanding. As we shall see later, this is the supreme task of hermeneutics when it functions as a critical reflection guided by an emancipatory interest.

The Dilthey-Winch solution to the problem of the social sciences is not only an unfortunate one, it is also an untenable one if the scientism, objectivism, and Cartesian dualism which it unquestioningly presupposes is itself questioned and no longer found acceptable.[10] And, indeed, it is Cartesianism, the nature-spirit opposition with its consequent objectivism that is the fatal victim of Husserl's radical phenomenology.

Husserl's great contribution to the debate as to the epistemological status of the social sciences was to have undermined the central categories of modern philosophy which make of the problem such an intractable one. The result of his far-reaching and radical reflections was in fact to have dissolved the *epistemological* problem itself. With Husserl the epistemological problem is dissolved because the very idea of science—the guiding ideal of modern philosophy—is called into question and discredited. To be sure, Husserl's effective contribution to the debate is not one he intended or would, no doubt, in any way have welcomed. Let us examine a bit more closely the momentous transformation in the problem effected by Husserl—in spite of himself.

Perhaps more than any other academic, professional philosopher, Husserl contributed directly to the demise of modern philosophy, of what, after Heidegger, we might want to call "metaphysics."[11] This is supremely ironic, since despite his conscientiously radical critique of the tradition, he viewed his own endeavor as an attempt to realize the inner entelechy, or *telos*, as he would have said, of this tradition. Husserl stated his philosophical goal quite clearly and unambiguously in his famous *Logos* article of 1911 ("Philosophie als strenge Wissenschaft"), and he never wavered in the pursuit of it, although he did at times undergo crises of doubt, crises from which nonetheless his faith emerged stronger and purer than ever. This goal was none other than the traditional goal of philosophy from Plato through Descartes to the present: to make of philosophy a *rigorous science*. In his *Cartesian Meditations* he explictly adopted as his own guiding idea "the Cartesian idea of a science that shall be established as radically genuine ultimately an all-embracing science."[12]

This last phrase is revealing: an all-embracing science. Husserl was at constant pains "to restore the most primoridal concept of philosophy—as all-embracing science in the ancient Platonic and again in the Cartesian sense."[13] In his eyes, phenomenology was to bring "to realization the Leibnizian idea of a universal ontology as the systematic unity of all conceivable *a priori* science."[14] He in fact defined phenomenology as "the *a priori* science of all conceivable existent beings, . . . the truly universal ontology."[15] Like the positivists, Husserl was obsessed by the idea of unified science. Like them he wanted to achieve a fundamental clarification and thereby an all-embracing unity of the sciences. It was not the positivistic project, the idea of universal commensuration, as Rorty would say, that Husserl objected to, only the positivist's way of pursuing the goal, which Husserl viewed as defective. "It is *we*," he said, "who are the genuine positivists."[16]

Husserl's conception of philosophy was thus fully traditional. Philosophy is the foundational discipline in regard to all of culture in that it adjudicates the claims to knowledge on the part of all the various modes of discourse, a task it assigns itself since it conceives of itself as the knowledge of the nature of knowledge and of the nature of the relation between mind and nature. If the word "representation" is appropriately qualified (to mean what in effect Husserl meant by "constitution"), the following remarks of Rorty's apply quite well to the way Husserl conceived of philosophy: "Philosophy's central concern is to be a general theory of representation, a theory which will divide culture up into areas which represent reality well, those which represent it less well, and those which do not represent it at all (despite their pretense of doing so)."[17] In particular, Husserl viewed all the particular sciences as forming a totality—or as having to form such a totality if the idea of science is to be fully realized—organized in a hierarchical order with phenomenology, the ultimate, self-grounding science, at its head. "In other words, *there is only one philosophy, one actual and genuine science*; and particular genuine sciences are only non-selfsufficient members within it."[18]

If, as he said in *Cartesian Meditations*, his goal was "to show the concrete possibility of the Cartesian idea of a philosophy as an all-embracing science grounded on an absolute foundation,"[19] then what Husserl needed to discover was just such an absolute foundation, a genuine *fundamentum inconcussum*. This of course, as we know, he believed that he had located in transcendental subjectivity. Husserl's relentless pursuit of "the fundamental" (to use an expression of Merleau-Ponty), his unceasing archaeological probings into the realm of transcendental life experience, led him in the end to his greatest discovery of all and one which was in fact to call into question the guiding idea of science which had led him to it: the *Lebenswelt*.

The *Lebenswelt* is nothing other than the immediate flow of unreflective life, the ground out of which arises all scientific thematization and theorizing. It is the world as we actually live it, a world, therefore, which precedes the Galilean and modern distinction between subjective and objective (primary and secondary qualities). The life-world is "the forgotten meaning-fundament [*Sinnesfundament*] of natural science."[20] It is the *prescientific* world of lived experience on which all scientific constructs are based and which they necessarily presuppose. Indeed, as Husserl again and again insisted, all scientific constructs are mere idealizations, abstractions *from* and interpretations *of* this prereflective world of immediate life. As David Carr remarks: "The scientific conception must be regarded as a view of the world, a certain way of looking at it and dealing with it which serves certain purposes."[21] The "objective" world of science is but an *interpretation* of the world of our immediate experience, the life-world, which transcends, or precedes, all objectivistic as well as all subjectivistic categories.[22]

The notion of the life-world, as that which is presupposed by all scientific theorizing, undermines the very claims of science to a mode of knowing which is truly presuppositionless and foundational. And yet Husserl seems clearly not to have wanted to accept this conclusion. Had death not put an end to his philosophical endeavors, he would undoubtedly have gone on to attempt to show how the life-world is itself something constituted in and by transcendental subjectivity. As Gadamer has remarked:

> Without any doubt the new way [through the *Lebenswelt*] leads to the old end of transcendental phenomenology, which is based in the transcendental ego. . . . This alone is rigorous science. . . . One hears there the old tones. The world of life in all its flexibility and relativity can be the theme of a universal science. . . . Nobody can doubt that here the tension between the running flux of time and life and the philosophical claim of eternal truth remains.[23]

The conclusion that Husserl was not prepared to accept is precisely the one that his successors were to draw from his work. From Husserl they learned something more than Husserl was prepared to teach. The ultimate lesson of Husserl's attempt to make of philosophy a rigorous science has been well summed up by Gadamer: "Philosophical thinking is not science at all. . . . There is no claim of definitive knowledge with the exception of one: the acknowledgement of the finitude of human being in itself."[24] This is pretty much what Merleau-Ponty, with the notion of the life-world in mind, meant earlier on by his somewhat cryptic assertion: "The most important lesson which the [phenomenological] reduction teaches us is the impossibility of a complete reduction."[25]

The consequence of philosophy's failure, its inability to make of itself a genuine and rigorous science is something we are still struggling to think today. If all scientific theorizing is but a matter of idealizing and interpreting a prescientific experience which does not contain within itself, and thereby neither dictates nor conclusively legitimates, any theories about it, what becomes of the philosophical-scientific attempt to express the "objective truth of things"? Does not everything become a matter of interpretation? Are we not obliged to agree with Nietzsche when he proclaimed that all being is interpreted being?[26] Certainly epistemology, as the foundational discipline guaranteeing to each particular science and mode of human discourse its quota of objective truth, would appear to be decisively discredited.

Since I cannot, here, possibly hope to put to rest once and for all the claims of epistemology, I shall simply ignore them, trusting that the moribund body of philosophical science will sooner or later be buried with the respect it deserves. Supposing, simply for the sake of argument, that in what we continue to call "philosophy" we have to do not with "objective realities and truths" but with idealizing interpretations and creative language games, there would still remain a great deal for "philosophers" to do. The name for this activity is *hermeneutics*. I shall attempt to indicate how hermeneutics may in fact have something to contribute to the problem of reason as it is instanced in the conflict between explanation and understanding, the *Naturwissenschaften* and the *Geisteswissenschaften*.

For the sake of the present discussion I shall understand hermeneutics to mean, very broadly, that reflective inquiry which is concerned with, in the words of Gadamer, "our entire understanding of the world and thus . . . all the various forms in which this understanding manifests itself."[27] Moreover, I accept here Gadamer's thesis as to "the essential linguisticality of all human experience of the world."[28] "Language," as he says, "is the fundamental mode of operation of our being-in-the-world and the all-embracing form of the constitution of the world."[29] If one accepts this, then it is clear that the proper object of hermeneutics is all the various language games by means of which people come to some understanding of the world and of themselves.[30]

When hermeneutics is defined in this way it is obvious that the natural sciences fall within the scope of hermeneutics, which is truly universal. It is obvious that science, whatever epistemological pretensions it may harbor, is one particular language game that humans engage in. It is, to be sure, a most momentous one, since it is not, like much of speculative metaphysics, an idle game but one that has extremely far-reaching consequences for the organization of our collective lives and for the mode of our being-in-the-world, which is to say, for our self-understanding. One of the concerns of hermeneutics in its emancipatory function is in fact to bring to consciousness those possibilities of being that the scientific-technological project, by reason of its necessary methodological abstraction from lived experience, necessarily conceals and closes off.

The hermeneutics of science is in no way a rival discipline to the traditional philosophy or epistemology of science. The latter is simply a metascientific, ancillary discipline which, for rhetorical or argumentative purposes, seeks to specify the supposed conditions under which utterances of a scientific sort can lay claim to "truth." Unlike traditional "philosophy of science," hermeneutics is not concerned with the so-called truth-value of science, but seeks simply to determine the actual mode in which scientific understanding occurs, the ways in which scientific theories (interpretations and idealizations of experience) are in fact put forward, defended, and believed in.

The revolutionary approach to science instituted above all by Thomas Kuhn typifies this kind of inquiry. Kuhn is representative of a current movement of thought which, as Richard Bernstein observes, can be seen "as contributing to the demise of the Cartesianism that has dominated and infected so much of modern thought."[31] What in particular Kuhn succeeded in undermining is the Cartesian view which has blinded philosophers of science to the way in which science is actually practiced (philosophers of science have traditionally ignored the hermeneutical question as to what scientists are actually doing, concentrating instead on the epistemological question as to what the criteria are which must be met if science is to count as a genuine "representation" of reality, "justified belief").[32] Kuhn's work, which he subsequently came to realize merits the label "hermeneutics," has had for its effect to throw open the whole question as to what "reason" in the case of science actually amounts to. Kuhn has drawn our attention to the essentially judgmental quality of scientific rationality. Scientific reasoning is not a matter of induction or deduction or demonstrative reasoning culminating in the adequate theoretical representation of "objective" reality but is, instead, in terms of actual scientific praxis, a matter of *interpretation* and *persuasion*.

This means, for one thing, that scientific reason is finally understandable only in terms of a speaking and writing community of people who are bound together and informed (in the literal sense of the term) by a particular *historical* and *cultural* tradition in terms of which alone their collective, conversational endeavor has meaning. Science is one particular way in which humans tell stories and refigure the world of lived experience, and the rules of this particular narrative genre or language game are determined not by nature but by culture. Now since the diverse ways in which people narrate the world is the proper object of hermeneutics, it follows that the inquiry into science is ultimately not a scientific or even epistemological undertaking but is, above all, a hermeneutical one.

This has important implications for the status of the social sciences, for, that is, their status vis-à-vis the natural sciences. When we take up a hermeneutical point of view, it becomes apparent that the human sciences are not only not reducible or even subordinate to the natural sciences but that the latter are in fact a proper object for the former, that the former in a sense encompass the latter. The passage from epistemology to hermeneutics, which in the discussion regarding science is what Kuhn in effect accomplished, has for one of its consequences to subvert the relation of dependency customarily supposed to exist between the two kinds of science. While from a merely epistemological point of view, the social sciences are indeed less methodologically secure, less well grounded, and less "scientific" than the natural sciences, from a hermeneutical point of view it is precisely the human sciences which enable us better to understand the exact significance of the natural sciences. If our ultimate goal is not simply to construct theoretical-instrumental interpretive theories about the natural world—whose ultimate "validity" lies in the enhanced power they confer on us to control the course of natural events— but if what we desire above all is to understand better what kind of self-understanding we may hope to achieve in this way, then the human sciences prove to be indispensable tools for attaining greater understanding.

What, for instance, the *sociology of science* can teach us is the actual meaning of "explanation" (scientific rationality) and its relation to "understanding." Simply by way of indicating what is at stake here, let me quote Rom Harré:

> That a sociological account of some paradigmatically rational discourses is essentially correct has been supported by the recent work of Latour and Woolgar, *Laboratory life*, and that of Knorr-Cetina, *The Manufacture of Knowledge*, on the way that the messy results of scientific research are brought together with fragments of the existing recognized corpus of scientific knowledge to create a scientific paper. These authors make a good case for the idea that "logic" is an artful insertion into a discourse through the effect of a collective criticism and evaluation of the structure of the paper during its composition. Its presence is called for by the practical necessity to cope with debates and disputes with other scientists, who will use accusations of "illogicality" to denigrate the contributions of their rivals. It is suggested that "logic" is not involved in the primary cognitive activity of "doing science."[33]

To realize that 'logic' is not involved in the primary cognitive activity of 'doing science' is to realize something very important. It discredits completely the prehermeneutical, epistemological account of science, typified, for instance, by R. B. Braithwaite, who defined science as "a deductive system . . . which is arranged in such a way that from some of the hypotheses or premises all the other hypotheses logically follow."[34] This epistemological account of science has been exposed for the myth it is by the physicist Gerald Holton of Harvard University in his investigations into the history of modern science, investigations which are themselves neither scientific nor epistemological but *Geisteswissenschaftlich*. As in the work Harré refers to, Holton, on the basis of his distinction between private science and public science, has sought to show how "scientific rationality" is in fact something imposed upon the results of individual research at the moment when a scientist addresses himself to the community of scientists, seeking their approval. As Holton says: " . . . in formalizing an individual contribution for publication, it is part of the game to cover up the transition from the private stage, to make the results in retrospect appear neatly derived from clear fundamentals."[35]

Hermeneutical inquiries such as these into the natural sciences on the part of the social sciences have a potentially very important lesson to teach regarding the status of the social sciences themselves, the relation between "understanding" and "explanation." It would be the task of philosophical hermeneutics to articulate what manifests itself here. The lesson seems to be something like this: Scientific "explanation" is not something opposed to, or more basic than, understanding. Scientific, causal, naturalistic explanations are simply one way of narrating the world, of ordering the chaotic flow of experience. Explanation is one particular language game, with its own rhetorical rules of genre, that humans have invented in order to achieve a sense of *understanding*. Scientific explanations are themselves interpretations of a sort, ones, however, which have the peculiar characteristic that in them the human subject or the author of the discourse does not show through.

On the face of it, explanation does appear to pose a threat to understanding. For a purely explanatory approach to human affairs is—whatever form it may take (physicalistic, structuralist, and so on)—inevitably reductionistic. To "explain" the human or the personal is to give an account of it in terms which are neither human nor personal (there are a great variety of subpersonal ways of accounting for personhood to choose from: materialist, physiological, environmental, behavioristic, cybernetic, logico-structuralist, functionalist, and so on). The curious fact about seeking understanding solely by means of explanation is that such an attempt makes it absolutely impossible to achieve any kind of genuine self-understanding, since the self is precisely that which eludes all explanation. As Husserl very pointedly observed in his famous Vienna lecture: " . . . the working subject is himself forgotten; the scientist does not become a subject of investigation."[36] As he also said:

> Our surrounding world [the *Lebenswelt*] is a spiritual structure in us and in our historical life. Thus there is no reason for him who makes spirit as spirit his subject matter to demand anything other than a purely spiritual explanation for it. And so generally: to look upon the nature of the surrounding world as something alien to the spirit, and consequently to want to buttress humanistic science with natural science so as to make it supposedly exact, is absurd.
>
> What is obviously also completely forgotten is that natural science (like all science generally) is a title for spiritual accomplishments, namely, those of the natural scientists working together; as such they belong, after all, like all spiritual occurrences, to the region of what is to be explained by humanistic disciplines. Now is it not absurd and circular to want to explain the historical event "natural science" in a natural-scientific way, to explain it by bringing in natural science and its natural laws, which, as spiritual accomplishment, themselves belong to the problem?[37]

Given the methodological naiveté of what Husserl calls "naturalism," it is understandable why Winch, for instance, should resist attempts to incorporate explanation into the social sciences and should maintain that we can hope to understand what is human only if we resist all attempts to explain it.

There can be no doubt that at the present time there are conflicting tendencies within the social sciences. While the anthropologist Clifford Geertz has attempted to work out what he calls an "interpretive theory of culture,"[38] other social scientists, who would like to approximate in their disciplines the "rigor" and "exactitude" that they imagine characterize the natural sciences, have continued to elaborate various purely naturalistic, reductionist strategies of an epistemological sort. The ongoing attempt to formulate a coherent cybernetic account of human consciousness and agency is a case in point.

And yet hermeneutical reflection clearly reveals the ultimate absurdity of all such attempts to conceive of understanding in purely explanatory terms. Can the scientist who attempts to explain everything that is in the world for him explain in this way his own attempt to explain everything? Can the neurophysiologist explain neurophysiology neurophysiologically? What is always left out in all attempts at total explanation is the *self* who does the explaining, the living discourse out of which are generated these explanations. Explanation, then, cannot explain understanding. It is simply one way in which people attain to a partial understanding of what it means for them to be, what it means that they are beings who exist in the mode of discourse and understanding.

From a hermeneutical point of view, therefore, explanation is not something purely and simply opposed to understanding nor is it something that could ever substitute completely for understanding. It is, rather, a legitimate, and no doubt necessary, stage in understanding whose ultimate goal is nevertheless always self-understanding. That branch of the *Geisteswissenschaften* known as interpretation theory or, more generally, literary criticism provides a useful model of what is involved here.

From the point of view of phenomenological hermeneutics, the task of textual interpretation is not to discover the psychological intentions of an author[39] but to explicate the type of being-in-the-world unfolded in and through the text. The ultimate goal of textual interpretation is the appropriation (*Aneignung*) of the text in the reading experience.[40] That is, it is that of actualizing the meaning of the text as it is addressed to a reader; the ultimate significance of the text is the heightened self-understanding that the reader acquires by means of his or her dialogical encounter with the text.

While the ultimate goal of interpretation is, therefore, "understanding," there is nevertheless, for phenomenological hermeneutics, a legitimate place for "explanation" in the reading process. For the initial stage in textual interpretation is precisely that of analyzing the text in terms of its formal organization, its internal relations, its structure. At this level of reading one will engage in a semiotic analysis of the text's linguistic and structural features and will, as well, take account of historical and philological, i.e., empirical, data. In short, one will will attempt to "explain" it as much as is possible.[41]

"Explanation" never furnishes us with the decisive "truth" about the text, however. Indeed, once epistemology is called into question, it becomes obvious that the traditional notion of truth is bound up with the modern subject-object dichotomy that epistemology, as well as all attempts at explanation, presuppose. When, as in hermeneutics, the modern conception of subjectivity (and objectivity) is abandoned and when, accordingly, the reader is viewed as a knowing player in the game of refiguration of the world that is occurring in the text, it becomes clear that, as Mario Valdés of the Centre for Comparative Literature at the University of Toronto says, "understanding must be self-understanding, that the truth of the text is in fact the truth of ourselves, or to put it in critical terms, the truth of the literary text is the world which it unfolds in the reader's appropriation."[42]

From a hermeneutical point of view, therefore, *interpretation* [*Deutung*], which Dilthey subsumed wholly under "understanding" (and which he thereby opposed to explanation), is not in fact something opposed to explanation. While it is true that the ultimate goal of all interpretation (whether of texts or lived experience) is self-understanding, and while it is true that such understanding irremediably transcends all forms of explanation, it is nevertheless clear, from the example of literary criticism, that explanatory procedures have their legitimate place in the overall interpretive process. They form one segment of what Ricoeur calls the *hermeneutical arc*.[43]

Over and above its crucial role in instituting universal mastery over nature, scientific explanation which, as Nietzsche observed, "may be the right imperative for a tough, industrious race of machinists and bridge-builders,"[44] is simply a limited and, ultimately, deficient way in which humans attempt to understand their place in nature ("Qu'est-ce que l'homme dans la nature?" as Pascal asked, is the overriding question for man). Explanation poses no problems for understanding when it is recognized for the partial, nontotalizable mode of understanding it is. The human sciences enjoy a unique and irreducible status vis-à-vis the natural sciences, not because they deal with a different object—"man" or "mind" as opposed to "nature"—but because in them the *self*, which is both the origin and the goal of all interpretations and all attempts at understanding, which is to say also, of all explanation, is no longer dissimulated behind the veil of methodological abstractions and "objective truths," behind the "garb of ideas" [*Ideenkleid, Kleid der Symbole*] that, as Husserl said, science throws over the life-world.

The ultimate significance of the discovery of the life-world for the social sciences is that it thoroughly discredits the natural-science model that for so long captivated the attention of social scientists and that, indeed, still continues to do so to a certain extent. The proper object of the social sciences is not primarily the validation and testing of hypotheses and theories designed to explain and predict social phenomena. Indeed, the proper object of the social sciences are not *facts*, in the scientific-positivistic sense of the term, but *interpretations*, the various means by which human beings achieve for themselves an understanding of what it means for them to be. The essential vocation of anthropology, for instance, is, as Clifford Geertz has said, "not to answer our deepest questions [the existential dilemmas of life], but to make available to us answers that others, guarding other sheep in other valleys, have given, and thus to include them in the consultable record of what man has said."[45]

Hermeneutics is not a science, and it is not epistemology, if by science one means, as the modern *epistemē* meant, the "correct" *representation* of "objective" reality and if by epistemology one means, as one usually does, a theoretical discipline whose function is to determine the epistemic conditions that must be met if any given discipline is to lay claim to truthful statements about reality. Hermeneutics is, rather, the reflective recognition of the finitude of all human claims to knowledge, of the historical and cultural relativity of all forms of human discourse. It is the rejection, the deconstruction, of what Rorty calls "the idea of universal commensuration." It is thus a rejection of the age-old metaphysical prejudice of "science."

Hermeneutics, it can therefore be seen, is part of the postmodern rejection of philosophy in the traditional metaphysical-epistemological sense of the term. However, unlike certain other forms of postmodern thought, such as post-structuralism or deconstruction, hermeneutics seeks to overcome not only objectivism but (to use Richard Berstein's term) relativism as well, including the nihilism that seems to accompany inevitably the latter. For hermeneutics, relativism is only the obverse, indeed the perverse, side of modern objectivism. Hermeneutics seeks not so much to reject the notion of reason and its universalist pretensions as it seeks to reconstruct radically our idea of what it means to be rational. For hermeneutics, to speak of "rationality" is simply an indirect way of referring to "the essential linguisticality of all human experience," which means: the fact that, when they so desire, humans can mediate their unending differences through conversation and dialogue aiming at agreement and common understanding.

Because of its essential linguisticality, that is, because there is no such thing as an ideal language which could ensure the commensurability of all partial discourses, human understanding is necessarily finite and pluralist. However, a hermeneuticist such as Gadamer does not see in this inescapable fact a justification for cultural relativism and the idea that human understanding is irremediably fragmented into a multitude of incommensurable, uncommunicating paradigms. In contrast to the cultural and epistemological relativists, Gadamer reminds us that although understanding is language-bound, "this assertion does not lead us into any kind of linguistic relativism."[46] As he goes on to say:

> While we live wholly within a language, the fact that we do so does not constitute linguistic relativism because there is absolutely no captivity within a language—not even within our native language . . . Any language in which we live is infinite in this sense [in that it opens us to the infinite realm of possible expression], and it is completely mistaken to infer that reason is fragmented because there are various languages. Just the opposite is the case. Precisely through our finitude, the particularity of our being, which is evident even in the variety of languages, the infinite dialogue is opened in the direction of the truth that we are.[47]

The supreme task of hermeneutics as a critical, emancipatory endeavor is precisely that of maintaining this openness of human discourse. "The primary human reality is persons in conversation," as Rom Harré says.[48] It is only through this ongoing conversation that anything like self-understanding is at all possible. Conversation, as Rorty says, is "the ultimate context in which

knowledge is to be understood."[49] The overriding task of philosophy conceived
of as hermeneutics is, therefore, as Rorty would say, that of sustaining and
furthering "the conversation of mankind."

Here hermeneutics joins up with, and reveals itself to be a continuation of,
the ancient, countertraditional tradition of *dialectics*. Ever since Protagoras and
the Greek sophists and rhetoricians, dialectics (in a strictly non-Platonic sense)
has amounted to the rejection of philosophy conceived of as a monological
enterprise, as the Platonic communion of the private, solitary soul with objective essences, of the frozen and authoritarian discourse of metaphysics. In the
place of monologue it seeks always and everywhere to institute dialogue, which
is precisely that which liberates us from the authoritarian claims of those-who-
are-in-the-know, who believe that they have somehow transcended the merely
human "realm of opinion." To conclude this paper I can do no better than to
quote the fine words of Pierre Aubenque in his article "Évolution et constantes
de la pensée dialectique":

> As the guardian of a higher rationality than scientific and technical rationality, it
> [dialectics] denounces the unreason that is concealed in the pretension on the part
> of the latter to reduce being, and along with it all aspects of human life, to what
> is objectifiable in them, which is to say ultimately to what is mathematizable in
> them . . . It thereby preserves intact, over and beyond momentary particular-
> izations and configurations, future possibilities for thought. . . . Dialectics is nei-
> ther science nor intuition: people engage in dialogue only to the degree that they
> do not see the being of which they speak and yet are not resigned to reducing it
> to the unilateral experience they have of it. . . . without the demand for [constant]
> overcoming which it upholds and with which it guides our conscience, there would
> have been in history neither spiritual mutations nor scientific revolutions nor per-
> haps even social and political revolutions. Without it, there would be no room in
> the current field of thought other than for an accumulation of fragmentary bits of
> knowledge and for no other kind of philosophy but that of their positivistic justi-
> fication. Finally, in the practical order, it alone can counteract the modern and
> subtle forms of oppression that, in the name of a certain cult of scientificity, are
> concealed in the increasing functionalization of social life.[50]

Notes

This paper was originally composed at the request of Klaus Nellen of the Institut für
die Wissenschaften von Menschen in Vienna, for inclusion in a projected volume on
the relevance of the notion of the life-world for the social sciences. Before being sent
off to Vienna, it was presented as a talk to the Philosophy Colloquium of Queen's
University (Kingston, Ontario), Fall 1985.

    1. Karl-Otto Apel, *Understanding and Explanation* (Cambridge, Mass.: MIT Press,
1984).

2. Richard Rorty, *Philosophy and the Mirror of Nature* (Princeton, N.J.: Princeton University Press, 1979), 210.

3. Rorty asks "whether there still remains something for epistemology to be" and says, "I want to urge that there does not" (ibid., p. 210).

4. Or, as Rorty says: " 'Hermeneutics,' as a polemical term in contemporary philosophy, is a name for the attempt to do so [to set aside epistemologically centered philosophy]" (ibid., p. 357). He says of his own position: "I am *not* putting hermeneutics forward as a 'successor subject' to epistemology, as an activity which fills the cultural vacancy once filled by epistemologically centered philosophy. . . . 'hermeneutics' is not the name for a discipline, nor for a method of achieving the sort of results which epistemology failed to achieve, nor for a program of research. On the contrary, hermeneutics is an expression of hope that the cultural space left by the demise of epistemology will not be filled" (ibid., p. 315). With this I fully agree (my expression "give way to" should not be read as "be replaced by").

5. See, for instance, the following writings of Winch: *The Idea of a Social Science and Its Relation to Philosophy* (London: Routledge and Kegan Paul, 1958); and "The Idea of a Social Science" and "Understanding a Primitive Society," both in *Rationality*, ed. B. R. Wilson (New York: Harper Torchbooks, 1971). Richard Bernstein writes: " . . . Winch's arguments about the logical gap between the social and the natural can be understood as a linguistic version of the dichotomy between the *Naturwissenschaften* and the *Geisteswissenschaften*. Even the arguments that he uses to justify his claims sometimes read like a translation, in the new linguistic idiom, of those advanced by Dilthey" (*Beyond Objectivism and Relativism* [Philadelphia: University of Pennsylvania Press, 1983], p. 30).

6. Winch, "The Idea of a Social Science," p. 15.

7. Winch, "Understanding a Primitive Society," p. 95 (emphasis added).

8. According to Wittgenstein, when one is confronted with a form of life, all that one can say is: "*This language-game is played*" (*Philosophical Investigations* [Oxford: Basil Blackwell, 1963], par. 64). As he also says: "The question is not one of explaining a language-game by means of our experiences, but of noting a language-game" (ibid., par. 655).

9. The famous English anthropologist E. E. Evans-Pritchard, who clearly did not advocate reductionist explanations, nonetheless observed: "Even in a single ethnographic study the anthropologist seeks to do more than understand the thought and values of a primitive people and translate them into his own culture. He seeks also to discover the structural order of the society, the patterns which, once established, enable him to see it as a whole, as a set of interrelated abstractions. Then the society is not only culturally intelligible, as it is, at the level of consciousness and action, for one of its members or for the foreigner who has learnt its mores and participates in its life, but becomes sociologically intelligible. . . . the social anthropologist discovers in a native society what no native can explain to him and what no layman, however conversant with the culture, can perceive—its basic structure. This structure cannot be seen. It is a set of abstractions, each of which, though derived, it is true, from analysis of observed behaviour, is fundamentally an imaginative construct of the anthropologist himself. By relating these abstractions to one another logically so that they present a pattern he can see the society in its essentials and as a single whole" (*Social Anthropology and Other Essays* [New York: Free Press, 1971], pp. 148–49; see also ibid., pp. 61–62). For a further discussion of this and related issues, see G. B. Madison, *Understanding: A Phenomenological-Pragmatic Analysis* (Westport, Conn.: Greenwood Press, 1982).

10. Gadamer speaks of an "inconsistency at the heart of Dilthey's thought" and attributes this to "his latent *Cartesianism*" ("The Problem of Historical Consciousness," sec. II: The Importance and Limits of Wilhelm Dilthey's Work, *Graduate Faculty Philosophy Journal*, New School for Social Research, Fall 1975, p. 20). At the end of his discussion of Dilthey, Gadamer remarks: "Dilthey's effort to understand the human

sciences through life, beginning from lived experience, is never really reconciled with the Cartesian concept of science which he did not know how to throw off. Emphasize as he might the contemplative tendencies of life itself, the attractions of something "solid" that life involves, his concept of "objectivity," as he reduced it to the objectivity of "results," remains attached to an origin very different from lived experience. This is why he was unable to resolve the problem he had chosen: to justify the human sciences with the express purpose of making them equal to the natural sciences" (ibid., p. 23). This text has been reprinted in *Interpretive Social Science: A Reader*, ed. P. Rainbow and W. Sullivan (Berkeley: University of California Press, 1979).

11. Ludwig Landgrebe, Husserl's late assistant and the compiler of Husserl's *Experience and Judgment*, says in this regard: " . . . in the later *Crisis* Husserl found himself forced to strike out on a new path (whose novelty is once again partially obscured by the self-interpretation he gave it); . . . here, before the eyes of the reader, occurs the shipwreck of transcendental subjectivism, as both a nonhistorical *apriorism* and as the consummation of modern rationalism. Today primarily as a result of Heidegger's work, the "end of metaphysics" is spoken of as if with a certain obviousness. We shall first properly understand the sense of such language if we follow closely how, in this work, metaphysics takes its departure behind Husserl's back. One can state quite frankly that this work *is* the end of metaphysics in the sense that after it any further advance along the concepts and paths of thought from which metaphysics seeks forcefully to extract the most extreme possibilities is no longer possible. To be sure, neither Husserl nor those who were his students at that time were explicitly aware of this, and it will still require a long and intensive struggle of interpretation and continuing thoughtful deliberation until we have experienced everything that here comes to an end" ("Husserl's Departure from Cartesianism," in *The Phenomenology of Husserl*, ed. R. O. Elveton [Chicago: Quadrangle Books, 1970], p. 261 ["Husserls Abschied vom Cartesianismus," *Philosophische Rundschau* IX, 1962]).

12. Husserl, *Cartesian Meditiations*, trans. D. Cairns (The Hague: Martinus Nijhoff, 1960), § 3, p. 7.

13. Husserl, "Phenomenology" (*Encyclopaedia Britannica* article), reprinted in *Phenomenology and Existentialism*, ed. R. Zaner and D. Ihde (New York: G. P. Putnam's Sons, 1973), p. 68.

14. Ibid., p. 66.

15. Ibid.

16. Husserl, *Ideas*, trans. W. R. B. Gibson (New York: Collier Books, 1962), § 20, p. 78.

17. Rorty, *Philosophy and the Mirror of Nature*, p. 3.

18. Husserl, *Formal and Transcendental Logic* (The Hague: Martinus Nijhof, 1969), § 103, p. 272.

19. Husserl, *Cartesian Meditations*, § 64, p. 152 [p. 178].

20. See Husserl, *The Crisis of European Sciences and Transcendental Phenomenology*, trans. D. Carr (Evanston, Ill.: Northwestern University Press, 1970), § 9.

21. David Carr, *Phenomenology and the Problem of History* (Evanston, Ill.: Northwestern University Press, 1974), p. 131.

22. As Carr observes: "Husserl's actual descriptions of the life-world at this stage in his argument proceed primarily by way of contrast to the mathematized world of the scientist. The scientific method is not an instrument for improivng our *sight*, something invented during the Renaissance along with the telescope, which enables us to put aside the world of appearances for good. It was and remains an idealizing construction *based upon* what is seen, and what is *seen* remains ever the same whether or not we are scientists who are engaged in such idealization. Above all, the life-world is a world of objects having both primary and secondary qualities, a world whose spatial features fall into vague and approximate types, not a world of geometrical idealities. While science operates with abstractions, the life-world is the concrete fullness from which these

abstractions are derived; science constructs, and the life-world provides the materials of construction; the ideal character of scientific entities precludes their availability to sense-intuition, while the life-world is the field of intuition itself, the 'universe of what is intuitable in principle,' the 'realm of original self-evidences,' to which the scientist must return in order to verify his theories. Science interprets and explains what is given; the life-world is the locus of all givenness. The emphasis here is on the *immediacy* of life-world experience in contrast to the mediated character of scientific thought. The life-world is prior to science, prior to theory, not only historically but also epistemologically, even after the advent and rich development of scientific theory in the West" (ibid., pp. 136–37).

23. Gadamer, "The Science of the the the Life-World," in *Analecta Husserliana*, ed. Tymieniecka (Dordrecht: D. Reidel, 1972), vol. 2: pp. 183–84.

24. Ibid., p. 185.

25. Maurice Merleau-Ponty, *Phenomenology of Perception* (London: Routledge and Kegan Paul, 1962), p. xiv.

26. In *Beyond Good and Evil* (trans. W. Kaufmann [New York: Vintage Books, 1966], § 14), Nietzsche remarked: "It is perhaps just dawning on five or six minds that physics, too, is only an interpretation and exegesis of the world (to suit us, if I may say so!) and *not* a world-explanation; but insofar as it is based on belief in the senses, it is regarded as more, and for a long time to come must be regarded as more—namely, as an explanation."

27. Gadamer, "On the Scope and Function of Hermeneutical Reflection," in *Philosophical Hermeneutics* (Berkeley: University of California Press, 1976, p. 18.

28. Ibid., p. 19.

29. Gadamer, "The Universality of the Hermeneutical Problem," in ibid., p. 3.

30. I use the word *understanding*, not *knowledge*, since *understanding* is a word which is phenomenologically intelligible in that it refers to a phenomenon in lived experience with which we are all familiar, whereas the word *knowledge* is a metaphysical-epistemological concept of dubious reference and usefulness.

31. Bernstein, *Beyond Objectivism and Relativism*, p. 71.

32. Kuhn's approach to science reflects the shift in hermeneutical theory as a whole away from the Enlightenment-Romantic tradition represented by Schleiermacher, Dilthey, Betti, and Hirsch, which is epistemological in the traditional sense to the movement of phenomenological hermeneutics represented by Gadamer, which is not a *de jure* inquiry into transcendental conditions of possibility but which seeks instead to determine what actually is the case and what has actually occurred when we claim to have understood.

33. Rom Harré, *Personal Being* (Cambridge, Mass.: Harvard University Press, 1984), p. 120. The works alluded to by Harré are B. Latour and S. Woolgar, *Laboratory Life* (Los Angeles: Sage, 1979) and K. Knorr-Cetina, *The Manufacture of Knowledge* (Oxford: Pergamon, 1981).

34. R. B. Braithwaite, *Scientific Explanation* (Cambridge, Eng.: Cambridge University Press, 1968), p. 12.

35. Gerald Holton, *Thematic Origins of Scientific Thought* (Cambridge, Mass.: Harvard University Press, 1973), p. 388.

36. Husserl, *The Crisis*, p. 295.

37. Ibid., pp. 272–73.

38. Geertz, *The Interpretation of Cultures* (New York: Basic Books, 1973).

39. See my article, "Eine Kritik an Hirschs Begriff der 'Richtigkeit,' " in *Seminar: Die Hermeneutik und die Wissenschaften*, ed. H.-.G. Gadamer and G. Boehm. (Frankfurt: Suhrkamp Verlag, 1978) (reprinted in this volume as essay 1).

40. See Paul Ricoeur, "Appropriation," in Ricoeur, *Hermeneutics and the Human Sciences*, ed. J. B. Thompson (Cambridge, Eng.: Cambridge University Press, 1981).

41. See Ricoeur, "What Is a Text? Explanation and Understanding," in ibid., p. 152,

where Ricoeur says: "What we have called the eclipse of the surrounding world by the quasi-world of texts engenders two possibilities. We can, as readers, remain in the suspense of the text, treating it as a worldless and authorless object; in this case, we explain the text in terms of its internal relations, its structure. On the other hand, we can lift the suspense and fulfil the text in speech, restoring it to living communication; in this case, we interpret the text. These two possibilities both belong to reading, and reading is the dialectic of these two attitudes." See also ibid., p. 158, where Ricoeur says that the goal of "interpretation" is *appropriation*, by which he means "that the interpretation of a text culminates in the self-interpretation of a subject who thenceforth understands himself better, understands himself differently, or simply begins to understand himself."

42. Mario Valdés, "The Phenomenological Hermeneutics of Paul Ricoeur as a Basis for Literary Criticism," unpublished paper (subsequently published in *Revue de l'Université d'Ottawa/University of Ottawa Quarterly*, vol.55, no.4, 1985; see p.124; this issue of the *Revue* comprises papers presented at the international conference held in honor of Ricoeur, "À la recherche du sens/In Search of Meaning," University of Ottawa, October 1983). As Ricoeur himself says: " . . . explanation is nothing if it is not incorporated as an intermediary stage in the process of self-understanding" ("What Is a Text?" p. 159).

43. See ibid., p. 161.

44. Nietzsche, *Beyond Good and Evil*, § 14.

45. Geertz, *The Interpretation of Cultures*, p. 30. In regard to the matter of "facts," Geertz says: " . . . what we call our data are really our own constructions of other people's constructions of what they and their compatriots are up to" (ibid., p. 9). Geertz explicity compares the task of the ethnographer with that of the literary critic and says: "Doing ethnography is like trying to read (in the sense of 'construct a reading of') a manuscript . . . " (ibid., p. 10). Geertz acknowledges his indebtedness to the work of Ricoeur.

46. Gadamer, "The Universality of the Hermeneutical Problem," p. 15.

47. Ibid., pp. 15–16.

48. Harré, *Personal Being*, p. 58.

49. Rorty, *Philosophy and the Mirror of Nature*, p. 389.

50. Pierre Aubenque, "Évolution et constantes de la pensée dialectique," *Les Études philosophiques*, juillet-septembre 1970, p. 301.

FOUR

Merleau-Ponty and Postmodernity

1

"Know thyself!" Ever since Socrates the admonition of the Oracle at Delphi has been been the admonition of philosophy itself and has conferred upon it its inescapable task. For the philosophizing subject, the subject who is reflexively conscious of himself, the task of responding to this admonition means that he must ask who in fact he is and how, precisely, he is conscious of himself as an existing subject. What does that mean? How is that possible? What does it mean to be a subject who is conscious of his own existence as a subject?

Philosophical inquiry has always been concerned with the problem of personal identity, using this term in a loose (nonanalytic) sense. And ever since antiquity the problem of personal identity has tended to be approached in terms of the metaphysical-anthropological problem of the union of body and soul (mind). (This has had for its effect to obscure the genuine philosophical problem, which is the hermeneutical one of self-understanding and personhood.) The mind-body problem (as we now call it) has been debated without letup by philosophers—without much success, it must be admitted.

At the beginning of the modern era, when the great and audacious syntheses of medieval philosophy had lost much of their persuasive power for thinking people, Pascal wrote:

> Who would not think, to see us compounding everything of mind and matter, that such a mixture is perfectly intelligible to us? Yet this is the thing we understand least; man is to himself the greatest prodigy in nature [*le plus prodigieux objet de la nature*], for he cannot conceive what a body is, and still less what mind is, and least of all how a body can be joined to a mind. This is his supreme difficulty, and yet it is his very being.

And then he added, quoting Saint Augustine, that unique individual who had his feet in two worlds, that of antiquity and that of premodernism: "The way in which minds are attached to bodies is beyond man's understanding, and yet this is what man is."[1]

An incomprehensible state of affairs, indeed, the more one thinks about it. And it does not appear that much progress in clarifying the matter has been made in philosophy since Pascal's time. It could even be said that the Cartesianism which permeates all of modern philosophy has made of the problem of the union of body and mind one which is altogether incapable of being resolved.

Indeed, if the terms "corporeal" and "spiritual" or "psychic" are taken to designate two kinds of substances—extended things and thinking things— which by reason of their own proper nature, i.e., conceptually speaking, are absolutely distinct from one another, how could they possibly ever be united so as to form not a mere juxtaposition of two disparate things but, as is— phenomenologically speaking—obviously the case, one single thing enjoying its own proper reality, namely, the human person? This mysterious unity can be brought about only through some kind of miracle—by divine fiat. However, to accord the secret to God is to take it away from men—who are most in need of knowing it. The outcome of Cartesianism is to set up, on the one hand, a totally objective nature which is fully intelligible in itself—since it is but matter in motion whose laws are capable of being discovered by the objective sciences of nature—and, on the other hand, conscious subjects who are nothing but pure interiorities and who, because they are but gazes [*regards*] *on* nature existing nowhere *in* this nature which is fully intelligible in itself, cannot be intelligible for themselves or the objects of any objective science.

A single word can serve to designate the essence of modern thought from Descartes to Sartre: *dualism*. And the result of dualism is *alienation*: the alienation of subject from object, of the psychic from the corporeal, and thus of man from nature as well as from his own proper nature. A consciousness which is alienated from itself is a consciousness which is split within itself, and such a consciousness, as we know from Hegel, is an unhappy consciousness.

The question which, with increasing vehemence, seems to be everywhere forcing itself on us today is: Is there any possibility or hope that postmodern humanity might discover the way of escaping from the unhappiness which is the result of the rupture between the subjective and the objective, the self and the world, the corporeal and the psychic, instituting thereby a new era in the history of thought? There is every indication that today philosophy is increasingly taking this to be its central task.

When one finds oneself in an impasse, as modern thought seems indeed to find itself, it is often because somewhere along the way a wrong turn was made. In such a situation the only remedy is to retrace one's steps. This is what psychoanalysis does in regard to the disoriented individual who has lost track of his own identity. By forcing him to relive the distorting experiences of his past, it enables him to make a new start in life.

What is to Husserl's great merit is that he sought to apply this kind of treatment to modern man. In the work he began on the eve of his death, *The Crisis of European Sciences and Transcendental Phenomenology*, Husserl undertook the project of a veritable *archaeology* of modern consciousness. The aim of this archaeology was to clarify the origin "of the modern opposition between physicalistic objectivism and transcendental subjectivism."[2] "What is clearly necessary," he said, " . . . is that we *reflect back*, in a thorough *his-*

torical and *critical* fashion, in order to provide, *before all decision*, for a radical self-understanding."[3] This *Rückfrage* on his part amounted to a veritable *deconstruction* of modern philosophy. In the words of his English translator and interpreter, David Carr: "It is an attempt to relive the tradition of which we are a part for the purpose of liberating us from the prejudices that are inherent in that tradition."[4]

One thing that Husserl succeeded in discovering through his archaeological investigations is how the origin of modern dualism coincides with the emergence of modern science and its viewing of nature as a self-contained world of mere, corporeal bodies. The consequence of this way of viewing nature is, so to speak, to split the world of ordinary, prescientific experience into two worlds, physical nature and the realm of the psychic:

> In general, we must realize that the conception of the new idea of "nature" as an encapsuled, really and theoretically self-enclosed world of bodies soon brings about a complete transformation of the idea of the world in general. The world splits, so to speak, into two worlds: nature and the psychic world, although the latter, because of the way in which it is related to nature, does not achieve the status of an independent world.[5]

"Natural-scientific rationality" thus makes possible psychology in the modern sense of the term whose object is the "psychical," as opposed to the "physical." The development of this psychology from Descartes through the British empiricists up to contemporary experimental psychology amounts to the development of a struggle between *objectivism* and *transcendentalism*. In the eyes of Husserl, phenomenology's historical vocation in this regard is to resolve this conflict by showing how the so-called objective world is precisely not self-sufficient but is rather something that is entirely relative and which in fact has its origin in transcendental subjectivity. It is the latter which itself constitutes the *Seinssinn* of the world, "the 'objectively true' world." The world of objectivistic science is nothing more than a structure of transcendental consciousness.[6]

We might well wonder, however, if Husserl genuinely overcame modern dualism or if he did not rather simply substitute for a dualism of substances (body, mind) an epistemological dualism (objectivism, transcendentalism). To be sure, naturalistic objectivity is in Husserl absorbed into transcendental subjectivity which is thenceforth conceived of as *omnitudo realitatis* or, as Husserl said in *Ideas*, the *only* universe which exists—all of which, it must be admitted, constitutes a kind of modern-style reductionism (corresponding to physicalism's reduction of the subjective to the objective). All forms of reductionism, nevertheless, presuppose dualism, conceptually speaking, and thus do not overcome it. It can therefore legitimately be wondered if Husserl's transcendental idealism which accords the decisive privilege to transcendental subjectivity is, when all is said and done, any more satisfactory than an objectivistic materialism which makes of consciousness a mere epiphenomenon of a physical body.

It would appear that Merleau-Ponty did not think so and that he was put off by Husserl's transcendental idealism. It is clear that he could not accept the notion of a transcendental Ego which does everything, which constitutes everything—in the first instance its own body as a wordly thing.[7] It is likely that the difficulty Husserl ran into in the Fifth Cartesian Meditation of defending himself in a fully convincing way against the objection of solipsism sufficed to convince Merleau-Ponty that Husserl's transcendental idealism was still a form of subjectivism—and thus a prisoner of modern dualism. He might well have said of Husserl what in fact he did say of Sartre: "For Sartre, it is always *I* who forms depth, who hollows it out, who does everything, and who closes from within my prison in upon myself—"[8]

For Merleau-Ponty there was never any question of a sovereign transcendental Ego or even, as Husserl would have said, of a "soul" or "spirit" which is somehow directly accessible by means of "internal perception." Referring in fact to Husserl, he stated: " . . . there is no inner man, man is in the world, and only in the world does he know himself."[9] And what his first great work, *Phenomenology of Perception*, aimed to show was that there is absolutely no dualism between me and my body, between this body that in fact I am and the world which it inhabits and animates, and between me and the other.

If modern dualism is but the result of a certain arbitrary way of viewing the world, if it is in fact the product of scientific abstraction and idealization, as in *Crisis* Husserl quite accurately said it was, then the rediscovery of the *Lebenswelt* underlying the objectifying thought of science furnishes us with the means of overcoming modern dualism. This is precisely the lesson Merleau-Ponty drew from Husserl. However, Husserl's (never fulfilled) aim was to go on to show how the *Lebenswelt* is itself the product of a constituting Ego, and this is something Merleau-Ponty refused to accept.

By reason of his attempt to overcome definitively modern dualism and subjectivism, Merleau-Ponty is fully a part of the mainstream philosophical current of our times. His philosophical effort is in this respect allied with that of Heidegger. One could even go so far as to ask whether Merleau-Ponty's attempt to overcome modern dualism does not make of him a postmodernist. The question is whether or not by destroying the primacy of consciousness and by deconstructing the Cogito, by insisting on the priority of the unreflected over reflection and on the fact that consciousness is not a constituting power but is rather given to itself out of the obscure life of the body, out of a polymorphous flesh which is a kind of confused anonymity and generality, Merleau-Ponty was not in fact a herald of that mode of thought which has flourished after his death and which has assigned itself the task of deconstructing the very notion of subjectivity, throwing overboard in the process all of modern thought and, in the first instance, the very idea of the rational and autonomous human subject, that is to say, "man."

Certain sociologists have used the term "postmodern" to refer to this mode of thought. Representatives of it everywhere abound at the present time. One such is the American writer Norman O. Brown, who in his books *Life against*

Death and *Love's Body* has celebrated polymorphous perversity and has proclaimed the superiority of the pleasure principle over the reality principle,
instinct over reason. Brown's effort was to dethrone consciousness in favor of
the dream. For him the essential thing was to dissolve the self into the body,
to eradicate all limitations, boundaries, and distinctions—between the self and
the body, between man and woman, between subject and object, between the
psychic and the physical, between man and nature. In his eyes these divisions
amounted to the Original Fall, the fall into divisions and lies, and what he
sought was the abolition of "all dualisms."

Michel Foucault, Jacques Derrida, Jean-François Lyotard, Gilles Deleuze,
and other poststructuralists and French Nietzscheans exemplify in their own
way various trends in postmodernity. What characterizes much of postmodernity is its refusal of all distinctions and all divisions—for example, between
body and spirit, the physical and the mental, reason and the irrational, the
intellectual and the sensual, the self and the other, nature and culture, reality
and utopia. On the one hand a rejection of order, limits, restrictions, the control
and *mesure* of reasonable consciousness, the apollonian and, in general, what
up to our times people generally referred to as "civilization," it is, on the other
hand, a celebration of the dionysian, delirium, the oneiric, the erotic, libidinal
sensuality, the instinctive and the spontaneous, narcissism. Being antinomian
and anti-institutionalist, utopic and anarchic, an appeal for the suppression of
oppressive consciousness, liberation of the instincts, emancipation of sensuality,
it forms a ready alliance with political radicalism.

The question I would like to consider here is how we should interpret
Merleau-Ponty's rejection of modern dualism and subjectivism. How, more
than twenty years after his death, should we situate him in regard to contemporary thought? Since human understanding is always retroactive (we live forward but understand backward, as Kierkegaard said), the way we understand
what was is by situating it in relation to what then did not yet exist, in relation
to what in fact has followed it in time and now is. Should we then view Merleau-
Ponty as a precursor of postmodernistic thinking? Or, on the contrary, should
we interpret his critique of modernism in quite another way, so as not to make
of him a mere "proto-poststructuralist"?

2

In his very first book, *The Structure of Behavior*, Merleau-Ponty assigned
himself the task "of understanding the relations of consciousness and nature."[10]
In other words, the relations between the objective and the subjective, the
exterior and the interior, the corporeal and the psychic. This problematic was
to remain the central problematic of all of his subsequent work. Let us therefore
take a brief look at how in his first two works the younger Merleau-Ponty
responded to the question.

It is worth noting, first of all, that in *The Structure of Behavior* he explicitly
dealt with the classical problem of the union between *soul* and *body*. And what

he categorically rejected was the idea that what is involved here is the union of two substances or two orders of reality, two worlds, as Husserl would say. This is to say that he completely relativized soul and body and insisted that they have absolutely no reality in and of themselves. What they are is rather two variable terms of a single structure which is nothing other than existence itself. The relation between the two is entirely dialectical: "It is not a question of two *de facto* orders external to each other, but of two types of relations, the second of which integrates the first" (*SB*, pp. 180–81).

It is nonetheless important for us to note that if here Merleau-Ponty rejects all *dualism* he is not for all that advocating a simple *monism*. The integration of body and soul is in no way a *fusion*. To be sure, there are not two substances in the human being, yet the human being is not a rigidly monolithic entity. There does indeed exist a "soul" and a "body," but the body is a *human* body only by being the very foundation of the soul, the visible expression of a "spiritual" life, and the soul is a soul only by means of a body which is, as it were, its own manifestation. Between soul and body there is something like a tensional polarity, and the total human being is nothing other than this tension which is continually renewed. Thus, if Merleau-Ponty categorically denies here all *dualism* in the human being, he nonetheless still insists that that there is a certain *duality* to that being. "There is always a duality," he says, "which reappears at one level or another." This is to say that "integration is never absolute and it always fails—at a higher level in the writer, at a lower level in the aphasic" (*SB*, p. 210).

It is also important to note that if soul and body are entirely relative and are but two moments of a single structure or Gestalt, this structuration is nevertheless *vertical*. This is to say that "soul" designates that which, at whatever level, pertains to what is superior in human behavior, "body" designates that which pertains to what is inferior. [11]

It is just as important to note that, in opposition to a certain persistent tendency in thought, Merleau-Ponty never attempts to explain the superior in terms of the inferior. The advent of the superior suppresses what is autonomous in the inferior by integrating it into an enlarged and more finely structured behavior. [12] Just as Husserl insisted that abnormality is but a variant of normality (and not the reverse, as some postmodernists would maintain), [13] Merleau-Ponty maintains that the abnormal and the pathological must be understood in terms of so-called normal behavior.

The conclusion we should draw from this is that at this time Merleau-Ponty had absolutely no intention of abolishing "all dualisms," at least in Norman O. Brown's sense of the term. How do matters stand in regard to the *Phenomenology of Perception*?

When one reads the report of the conference Merleau-Ponty gave under the title "The Primacy of Perception and Its Philosophical Consequences," in which he discussed the main theses of the *Phenomenology*, it is clear that many of his listeners thought that he wanted to dissolve the Cogito in the anonymous existence of the body—in the *Lebenswelt*—and that he was denying the existence of the rational, autonomous subject. Did he not want to celebrate what he called "la spontanéité enseignante du corps" at the expense of the arduous work of rational reflection?

The Merleau-Ponty of the *Phenomenology* was nevertheless not an advocate for the irrational or the unreflected, and it is a bit ironic that some sought to criticize his central project, that of reflecting on the unreflected as such, by saying that it was a contradiction in terms, since the moment the unreflected is laid hold of by reflection it ceases to be, precisely, unreflected. It is impossible to return to and coincide with the unreflected as such. The irony is that Merleau-Ponty never proposed to make reflection coincide with the unreflected. His philosophy was a properly reflective philosophy, in the strict sense of the term, and he never maintained that the important thing is to return to merely lived experience in order to remain there. Philosophy was for him a reflective enterprise, thus something altogether different from experience straightforwardly lived-through in an unreflective way. What he wanted to do was something properly apollonian; he did not want to renounce reason but wanted rather to enlarge it. Referring to Hegel, that great Apollo of modern times, he said that "the task of our century" is "to explore the irrational and integrate it into an expanded reason."[14] What he wanted to understand was rational consciousness itself—insofar, precisely, as it possesses itself only on the basis of an unreflected existence from which it emerges, but which it also transcends (which is to say, therefore, to which it is absolutely irreducible).

The two following texts say just about everything that needs to be said on the subject:

> Assuredly a life is not a philosophy. I thought I had indicated in passing that description is not the return to immediate experience; one never returns to immediate experience. It is only a question of whether we are to try to understand it. I believe that to attempt to express immediate experience is not to betray reason but, on the contrary, to work toward its aggrandizement.[15]

> Far from thinking that philosophy is a useless repetition of life I think, on the contrary, that without reflection life would probably dissipate itself in ignorance of itself or in chaos.[16]

Since by his own account he was working for the enlargement (*agrandissement*) of reason and was opposed to the dissipation of consciousness in ignorance of self and in chaos, the younger Merleau-Ponty, we are obliged to conclude, was in no way a prophet of that new Dionysus, postmodernistic man, the man who seeks to dwell in the realm of dream and desire and who is at last liberated from the tyranny of self-consciousness (which means, of course, the consciousness of his separation from himself, from nature, and from others).

3

Can we say as much for the later Merleau-Ponty? Is it not rather the case that in *The Visible and the Invisible* everything has been turned upside down and set adrift? Does he himself not say there that it is necessary for philosophy to "recommence everything (*tout reprendre*), reject the instruments reflection and intuition had provided themselves, and install itself in a locus where they have not yet been distinguished, in experiences that have not yet been 'worked over,' that offer us all at once, pell-mell, both 'subject' and 'object,' both existence and essence, and hence give philosophy resources to redefine them" (*VI*, p. 130)? When he recognized the "Necessity of a return to ontology," an "ontology of brute Being" (*VI*, p. 165), to the "barbaric principle which Schelling spoke of," was it not all dualisms that he then wanted to overcome, and in a decisive way?

In any event, it is evident that he believed that this new ontological interrogation would have important ramifications on "the subject-object question," "the question of inter-subjectivity," "the question of Nature" (*VI*, p. 165). Is it thus not the case that in plunging into "the basement of phenomenology"[17] of consciousness, into the obscure realm of the unconscious (whose existence he had formerly, somewhat like Sartre, denied), Merleau-Ponty found himself on the other side of the barricade, the other side of all philosophy of consciousness and of subjectivity itself? It seems that this was more or less the impression Sartre had. "In one sense," the latter said, "nothing in the ideas that he defended in his thesis [*PhP*] has changed; in another sense everything is unrecognizable. He has plunged into the night of non-knowledge [*non-savoir*], in quest of what, now, he calls the 'fundamental.'"[18] Is it possible that in the end Merleau-Ponty had become a disciple of that great precursor of postmodernity, Baudelaire, who had written at the end of his poem *Le Voyage*:

Nous voulons, tant ce feu nous brûle le cerveau,
Plonger au fond du gouffre, Enfer ou Ciel, qu'importe?
Au fond de l'Inconnu pour trouver du *nouveau*!

In any event, to the new "fundamental" that Merleau-Ponty discovered in his descent into the basement of consciousness he gave a name: the *flesh*. It is undeniable that the flesh is not simply another name for what traditional philosophy has called the body; "one knows," he said, "that there is no name in traditional philosophy to designate that" (*VI*, p. 139), to designate what this philosophically unheard-of word is meant to designate: the flesh. Thus the exploration of the flesh was inevitably to lead Merleau-Ponty to some "extravagant consequences" (*VI*, p. 140).

It was in fact to lead him to a kind of philosophical monism beyond all dualisms. Being neither the objective body nor the body which the soul thinks of as its own, the flesh is rather the sensible itself, "the sensible in the twofold sense of what one senses and what senses" (*VI*, p. 259). The flesh is the formative milieu of both the corporeal and the psychic, of object and subject; it is the undivided Being (*l'Être d'indivision*) existing before the consiousness-object split. It is the "generality of the Sensible in itself, this anonymity innate to

Myself" (*VI*, p. 139). In a working note of November 1960 Merleau-Ponty wrote:

> The *antecedent* unity me-world, world and its parts, parts of my body, a unity before segregation, before the multiple dimensions—and so also the unity of time— Not an architecture of noeses-noemata, posed upon one another, relativizing one another without succeeding in unifying themselves: but there is first their underlying bond by *non-difference*—. (*VI*, p. 261)

The discovery of the flesh calls for nothing less than a "complete reconstruction of philosophy" (*VI*, p. 193). Philosophy can no longer be mere psychological reflection or even transcendental reflection (*VI*, p. 158). The entire vocabulary of traditional psychological reflection is to be rejected. "We must, at the beginning, eschew notions such as 'acts of consciousness,' 'states of consciousness,' 'matter,' 'form,' and even 'image' and 'perception' " (*VI*, pp. 157–58). In his late philosophy, Merleau-Ponty even goes so far as to reject the key term of his earlier thought, *perception*!

What he calls for is a "complete reconstruction" of our language itself. "Language is a power for error," he says, "since it cuts the continuous tissue that joins us vitally to the things and to the past and is installed between ourselves and that tissue like a screen" (*VI*, p. 125). Postmodernist thought is perhaps right in thinking that subjectivity and language are inseparably bound together and that if the former is to be abolished, the latter must be radically transformed. What Merleau-Ponty sometimes appears to be saying at this late moment in his life is that the language philosophy must search for is "a language of coincidence, a manner of making the things themselves speak. . . . It would be a language of which he [the philosopher] would not be the organizer, words he would not assemble, that would combine through him by virtue of a natural intertwining of their meaning, through the occult trading of the metaphor [*le trafic occulte de la métaphore*]—where what counts is no longer the manifest meaning of each word and of each image, but the lateral relations, the kinships that are implicated in their transfers and their exchanges." Is not this language which has been liberated from the stranglehold of calculative and manipulative consciousness, from its clear and distinct meaning-intentions, this metaphorically wild language which speaks when to all appearances nothing is really said, which speaks in occult suggestions, is this not precisely that language fashioned by those philosophers and writers who have come to occupy the front stage of our culture since Merleau-Ponty's death? Is not the "complete reconstruction" called for by Merleau-Ponty that complete destruction wrought by various postmodernists?

However that may be (we shall return to the question), it is necessary to recognize that the discovery of the flesh and of brute or wild being led Merleau-Ponty to say things which from a traditional point of view are indeed "*extravagant*." He says, for instance, that "the things have us, and that it is not we who have the things. . . . That language has us and that it is not we who have language. That it is being that speaks within us and not we who speak of being" (*VI*, p. 194). The point of view of the speaking and thinking *subject* seems at last to have been fully left behind: " . . . things *are said* and *are thought* by a Speech and by a Thought which we do not have but which has us."[19]

Even the idea of man seems to have dropped out of the picture, since it is no longer he who, strictly speaking, *does* anything. "It is not we who perceive, it is the thing that perceives itself yonder—it is not we who speak, it is truth that speaks itself at the depths of speech— Becoming-nature of man which is the becoming-man of nature—" (*VI*, p. 185). As in postmodernity, the distinction man/nature seems to have been abolished and man is reintegrated into *la nature naturante*. Anthropology has been deconstructed. "When we speak of the flesh of the visible," he insists, "we do not mean to do anthropology . . . " (*VI*, p. 136). Merleau-Ponty's late philosophy would indeed seem to be no longer a philosophy of man but the thought of a polymorphous or amorphous being, a being of promiscuity and transitivism.[20] Merleau-Ponty states that his philosophy would have to work itself out "without any compromise with *humanism*" and that "*the visible* has to be described as something that is realized through man, but which is nowise anthropology" (*VI*, p. 274).

An overcoming of all dualisms of this sort would be such as to effect a cure for the unhappiness of modern consciousness brought about by subjectivism and the separation of consciousness from Nature, which is "the flesh, the mother" (*VI*, p. 267), "polymorphic matrix" (*VI*, p. 221), "Being in indivision [*Être d'indivision*]" (*VI*, p. 208), "*pregnancy* of possibles" (*VI*, p. 250). A cure by means of a return to the maternal womb and to the union before separation.

In this way that most painful separation of all would be overcome, the separation between the self and the other. "There is here no problem of the *alter ego*," he says, "because it is not *I* who sees, not *he* who sees, because an anonymous visibility inhabits both of us, a vision in general . . . " (*VI*, p. 142); "there is transitivism by way of generality" (*VI*, p. 269). Myself and the other, "we function as one unique body" (*VI*, p. 215); "he and I are like organs of one single intercorporeality" (*S*, p. 168). If there is a break," he says, "it is not between me and the other person; it is between a primordial generality we are intermingled in and the precise system, myself–the others" (*S*, p. 174). What basically exists is a "corporeality in general," which, like "the child's egocentricity," is "transitivity and confusion of self and other" (*S*, p. 174). As civilized adults who have learned to view our lives "as a series of private states of consciousness" (*S*, p. 175), we have also "learned to distribute the pains and pleasures in the world among single lives. But," Merleau-Ponty insists, "the truth is not so simple" (*S*, p. 175). Thus his conclusion: "We must conceive of a primordial *We [On]* that has its own authenticity and furthermore never ceases but continues to uphold the greatest passions of our adult life and to be experienced anew in each of our perceptions" (*S*, p. 175). Husserl's "egology" and "sphere of ownness" are thereby dissolved in favor of "attaches primordiales." And thus "the compresence of my 'consciousness' and my 'body' is prolonged into the compresence of my self and the other person"; the presence of me to myself and the presence of me to the other are "substitutable in the absolute presence of orgins" (*S*, p. 175). The flesh is therefore not *my* flesh or *your* flesh but the indivisible flesh of the world, of a brute and wild Being, of the Earth Mother which englobes us all.

Time itself, lastly, is abolished, the time of the man who is wakeful and conscious of himself, the source of all distinctions and all suffering, the *Es war* of Nietzsche, origin of resentment. "It is a question of finding in the present, the flesh of the world (and not in the past) an 'ever new' and 'always the same'— A sort of time of sleep. . . . The sensible, Nature transcend the past present distinction, realize from within a passage from one into the other   Existential eternity. The indestructible, the barbaric Principle" (*VI*, p. 267).[21]

Such, then, is the philosophically unusual and, indeed, extravagant mode of discourse adopted by the later Merleau-Ponty. It must be admitted that it is such as to be somewhat disconcerting for a philosophy of the subject which, while rejecting—like Merleau-Ponty—modern dualism and subjectivism, refuses nonetheless to be drawn into the postmodernistic dissolution of the subject itself—which, indeed, refuses to believe that the concept of "self" is nothing more than an arbitrary and groundless creation of the modern *epistemē*. The moment has therefore arrived to raise the question as to the exact signficance of the later Merleau-Ponty's seeming rejection of "all dualisms."

What must first be noted in this regard is that if Merleau-Ponty wanted— as, indeed, it is clear he did—to overcome decisively modern dualism, there is yet no evidence to indicate that he was prepared to deny all dualities and to abolish all distinctions (viewing them, as postmodernists would, as artificial, repressive limitations imposed on the fullness of lived experience). The flesh is not the key notion of a philosophy of Identity beyond all Difference. To say that two things are inseparable is not to say that they are one and the same thing. It is true, of course, that the flesh is not the "body" (as modernism calls it). It is, rather, that which contains both the corporeal and the psychic; it is the unique reality of which soul and body, subject and object are but "total parts." If, however, one can even speak of "total parts," it is because the words *corporeal* and *psychic* still retain a meaning; they continue to designate something—not, to be sure, two substances[22] but, rather, two irreducible *dimensions* of a being which is conceived of as dimensionality itself. The flesh is nothing other than the fact that between the psychic and the corporeal, between the subject and its body, between it and the world, between the self and the other, there exists a relation of circularity and even of reversibility. However, reversibility is not coincidence. "It is time to emphasize," he wrote, "that it is a question of a reversibility always imminent and never realized in fact." When one of my hands touches the other when it is in the process of touching a thing, "I never reach coincidence." This coincidence is always aborted, and thus there remains something like a "hiatus" between the two sides of the lived body (*le corps propre*), the "subject" side and the "object" side (*VI*, p. 147).

In his late philosophy, therefore, Merleau-Ponty does not attempt to *suppress* the subject-object duality. Rather, he *overcomes* it by conceiving of the intentional relationship, the relationship consciousness-object, as one which takes place inside of Being itself, a Being which in its own regard transcends the consciousness-object distinction.[23]

If, then, there exists neither identity, fusion, nor coincidence between the psychic and the corporeal, the goal of philosophy itself cannot be that of enabling us to coincide with "the absolute presence of origins." Its task cannot be that of effectuating a fusion with the sensible, with an undivided Being (*un Être d'indivision*) beyond the subject-object split. We are thus perhaps in a position now to understand that strange passage in *The Visible and the Invisible* where Merleau-Ponty spoke of "a language of coincidence" and said that the philosopher must deliver up his language to the "occult traffic of metaphor" (*VI*, p. 125). Indeed, at the end of this passage he added a remark which I did not quote above and which changes everything. If the philosopher lays claim to a language of this sort, "we have to recognize," Merleau-Ponty says, "the consequence: if language is not necessarily deceptive, truth is not coincidence, nor mute" (*VI*, p. 125).

It would thus appear that Merleau-Ponty was in no way proposing that the philosopher "should keep silent, coincide in silence, and rejoin in Being a philosophy that is there ready-made" (*VI*, p. 125). The situation would actually seem to be something quite different for him. The language of the reflective subject is not a *coinciding* with the flesh but rather its *sublimation*, which is something else altogether. The thematization of perceptual meaning (*sens*) or of the *Lebenswelt*—the goal of philosophy—must be understood as "a behavior of a higher degree" (*VI*, p. 176). There is, he says, a dialectical relation between the silence of the origins and the language of reflection: "language realizes, by breaking the silence, what the silence wished and did not obtain" (*VI*, p. 176). And as he also says, in as clear a way as could be desired, the "very description of silence rests entirely on the virtues of language. The taking possession of the world of silence, such as the description of the human body effectuates it, is no longer this silence, it is the world articulated, elevated to the *Wesen*, spoken" (*VI*, p. 179). The silence which follows upon language is not the silence which precedes it; it is a product of the work of reflection. Philosophy, therefore, is not useless, mere subjectivistic vanity, since, without it, one would not *know* what our inherence in the flesh of the world *means*.

Merleau-Ponty had no intention, therefore, of suppressing self-consciousness, reflection, science, and philosophy. He was no harbinger of the movement toward antiphilosophy. In a working note entitled "Science and philosophy," in which he attacks modern scientism and the philosophy of *Erlebnisse*, the philosophy of mere consciousness, he also attacks, significantly enough, that "primitivism" so celebrated by postmodernistic opponents of the scientific ideal. He writes:

> The search for the "wild" view of the world nowise limits itself to a return to precomprehension or to prescience. "Primitivism" is only the counterpart of scientism and is still scientism. The phenomenologists (Scheler, Heidegger) are right in pointing out this precomprehension which precedes inductivity, for it is this

that calls in question the ontological value of the *Gegen-stand*. But a return to prescience is not the goal. The reconquest of the *Lebenswelt* is the reconquest of a *dimension*, in which the objectifications of science themselves retain a meaning and are to be understood as *true*. . . . —the pre-scientific is only an invitation to comprehend the meta-scientific and this last is not non-science. It is even disclosed *through* the constitutive movements of science. . . . (*VI*, p. 182)

Because he had no desire to suppress scientific and philosophical reflection, he had, as well, absolutely no intention of suppressing what he had called "the thought of the subjective." He had, in other words, no intention of rejecting that *subjectivity* which was the great discovery of modern philosophy. He was quite clear on this score. In a reference to Heidegger, who, as is well known, castigated "humanism" and wanted to get rid of subjectivity or self-consciousness since, as he thought, it conceals Being from us, Merleau-Ponty insisted, on the contrary: "the thought of the subjective [*la pensée du subjectif*] is one of these solids that philosophy will have to digest. Or let us say that once 'infected' by certain ways of thinking, philosophy can no longer annul them but must cure itself of them by inventing better ones. . . . There are some ideas which make it impossible for us to return to a time prior to their existence, even and especially if we have moved beyond them, and subjectivity is one of them" (*S*, p. 154). There is no absolutely no trace in Merleau-Ponty of any question as to "the death of man," and, unlike a number of postmodernistic thinkers, he did not talk about ridding us of self-consciousness.

Indeed, he seems fully to have realized that the malaise of contemporary man is not something for which one can, or should, attempt to find a definitive "cure." While it is both possible and desirable to undo certain distortions in our self-consciousness, to overcome certain forms of alienation and to render human relations freer and less opaque, it is neither possible nor desirable to overcome alienation as such. To be alienated, separated from oneself, to be, as it were, a stranger to oneself, to be at odds with, indeed, not only ourselves but with nature and and with others as well—this is the very definition of what it means to be human. It could perhaps be said with Hegel that a split consciousness may possibly be said to be an unhappy consciousness and man may be, as Nietzsche said, the "sick animal," but because animals, while they might in one sense be said to be "conscious," are nevertheless not self-conscious, i.e., conscious of themselves as something *other* than the world of which they are a part, are neither happy nor unhappy. They simply are—and are nothing other than what they are. Moreover, they are not conscious of a *Welt* but exist merely in an *Umwelt*. If humans did not experience unhappiness—which means, if they were not animated in their being by the realization that it is always possible for them to be more and to be other than whatever they simply happen to be and if they were not conscious of the fact that the world in which they exist could be other than it is—they would not be human. While utopianism is, on the whole, simply the manifestation of a deluded consciousness, the fact remains that only the human being constructs utopias.

Nor would humans be human were they not "rational," as the ancients fully realized when they defined the human animal as *animal rationale, zoon logon ekon*. Since reason is an essential characteristic of human being, it is something which, strictly speaking, has no "essence" but exists only in its interpretation. We all know how modern thought, faithful to its Platonic heritage, interpreted it, and we know now how arbitrary this interpretation was.

Reason, it was generally thought, is that component part of man's being, that "faculty," by means of which the solitary, private individual is able to intuit or otherwise discover the true, inner "natures" of things. Reason is that which guarantees that between words and things there exists a strict correlation. Such a view of reason is to be found still in Husserl,[24] and it is one which is part and parcel of what Merleau-Ponty called "la pensée objective," i.e., objectivism, or again: "la pensée de l'absolu," "la pensée du survol"—or what today we might refer to as the "metaphysics of presence."

Throughout his entire career Merleau-Ponty waged a ceaseless and uncompromising battle with this form of thought. The question of reason or rationality is thus central to all of his work; what he was seeking to accomplish was, in effect, a *refonte* of our conception of what it means to be rational. It is, therefore, unfortunate that he never really dealt with the problem in a fully explicit and systematic way. There are, nevertheless, a few texts which reveal rather well the decidedly postmodern conception of reason he was striving to formulate.

In the following text, for instance, Merleau-Ponty speaks of the "universality of knowledge" and in effect says that what makes a thought rational is that it can be universalized. It is clear, however, that he is effecting a decisive break with the traditional way of conceiving of the "principle of universalizability" (which itself is synonymous with "rationality") when he writes:

> The universality of knowledge is no longer guaranteed in each of us by that strong-hold of absolute consciousness in which the Kantian "I think"—linked as it was to a certain spatio-temporal perspective—was assured *a priori* of being identical to every other possible "I think." The germ of universality or the "natural light" without which there could be no knowledge is to be found ahead of us, in the thing where our perception places us, in the dialogue into which our experience of other people throws us by means of a movement not all of whose sources are known to us. (*SNS*, p. 93)

When Merleau-Ponty says that it is in dialogue that the germ of universality is to be found, he is rejecting the modern rationalist idea that an idea is rational only if it can be generalized without limit and possesses a uniform (univocal) value in all situations, thereby making contact with some kind of objective absolute (the idea of universal commensuration, as Richard Rorty has more recently called it). For Merleau-Ponty, in contrast, human beings are rational, not because what they say and do has a transcendent guarantee in things, but simply because of the fact that, despite all the differences which set them apart, they can still, if they make the effort, communicate with and understand one another. Rationality has no other foundation than the uncertain communication among people whereby they succeed in working out mutual agreements:

> It remains just as hard to reach agreement with myself and with others, and for all my belief that it is in principle always attainable, I have no other reason to affirm this principle than my experience of certain concordances, so that in the end whatever solidity there is in my belief in the absolute is nothing but my experience of agreement with myself and others. (*SNS*, p. 95)

On the same page Merleau-Ponty speaks in one and the same breath of "rationality or communication" and, as he goes on to say, the foundation of truth or rationality is this "progressive experience," this "experience of agreement with myself and others." The universality of thought, as he says elsewhere, is always "presumptive." It is "never the universality of a pure concept which would be identical for every mind. It is rather the call which a situated thought addresses to other thoughts, equally situated, and each one responds to the call with its own resources."[25]

It could thus be said that for Merleau-Ponty rationality is a matter of "taking the risk of communicating" (*PriP*, p. 9). It has absolutely no guarantee in being and depends solely on the *good will* of men. Reason is a power not of discovering the "truth" but of "going further" in what is called the search for truth, which means: the search for mutual agreement and understanding. It is what maintains that great, always interrupted and always rebegun conversation that we call Culture. It is also what thereby makes it be that there is "a history of humanity or, more simply, *a* humanity. In other words, granting all the periods of stagnation and retreat, human relations are able to grow, to change their avatars into lessons, to pick out the truth of their past in the present, to eliminate certain mysteries which render them opaque and thereby make themselves more transparent" (*PriP*, p. 9). For Merleau-Ponty, "Our life is essentially universal," although he rightly insists that "this methodological rationalism is not to be confused with a dogmatic rationalism which eliminates historical contingency in advance by supposing a 'World Spirit' (Hegel) behind the course of events" (*PriP*, p. 10).

What is interesting from our present-day point of view is that this properly *postmodern* conception of reason has nothing *postmodernistic* about it, by which I mean that it in no way involves a rejection of reason or a disavowal of the overriding importance that the Western tradition has always placed on reason. Merleau-Ponty never suggested that "reason" is nothing more than the idea-product of one particular historical tradition, merely a cultural bias of Western man. He was most definitely not opposed to the traditional and, in particular, Enlightenment stress on rationality. He wanted neither to reject rationality nor, like Heidegger, to transcend it, as the latter said in his *Zur Seinsfrage*, toward a "Λόγος, whose essence logic and dialectics, which stem from metaphysics, are never able to experience." Certainly, the effect of Merleau-Ponty's philosophical endeavors was to subvert the traditional modern conception of reason described above. But this subversion is to be understood not as an abandonment of reason or rationality but as an attempt to work out a new conception of reason, to arrive at "an enlarged reason."

By "rationality" Merleau-Ponty understood basically what might be called "reasonableness": the attempt to reach uncoerced agreement with others by means of unrestricted dialogue. This is a conception of reason that, interestingly enough, is remarkably akin to the conception of reason that a thinker such as Jürgen Habermas has in recent years diligently labored to articulate and which he refers to as "communicative rationality." It is a properly hermeneutical conception of reason.

In his relentless struggle to overcome modernism, Merleau-Ponty remains for us, today still, a source of continuing inspiration. He has indeed become what he himself would have called a "classic."[26]

In the first part of this paper, I mentioned that in political matters postmodernistic thought readily allies itself with radicalism or revolutionism and that it is characterized by antinomianism and anti-institutionalism, by a belief in utopia and anarchy. The position that the later Merleau-Ponty came to adopt in political matters should serve to confirm the fact that—while he is indeed postmodern—he is not to be counted among the ranks of the postmodernistic thinkers. For at the end of his life, more so than ever before, he absolutely did not subscribe to utopianism and had abandoned whatever belief he might have had in the possibility of some kind of definitive resolution of the differences and conflicts that separate people, and this, of course, is why he clearly took up his distance from Marxism.

In *The Adventures of the Dialectic*, Merleau-Ponty decisively rejected revolutionary ideology and affirmed his solidarity with the liberal tradition of the West. In this work he said that "the revolution which would recreate history is infinitely distant,"[27] and he characterized as "fictions" the idea of proletarian power, direct democracy, and the withering away of the State (*AD*, p. 222).

Far from being anti-institutionalist ("antiestablishment"), Merleau-Ponty, exactly like Camus before him, insisted that without liberal institutions there can be no real freedom, and that without freedom, no acceptable solution to the human and social problem. If the problems which disturb us today have a solution, he said, "it is a liberal one" (*S*, p. 348). The important thing in his eyes was that we should discover "institutions which implant this practice of freedom in our customs" (*S*, p. 349). For, as he said, " . . . freedom requires something substantial; it requires a State, which bears it and which it gives life to" (*S*, p. 349). As is clear from the text, when Merleau-Ponty speaks of "institutions" he means *liberal* institutions. In his political thought Merleau-Ponty in the end adhered steadfastly to the essentials of the traditional liberalism of our Western democracies, based as it is on the idea of the autonomous and responsible Individual, the importance of limits and forms (the prime targets of antinomian revolutionism and of utopian believers in direct democracy). His hope, as he expressed it in the very last lines of the *The Adventures of the*

Dialectic, was to "inspire a few—or many—to bear their freedom, not to exchange it at a loss; for it is not only their own thing, their secret, their pleasure, their salvation—it involves everyone else" (*AD*, p. 233).

A rejection of Utopia of this sort amounts to a reaffirmation of *history*, that same history that postmodernistic writers, advocates of revolutionism and the psychoanalysis of coincidence or of polymorphous perversity, would like to do away with. It was no praise of primitivism or of the "natural" that Merleau-Ponty made when, having recently returned from a stay in Madagascar in 1957, he responded to the questions put to him by a journalist. At the end of the interview, the journalist said to him: "You seem to believe that our values, the values of Western civilizations, are superior to those of the underdeveloped countries." Merleau-Ponty replied with the following remarks, which merit being quoted at length, since they are largely ignored today, a result no doubt of the postmodernistic, guilt-ridden fascination with the "Third World":

> Certainly not in respect to their moral value, and even less to their superior beauty, but, how shall I put it, in respect to their *historical* value. In landing at Orly in the morning twilight, after a month in Madagascar, how amazing to see so many roads, so many objects, so much patience, labor, knowledge; to make out in the switching on of lights so many individual lives arising in the morning. This great feverish and crushing arrangement of what is called developed humanity is, after all, what will one day enable all men on earth to eat. It has already made them exist in one another's eyes, instead of each proliferating in his country like trees. They have met in blood, fear, and hatred, and this is what must stop. I cannot seriously consider this encounter an evil. In any case, it is something settled; there can be no question of recreating archaism; we are all embarked and it is no small matter to have begun this game [*d'avoir engagé cette partie*].(*S*, p. 336)

Merleau-Ponty most assuredly did not believe that Western civilization and its traditional values was something that had to be deconstructed. He adhered instead to the spirit of enlightened, modern, critical liberalism. We are all underway [*embarqués*] together and have no other option than to continue with the game [*partie*], improving on it wherever possible. For the name of the game is that without which the human being would not be human: *Liberty*.

4

To affirm history in this way amounts to a recognition that there is no definitive solution to human problems. It amounts therefore to a rejection of the utopian belief in some kind of trans- or metahistorical salvation, the desire, avowed or unavowed, on the part of much of postmodernity for a saving god, for the overcoming of all alienation. The conclusion of a reflection on history, Merleau-Ponty said, "does not lie in rebellion, but in unremitting *virtù*." (*S*, p. 35). The conclusion is a prudent and reasonable belief in the possibility of a certain *progress*. The conclusion, as he stated in a superb text which we have already had the occasion to quote, is to believe that, "granting all the periods of stagnation and retreat, human relations are able to grow, to change their avatars into lessons, to pick out the truth of their past in the present, to eliminate certain mysteries which render them opaque and thereby make themselves more transparent" (S, p. 9).

If it is likewise possible to speak of progress in philosophy, it is not in the sense in which philosophy might one day discover the answers to the questions it raised at its beginning, such that it could, as Hegel said, "ihren Nahmen der Liebe zum Wissen ablegen zu können und wirkliches Wissen zu seyn"[28] If there is any progress in philosophy, it is rather in the sense that it sometimes succeeds in better formulating its questions, in better understanding the real meaning of its questions, and in eliminating a certain number of false questions, such that it is no longer obliged to continue repeating them or dealing with them in the way in which it did in the past. The progress of philosophy consists, precisely, as Merleau-Ponty would say, in occasionally being able to turn its avatars into lessons.

This applies in particular to the very old problem of the union of body and mind. Modern philosophy's failure to solve this problem is such as to teach us that it was a false problem from the start or, at least, a problem which was posed in the wrong way. What we have learned from the failure of modern philosophy is that it was a mistake even to speak in terms of mind or soul and body, as if these were two things whose existence was self-evident. As a matter of fact, as we know now, these notions correspond to nothing absolute or self-evident, certainly to nothing in our actual experience—Husserl already taught us as much.

Can one, however, say the same for the modern notions of subjectivity and consciousness? Are these nothing more than purely arbitrary inventions of the modern epistemē which today conceal Being from us and are therefore to be deconstructed? Is there no truth in these notions of the past which cannot be gathered up in the present? Are they but names for problems that need to be not so much taken up in an Aufhebung as deconstructed in a Niedergang?

If the latter were the case and if the great discoveries of modern philosophy—subjectivity, consciousness—were, like Nietzsche's "last man," abandoned and left behind, philosophy would have made so much "progress" that it would actually have ceased to exist. The result would be the deconstruction of philosophy itself. And, indeed, we hear every day more and more references to the "end of philosophy."

That philosophy, like "man" himself, finds itself today in a state of crisis is not to be doubted. Indeed, already in 1959 Merleau-Ponty wrote in the first of his working notes included in The Visible and the Invisible: "Our state of non-philosophy— Never has the crisis been so radical—" "End of philosophy or rebirth?" he asked. The Visible and the Invisible was itself the response to his conclusion that what is needed is "a return to ontology" (VI p. 165).[29]

The dissolution of subjectivity and the "death of man" would spell the end of philosophy, for, ever since Socrates, the chief object of philosophy has been man himself. "The philosopher," Merleau-Ponty said, "is the man who wakes up and speaks."[30] Philosophy is the reflective interrogation that that man who has woken up to the fact of his existence pursues. Philosophy springs up at that moment when a subject becomes conscious of himself as a subject and discovers in front of him as his counterpart (*Gegen-stand*) an opaque world which, like a clouded mirror, sends back to him a confused reflection which is the enigma of his own existence. We ourselves are, as Merleau-Ponty wrote, "one sole continued question, a perpetual enterprise of taking our bearings on the constellations of the world, and of taking the bearings of the things on our dimensions" (*VI*, p. 103).

This last remark of Merleau-Ponty's points to a most interesting characteristic of human understanding. When Merleau-Ponty speaks of "a perpetual enterprise of taking our bearings on the constellations of the world, and of taking the bearings of the things on our dimensions," what he is describing is nothing other than *metaphor*. For the essence of the metaphorical process is that it enables us to understand one thing better by likening it to something it is not. As Bruno Snell pointed out in his now classic study, *The Discovery of the Mind*, one object is capable of casting fresh light upon another in the form of a metaphor only because we read into the object the very qualities which it in turn illustrates. Snell observed how it is a peculiar characteristic of all Homeric similes and, indeed, of all genuine metaphors that they illuminate human behavior only by referring to something else, such as a boulder in the pounding surf, which is in turn explained by analogy with human behavior. It is only in this way, by listening to an echo of ourselves in the world, that we are able to know ourselves.[31]

As Snell's work itself suggests, what we have learned to call the "self" may itself be the product of a certain creative, metaphorical use of language. The unconscious may, as Lacan insists, be structured like a language; consciousness, in any event, *is* language (it is, as everyone will admit, inconceivable apart from language, which amounts, once more, pragmatically speaking, to saying that it is language). Thus, as something linguistic in its very essence, the "self" is, as well, something whose existence can be assigned historical dates. As Merleau-Ponty himself remarked: "Man is a historical idea and not a natural species" (*PhP*, p. 170).

Since, in the realm of human understanding, that which understands and that which is understood are inseparable, are in fact one and the same, it makes perfectly good sense to say that the "self" which we interrogate in order better to understand it is itself a product of this interrogation, of what Merleau-Ponty referred to as "the occult traffic of metaphor." As he himself observed: " . . . there is no experience without speech, as the purely lived-through has no part in the discursive life of man" (*PhP*, p. 337). And again: " . . . speech itself *brings about* that concordance between me and myself, and between myself and others, on which an attempt is made to base thought" (*PhP*, p. 392).

Does this mean that the "self" is a mere "fiction," having no genuine ontological reality or significance, the illusion of a particular culture or *epistemè*? This is no doubt what a number of postmodernistic writers would conclude.

And yet such a conclusion is not warranted. In fact, a relativistic, nihilistic conclusion of such a sort seems only to be the reverse, indeed the perverse counterpart, of modern objectivism. If "self-consciousness"—thus the very notion of the self—has any meaning, it is the reflective presence of the self to itself. The notion of *absolute presence* may be, as Derrida has insinuated, meaningless, but that of presence itself is not—so long as we recognize that the presence of the self to itself is a mediated presence, mediated by language, precisely. As Merleau-Ponty remarked: "it is true that the subject as an absolute presence to itself is something we cannot circumvent. . . . It is also true that it provides itself with symbols of itself in both succession and multiplicity, and that these symbols *are* it, since without them it would, like an inarticulate cry, fail to achieve self-consciousness" (*PhP*, pp. 426–27). Speaking of Merleau-Ponty, Cornelius Castoriadis says that the subject is "a being who can become what he will have been only in speaking of it."[32]

That all genuine understanding is linguistic through and through, as Merleau-Ponty always insisted, and is, moreover, the consequence of a certain creative, metaphorical use of language does not, of itself, mean that all understanding is illusory. Rather, if it is indeed the case that, as post–Merleau-Pontyian, hermeneutical phenomenology has taught us, to understand something is not to form a representation of it but creatively to transform it, this should serve to indicate that we need to conceive of human understanding—of that which we ourselves are—in terms which effect a decisive break with modern objectivism. It does not seem that many postmodernistic thinkers have yet made such a break.

When all is said and done, what, really, is man in nature, as Pascal asked? What precisely is that being which, as he observed, is everything in regard to nothing, a nothing in regard to the all, a mean between everything and nothing? What is it to be an object which is at the same time a subject, a subject which is simultaneously an object, a thing visible which is also seeing (*un visible qui est aussi voyant*), a seer (*voyant*) which is also visible, neither a mere part of the (in itself) world nor a pure (for itself) gaze on the world, but the two at once, since it could not see were it not also visible? What is that strange intertwining (*entrelas*) or chiasm between the sensing (*le sentant*) and the sensible in the flesh of the world that is the human individual? As Merleau-Ponty said of the perceiving subject whose body is a spontaneous power of expression: "There is no doubt that this marvel, whose strangeness the word *man* should not hide from us, is a very great one" (*S*, p. 66).

All of the questions of science or of mere curiosity are internally animated, Merleau-Ponty says, by "the fundamental interrogation which appears naked in philosophy" (*VI*, p. 103). Man is for himself a question and "Who am I?"—"What is man's place in nature?"—is the central question of philosophy. Philosophy is the answer, sometimes triumphant and confident, sometimes hesitant and cautious, that throughout the ages man has formulated in response to the clear *consciousness* he has of his obscure *existence*. The question that, at bottom, the individual raises—above all in exceptional moments of his life, that the sick person raises (but in a sense is not man himself, as we have seen Nietzsche say, the sick animal?)—is, as Merleau-Ponty formulated it: " . . . why am I myself? How old am I really? Am I really alone in being me? Have I not somewhere a double, a twin?" "Every question," he said, "even that of simple cognition is part of the central question that is ourselves. . . . " (VI, p. 104). The question of personal identity is indeed the central question of philosophy.

If Merleau-Ponty contributed something to the thought of our epoch and made some contribution to the progress of philosophy, it is, I suggest, in regard to this question, this problem of personal identity. To be sure, he did not bequeath us a solution to the problem of subjectivity and the relation between the psychic and the corporeal, but at least he did not simply skirt the issue by boldly proclaiming the dissolution of all dualities. The problem of subjectivity may be a kind of Gordian knot, but if it can be "solved" at all, it is only by a painstaking attempt to unravel it; it cannot simply be cut in one fell swoop, as many a postmodernistic pseudo-Alexander might attempt. This is something that Merleau-Ponty realized full well. The important thing for him was not to dissolve subjectivity but to conceive of it afresh, in a less metaphysical way than philosophy had done in the past. If this concern on his part for "man" could be labeled "humanistic," then Merleau-Ponty was undeniably a "humanist." Had he not died such an untimely death, there is every likelihood that in this postmodern era that is dawning he would have been a staunch anti-antihumanist.

In the last analysis, what Merleau-Ponty succeeded perhaps in doing is to have turned the failure of the modern problem of the union of body and mind into a lesson. Husserl had already exposed the artificiality of conceiving of the relation between the psychic and the corporeal as a relation between two worlds, but Merleau-Ponty, who always attempted to remain faithful to Husserl, even when he subjected Husserl's philosophy of consciousness to a pitiless critique, contributed to the advancement of phenomenology by frankly rejecting all "egology" and the Husserlian notion of a "sphere of ownness." What he did thereby was to rid us of all the bric-a-brac, as he put it, of psychological or even transcendental reflection: the states of consciousness, acts of consciousness, noeses, noemas, images, hyletic data, and all those other cherished relics of the metaphysics of presence with which even Husserl had attempted to construct—or as he would have said, constitute—the world.

By attempting not to deconstruct the subject but to eliminate a certain way of formulating the problem of personal identity or subjectivity whose effect has been to make us obscure to ourselves, Merleau-Ponty has enabled us to raise anew the question of subjectivity in a way which might enable us to preserve, in a less speculative and metaphysical understanding, the truth of our past.

Above all, Merleau-Ponty has helped us to liberate ourselves from the idea that philosophy, conceived of as a reflection on subjectivity, can or should compete with the physical sciences. He contributed in a direct way to the demise of the modern, metaphysical idea that philosophy must, or even can, be a science, the superscience that Husserl continually sought—which only serves to show that despite the philosophical "radicalism" he espoused, Husserl remained to the bitter end a prisoner of modern rationalism, of metaphysics.[33] If the vocation of philosophical reflection is to become a rigorous science, then, in Husserl's own words, the dream has been dreamed out and is indeed over, and philosophy has reached its end. However, there is no reason why the abandonment of philosophy conceived of as rigorous science should spell the end of philosophy conceived of as a form of rigorous and methodical interrogation—and it is indeed this historical vocation of philosophy that Merleau-Ponty reclaimed and defended. He wanted not to deconstruct philosophy but to lead it back to "its vital sources" (TFL, p. 100). As he said toward the end of his life, in pursuing his own archaeological endeavors: "It is the aim of an inquiry such as we have pursued here on the ontology of Nature to sustain through contact with beings and the exploration of the regions of Being the same attention to the fundamental that remains the privilege and the task of philosophy" (TFL, p. 112).

In battling mercilessly with the conceptual and metaphysical avatars of our past, Merleau-Ponty may well have contributed to our being in a better position in this new postmodern period to tame the sphinx and to respond, with less indirection and deviousness than philosophy traditionally has done, to the enigma she confronts us with, which is that of our own being in the world.

Notes

This essay appears here in English for the first time. On the basis of a sketchy prototype given in English in the form of a commentary to a paper presented by Ernest Sherman at a meeting of the Merleau-Ponty Circle, it was completely and extensively rewritten in French for presentation at the Xᵉ Colloque International de Phénoménologie organized by Anna-Teresa Tymieniecka on the theme "Maurice Merleau-Ponty: Le psychique et le corporel," University of Paris (Sorbonne), May 1981. It was subsequently published in the form in which it was read under the title "Du Corps à la chair: Maurice Merleau-Ponty," in *Analecta Husserliana*, vol. XXI, 1986. It had appeared in the meantime—in another heavily reworked version and in a quite different form—under the title "Merleau-Ponty und die Postmodernität," in *Leibhafige Vernunft: Spüren von Merleau-Pontys Denken*, ed. A. Métraux and B. Waldenfels (Munich: Wilhelm Fink Verlag, 1986). In still another, abbreviated and otherwise modified version—this time in English—the text was read to a meeting of the Merleau-Ponty Circle held at the State University of New York at Binghamton, September 1982. The present English version is a transformative translation of the German (itself a decidedly original version of the text based on an English translation of the French version). A truly original version of this text—in whatever language—does not exist, and never has—unless it be the present one.

1. Pascal, *Pensées*, trans. A. J. Krailsheimer (Harmondsworth, Eng.: Penguin Books, 1966), no. 199 (Lafuma), no. 72 (Brunschvicg).
2. Husserl, *The Crisis of European Sciences and Transcendental Phenomenology*, trans. D. Carr (Evanston, Ill.: Northwestern University Press, 1970), p. 20.
3. Ibid., § 7.

4. David Carr, *Phenomenology and the Problem of History* (Evanston, Ill.: Northwestern University Press, 1974), p. 120.

5. Husserl, *The Crisis*, § 10.

6. Ibid.

7. See Husserl, *Cartesian Meditations*, trans. D. Cairns (The Hague: Martinus Nijhoff, 1960), § 44.

8. Merleau-Ponty, *The Visible and the Invisible (VI)*, trans. A. Lingis (Evanston, Ill.: Northwestern University Press, 1968), p. 237.

9. Merleau-Ponty, *Phenomenology of Perception (PhP)*, trans. C. Smith (London: Routledge and Kegan Paul, 1962), p. xi.

10. Merleau-Ponty, *The Structure of Behavior (SB)*, trans. A. L. Fisher (Boston: Beacon Press, 1963), p. 3.

11. See G. B. Madison, *La phénoménologie de Merleau-Ponty* (Paris: Editions Klincksieck, 1973), p. 34 (English trans., *The Phenomenology of Merleau-Ponty* [Athens, Ohio: Ohio University Press, 1981], p. 12).

12. "There is the body as mass of chemical components in interaction, the body as dialectic of living being and its biological milieu, and the body as dialectic of social subject and his group; even all our habits are an impalpable body for the ego of each moment. Each of these degrees is soul with respect to the preceding one, body with respect to the following one. The body in general is an ensemble of paths already traced, of powers already constituted; the body is the acquired dialectical ground upon which a higher 'formation' is accomplished, and the soul is the meaning which is then established" (*SB*, p. 210).

13. See Husserl, *Cartesian Meditations*, § 55.

14. Merleau-Ponty, *Sense and Non-Sense (SNS)*, trans. H. L. Dreyfus and P. A. Dreyfus (Evanston, Ill.: Northwestern University Press, 1964), p. 63.

15. Merleau-Ponty, "The Primacy of Perception and Its Philosophical Consequences," in *The Primacy of Perception (PriP)*, trans. J. M. Edie (Evanston, Ill.: Northwestern University Press, 1964), p. 30.

16. Ibid., p. 19.

17. See Merleau-Ponty, preface, in Dr. A. Hesnard, *L'Oeuvre de Freud* (Paris: Payot, 1960), p. 8.

18. J.-P. Sartre, "Merleau-Ponty," in *Situations IV* (Paris: Gallimard, 1964), p. 266.

19. Merleau-Ponty, *Signs (S)*, trans. R. C. McCleary (Evanston, Ill.: Northwestern University Press, 1964), p. 19.

20. See *VI*, p. 270.

21. The resemblance of certain remarks of the later Merleau-Ponty to those of a postmodernist writer such as Norman O. Brown is at times as striking as it is disconcerting. See, for instance, the following texts of Brown, selected at random from his book *Love's Body* (New York: Vintage Books, 1966): "Psychoanalysis can be used to uncover the principle of union, or communion, buried beneath the surface separations, the surface declarations of independence, the surface signs of private property. Psychoanalysis also discloses the pathology of the process whereby the normal sense of being a self separate from the external world was constructed. Contrary to what is taken for granted in the lunatic state called normalcy or common sense, the distinction between self and external world is not an immutable fact, but an artificial construction. It is a boundary line; like all boundaries not natural but conventional; like all boundaries, based on love and hate" (p. 142); "The boundary line between self and external world bears no relation to reality; the distinction between ego and world is made by splitting out part of the inside, and swallowing in part of the outside" (p. 143; in what follows Brown quotes Malanie Klein, to whom Merleau-Ponty also frequently referred); "The net-effect of the establishment of the boundary between self and external world is inside-out and outside-in confusion. The erection of the boundary does not alter the fact that there is, in reality, no boundary. The net-effect is illusion, self-deception; the big lie. Or aliena-

tion. 'Le premier mythe du dehors et du dedans: l'aliénation se fond sur des deux termes.' " (pp. 143–44; the internal quotation is from Merleau-Ponty's close friend and associate, Jean Hyppolite); "Symbolism is polymorphous perversity, the translation of all of our senses into one another, the interplay between the senses, the metaphor, the free translation. The separation of the senses, their mutual isolation, is sensuality, is sexual organization, is bondage to the tyranny of one partial impulse, leading to the absolute and exclusive concentration of the life of the body in the representative person" (p. 249); "Knowledge is carnal knowledge, a copulation of subject and object, making these two one"(p. 249); "Knowledge is carnal knowledge. A subterranean passage between mind and body underlies all analogy; no world is metaphysical without its first being physical; and the body that is the measure of all things is sexual" (p. 249); "Get the nothingness back into words. The aim is words with nothing to them; words that point beyond themselves rather than to themselves; transparencies, empty words. Empty words, corresponding to the void in things" (p.259); "It cannot be put into words because it does not consist of things. Literal words always define properties. Beyond the reality-principle and reification is silence, the flesh. Freud said, Our god Logos: but refrain from uniting with words, in order to unite with the word made flesh" (p. 265); "The antinomy between mind and body, word and deed, speech and silence, overcome. Everything is only a metaphor; there is only poetry" (p. 266).

22. "We must not think the flesh starting from substances, from body and spirit—for then it would be the union of contradictories—but we must think it, as we said, as an element, as the concrete emblem of a general manner of being" (VI, p. 147).

23. See Madison, La Phénoménologie de Merleau-Ponty, pp. 223–24 (The Phenomenology of Merleau-Ponty, pp. 210–11.).

24. See, for instance, Ideas, § 135.

25. "An Unpublished Text by Maurice Merleau-Ponty," in The Primacy of Perception, p. 8.

26. See Signs, p. 11.

27. Merleau-Ponty, Adventures of the Dialectic (AD), trans. J. Bien (Evanston, Ill.: Northwestern University Press, 1973), p. 220.

28. Hegel, Phänomenologie des Geistes (Hamburg: Felix Meiner Verlag, 1980), p. 11.

29. In the summary of one of his lectures at the Collège de France in 1958–1959, to which the title "Possibilité de la philosophie" has been attached (appearing in English as "Philosophy as Interrogation"), Merleau-Ponty wrote: "With Hegel something comes to an end. After Hegel, there is a philosophical void. This is not to say that there has been a lack of thinkers or of geniuses, but that Marx, Kierkegaard, and Nietzsche start from a denial of philosophy. We might say that with the latter we enter an age of non-philosophy. But perhaps such a destruction of philosophy constitutes its very realization. Perhaps it preserves the essence of philosophy, and it may be, as Husserl wrote, that philosophy is reborn from its ashes" (Themes from the Lectures at the Collège de France, 1952–1960 [TFL], trans. John O'Neill [Evanston, Ill.: Northwestern University Press, 1970], p. 100). A couple of paragraphs further on, he said: "For us who have to deal with the bewitched world foreseen by Marx and Nietzsche their solutions are inadequate to the nature of the crisis. In place of a philosophy which—at least in principle and ex officio—stood for clarity against possibly different replies to the same problems, we see more and more a history of non-philosophy whose authors have as their sole common denominator a certain modern obscurity, a pure interrogation. We shall not find the new philosophy already developed in Marx or in Nietzsche. We have to create it, taking into account the world in which we live where it becomes clear that their negation of metaphysics cannot take the place of philosophy" (ibid., pp. 101–102).

30. Merleau-Ponty, In Praise of Philosophy, trans. J. Wild and J. M. Edie (Evanston, Ill.: Northwestern University Press, 1963), p. 63.

31. For a detailed treatment of the metaphorical, creative nature of human understanding, see G. B. Madison *Understanding: A Phenomenological-Pragmatic Analysis* (Westport, Conn.: Greenwood Press, 1982).

32. C. Castoriadis, "The Sayable and the Unsayable," in *Crossroads in the Labyrinth*, trans. K. Soper and M. H. Ryle (Cambridge, Mass.: MIT Press, 1984), p. 143.

33. See G. B. Madison, " 'Phenomenology and Existentialism': Husserl and the End of Idealism," in *Husserl: Expositions and Appraisals*, ed. F. A. Elliston and P. Mc-Cormick (Notre Dame, Ind.: University of Notre Dame Press, 1977).

FIVE

Ricoeur's Philosophy of Metaphor

Paul Ricoeur's latest book, *La Métaphore vive* (Éditions du Seuil, 1975; published as *The Rule of Metaphor*, University of Toronto Press, 1977) is without a doubt one of the most important studies on metaphor to date. It is a very thorough study, dealing both with the history of the subject and with various contemporary theories of metaphor. Accordingly, rather than summarize Ricoeur's very detailed and masterful analyses, I propose to take a different approach by setting down a few of the *questions* which its reading provoked in me.

One of Ricoeur's principal goals in this book is to justify, in opposition to positivism, the notion of *metaphorical truth*. What is interesting to note is that in order to do this he feels that it is necessary to rehabilitate, with regard to metaphor, the notion of *reference*, as formulated by the German logician Gottlob Frege, a notion which has had an enormous influence on English-language philosophy in particular. Not only do metaphors and poetic texts say something, but they say something about reality; they have not only *sense* but also *meaning*, i.e., *reference*. In saying this Ricoeur appears to accept at the outset as valid the Fregean—as well as positivistic—distinction betweeen sense and reference and agrees that metaphorical discourse can lay claim to truth only if there is a reality which it can be said to describe or denote. This is why he objects to what he calls the "conventionalistic nominalism" (*MV*, p. 294; *RM*, p. 233) of a writer such as Nelson Goodman (*Languages of Art*). Ricoeur argues that if one holds to a kind of nominalism, such as Goodman's, for which the literal application or meaning of terms is determined solely by usage and convention and for which metaphor is but the unusual usage of terms which conflicts with their customary usage, then one cannot account for the "appropriate" character of metaphorical discourse or, for that matter, for the literal application of terms (*MV*, p. 301; *RM*, p. 239). How, Ricoeur asks, can one account in this way for the sort of "fitness" which certain linguistic innovations seem to have? Does not the "seemliness," the "appropriate" character, of certain terms indicate that the function of language is referential, that language reveals "a way of being of things which is brought to language, thanks to semantic innovation?" (*MV*, p. 301; *RM*, p. 233). Metaphorical discourse is indeed creative and inventive, and yet, this *creation* is a *discovery*. Ricoeur seems to be saying that there are, in some sense or other, certain objective "essences" which language articulates—although it may only be able to do so in certain cases when it is used creatively, innovatively.

Having in me something of a nominalist and pragmatic strain, I must admit that I am not nearly as concerned as is Ricoeur to object to the nominalist view of meaning present in Goodman or, for that matter, to the conventionalism of the later Wittgenstein. In fact, it seems to me that conventionalism is a perfectly adequate way of describing the way in which both literal and metaphorical languages function. If one is merely describing the *use* of language, how language in fact functions, does one need to appeal to extralinguistic reality, to essences? I wonder if Ricoeur would not agree that, for purely descriptive purposes, such an appeal is indeed superfluous.

However, I would wish to maintain with Ricoeur that meaning cannot be *reduced* to mere use—as Wittgenstein tends to do. With Ricoeur I firmly believe that there is a meaning-intention which, in some sense, transcends language. But for my part I do not believe that this "intended meaning" is the extralinguistic reality to which language is said by the positivists to refer. Thus I do not know if what I have just called the "meaning-intention" is the same as what Ricoeur calls the "intended." In fact, I am not altogether clear as to what exactly he means by this provocative term. Is the "intended" of discourse nothing more or nothing other than the extralinguistic reality to which a text is said to refer? What is the relation between Ricoeur's "intended" and Frege's "referent"? At one point (*MV*, p. 273; *RM*, p. 216), Ricoeur compares the intended with what Ferdinand de Saussure called the "signified." He seems to be saying that just as the signified is the counterpart (the "correlate") of the signifier, so the intended is the counterpart of the entire sentence. But this would make of the intended an *intra*linguistic thing, for Saussure's signified is an internal element of the semiotic unit (of the linguistic sign)—in which case the intended could not correspond to Frege's referent, i.e., it could not be the *extra*linguistic reality which Ricoeur says language intends or refers to. Perhaps I have failed to understand properly the meaning that Ricoeur attaches to the notion of the "intended," but in any event I feel that this is one question which calls for further clarification.

To return to the notion of reference, I must confess that at times I feel a bit uneasy when Ricoeur, like an English philosopher, speaks of an extralinguistic reality which language refers to or denotes. Is there such a reality? Phenomenology tells us that the way the world appears to us—what the world *is* for us, its meaning—is in fact a function of the way in which consciousness intends it; it is what it is only as an object of and for belief. "The world," as Husserl says, "is a meaning, an accepted sense." Now I'm wondering if we could not extend what Husserl says about the relation between consciousness and reality (this being a relation *within* consciousness) to the relation between language and reality. If we could, we would then have to say something like this: The world referred to by language is what it is only because of the way it is linguistically referred to. The world, in short, is a function of language. But were we to say this, *we could no longer accept the traditional, Fregean distinction between sense and reference* (no more than in phenomenology we can accept the natural distinction between consciousness and reality). Strictly speaking, there would no longer be any extralinguistic reality to which language could be said to refer; reality would be constituted differently in accordance with the different ways we use to speak about it, and, in the final analysis, there would be as many "realities" as there are languages.

It will be recognized that this view pretty much coincides with the "theory of linguistic relativity" put forward by Edward Sapir and Benjamin Lee Whorf. And this is enough, I suspect, for Ricoeur to express reservation in going along with it (in *MV*, p. 385, n.1; *RM*, p. 364, n.85, Ricoeur hints at an opposition to Whorf). He would no doubt see in it a ruinous relativism which is incompatible with the ontological pretensions of language, its built-in claim to say something meaningful and true about reality itself as it is apart from language. Now while I would agree with Ricoeur that relativism, as a *philosophical* position, is unacceptable, I do not think that if we reject the traditional sense-reference distinction we need fall into relativism, and I shall suggest why in a moment. What I want to point out now is the grounds I find *within Ricoeur himself* for revising radically the traditional sense-reference distinction (or for abandoning it altogether).

The notion of an extralinguistic "referent" makes genuine sense only if we suppose that this referent is *what it is* independently of language, only, that is, if we suppose that the structure of reality—and we must assume, in this case, that reality *does* have an objective, essential structure—is itself independent of language. But what if it were actually the case that the categorial structures reality is said to have were in the first instance engendered by language itself? Ricoeur actually seems to suggest as much when he speaks of his "most extreme hypothesis: namely that the 'metaphorical' which transgresses the categorial order also begets it" (*MV*, p. 34; *RM*, p. 24)

> In other words, the power of metaphor would be to break an old categorization, in order to establish new logical frontiers on the ruins of their forerunners. . . . can we not hypothesize that the dynamic of thought that carves its way through already established categories is the same as that which engenders all clasifications? . . . one can propose that the figure of speech we call metaphor, and that appears first of all as a phenomenon of deviation in relation to an established usage, is homogeneous with a process that has given rise to all the "semantic fields," and thus to the very usage from which metaphor deviates. (*MV*, pp. 251–52; *RM*, pp. 197–98)

I am quite ready to entertain this hypothesis of Ricoeur's in all seriousness. But if one does entertain it, it would seem to me that one can no longer maintain that language refers to an extralinguistic reality (in the strict sense in which Frege maintains this). From a purely descriptive point of view and with regard to literal usage, one must say with Gilbert Ryle that a metaphor is a "category mistake," since it violates established categories. But it must be realized that this is actually an *improper* way of characterizing metaphor, *since the established categories that a new metaphor violates are themselves products of previous metaphorical discourse.* What one normally takes to be the objective referent of language is in actuality the correlate of a dead metaphor! Reality is nothing other than a metaphor which is taken literally and is *believed* in. As Wallace Stevens says: "Reality is a cliché from which we escape by metaphor." Metaphors are not so much the means for allowing us to perceive new resemblances which previous classifications prevented us from seeing, therefore, as they are the means whereby these new resemblances are created in the first place. If, as Ricoeur remarks, everything is in a sense like everything else, then there can be no antecedent reason why in a metaphor we should compare any one particular thing with any other. And thus to be able to coin a good metaphor does not require, as Aristotle would say, that one have the eye for *discerning* resemblances so much as the imaginative talent for *inventing* them.

Thus when Ricoeur argues that "suspension of real reference is the condition of access to the virtual [poetic, literary] mode of reference" (*MV*, p. 288; *RM*, p. 229), it would seem that he is really describing the way in which, *as a matter of fact*, we happen to encounter and come to understand literary texts—starting as we do with the ingrained prejudice of a literal understanding of things— rather than the actual relation that holds between literal and metaphorical language. In actuality, the relation between the two would be just the opposite. Thus I wonder whether the validity of an attempt to defend the truth-value of metaphorical discourse by arguing that this mode of discourse has a higher- level referent than has literal, scientific discourse is not limited to a treatment of metaphor from the point of view of our reaction to it rather than to what it is, so to speak, in itself. To employ a traditional distinction, does it not have to do with the *ordo cognoscendi* rather than the *ordo essendi*? This, then, is another question I would like to address to Ricoeur.

Although I am very wary when it comes to the Fregean notion of reference— since it seems to me to be basically a positivistic and rationalist notion—I am in full agreement with Ricoeur as regards the truth-value of metaphor. Meta- phors, I believe, can tell us something about the really important things human beings are concerned with, "things" such as the self or the soul, human freedom, Being, God, and so on. Not only does metaphorical discourse have something to say about these "things," it is, I further believe (though here I go beyond Ricoeur), the *only* means for talking about them meaningfully and truthfully and in a direct and straightforward fashion. And the reason, I think, is this: Only metaphorical discourse can say something about something without hy- postatizing that about which it speaks. When, for instance, in religious discourse we call God a "father," it is understood that he is not really a father in the usual, literal sense of the term. And yet in another sense he is. Metaphorical assertions are truthful, yet qualified assertions.

I wonder if Ricoeur would not agree with this, at least in part. For does it not correspond to that unique feature of metaphorical predication which he has himself emphasized: the fact that every metaphorical assertion is a qualified one and that the metaphorical "is" always includes an "is-not"? (see *MV*, pp. 11, 272, 282, 312, 321, 376, 388; and *RM*, pp. 6–7, 214–15, 223–34, 248, 255–56, 296–97, 306)? Metaphorical truth, as Ricoeur says, is a "tensional" truth. Shouldn't we say, therefore, that metaphors don't "really" mean what they say, that they are *ironic* and *paradoxical*?

But if this is the case, don't we have to go further and say—and wouldn't Ricoeur have to agree—that *what* a metaphor apparently refers to *does not really exist*? If, for instance, we are doing ontology and are speaking about Being, don't we have to admit that the "referent" of our discourse doesn't really exist, that Being both is and is not? Interestingly enough, this is exactly what Heidegger says ("Being *is* not").

This leads me to two final points (which I put forward tentatively and as, so to speak, hypotheses). If the referent of a metaphor doesn't really exist, then metaphors can't really be said to *refer* to anything. They still *mean* something, though, and this meaning is more than the mere *sense* of the utterance; it is the "intended," by which I mean our preverbal, lived experience, the experience we all have of what can only be called the basic "meaningfulness" of existence. That is, the "intended" is not the extralinguistic and extra-experiential reality to which language is so often said to refer. It lies, so to speak, on this side, the inner side of language, not on the other, the outer, side. Instead of speaking of the relation between language and an extralinguistic reality, I would prefer to speak, as Ricoeur himself does in another work, of the relation "between language and lived experience." That is, I would indeed say, with Ricoeur, that there is an "overture of language towards the other-than-itself," and I would also speak of the "nonlinguistic," but it seems to me that a distinction should be made between two kinds of "other." There is the preverbal meaning-intention which is the source of the meaning of language, and there is the extralinguistic "referent," but this latter is a product of language and a function of its "sense."

Unlike language when it is viewed from a merely linguistic or semiotic viewpoint, human discourse is *overdetermined*; it contains, so to speak, an excess or surplus of meaning. As the literary critic George Steiner remarks: "language generates—grammar permitting, one would want to say 'language is'—a surplus of meaning (meaning is the surplus-value of the labor performed by language)." Now my hypothesis is that it is precisely this overdetermination of living language (in a discourse or a text), this intentional excess, which is what, in philosophy, we mean by "reality." To paraphrase Merleau-Ponty, I would say that the dimension of reality that language does not so much "refer" to as express is "l'excès de ce que nous vivons sur ce qui a été déjà dit."

This is to say that reality in the ordinary sense, the so-called extralinguistic referent of language, is thoroughly relative to language itself and is its "product," but reality in the deepest sense (what we might call "being") is not determinate (has no essence) and is not the product of language but is its creative source. And this source is to be located in the lived experience which all humans share in, in one form or another. It is the "intention" which motivates all discourse. It is not so much what language refers to as what it makes manifest in the very fact that it is creative and is constantly throwing off categories, essences, and "real entities." It seems to me that this view has the merit of being able to assimilate nominalism and conventionalism while not succumbing for all that to relativism, for when ultimate reality or true being is viewed, not as the fixed referent of language, but as its creative source, it can be said to be what is *analogically* common to all the creative or metaphorical, i.e., "analogical," uses of language. In this way we could arrive at a genuine *analogia entis* (Ricoeur discusses at length this latter notion in Study VIII).

But, I admit, and this is my final point, such a view does have as its ultimate consequence the rendering impossible of a specifically philosophical, by which I mean here metaphysical, mode of discourse over and above the poetic and mythic. Now this is a conclusion which I'm afraid Ricoeur would not wish to accept, for the entire last study of his book is a plea "for the discontinuity between speculative [philosophical] and poetic discourse" (*MV*, p. 324; *RM*, p. 258). I really don't see, though, how it can be avoided if, with Ricoeur, we recognize that metaphorical truth is a creative, "tensional" sort of truth. Truth, it would seem, is either literal or metaphorical. If metaphorical, it is again of two kinds: mythic and poetic. What characterizes both literal, including scientific, truth and metaphorical truth in the mode of myth is that what is said and what in this saying is posited as real (as the referent of discourse) is an object of *belief*. As Ricoeur says: "The myth, in fact, is 'believed poetry (poetry *plus* belief)—metaphor taken literally, I would put it. Now, there is something in the use of metaphor that inclines it towards abuse, and so towards myth" (*MV*, p. 316; *RM*, p. 251). Could it not be said that literal truths are simply metaphorical truths which are taken literally, i.e., believed in? Can we not say in fact that all literal truths, including scientific truths, are *myth*? The peculiar feature of poetry is that here belief is suspended and the reality talked about is not actually posited as real; the poetic object is a quasi object, an irreal object, as Husserl would say. Its mode of existence is that of the *as if*.

Now it is hard to see where traditional, systematic metaphysics, which claims to say something definite about being—namely, *what* it is—fits in here, between what Ricoeur calls "poetic metaphor and transcendental equivocity" (*MV*, p. 324; *RM*, p. 258). If systematic metaphysics is something more or something other than poetry, something more than the pure imaginative use of metaphorical language, as Ricoeur wants to say, it would seem that it would have to be the *abuse* of metaphor, in which case it would be a form of myth, and the truths of metaphysics would be believed-in, dead metaphors. But this, too, Ricoeur refuses to accept (see Study VIII, sec. 3). Conceptual truth is not "tensional" truth, he says (*MV*, p. 375; *RM*, p. 296). I take this to mean that conceptual, speculative truths are not qualified assertions where the "is" in-

cludes an "is-not." Conceptual vision, if it is not then a "stereoscopic," metaphorical double vision, must be the straightforward intuition of an unequivocal
essence; here one sees not "likeness" but "identity" (see *MV*, p. 376; *RM*,
pp. 296–97). But this would be tantamount to saying that philosophical, speculative truths are literal (univocal) ones and that philosophical understanding
is of the same sort, basically, as scientific understanding. I find this hard to
accept, since it carries along with it the traditional rationalist prejudice that
philosophy is or can be a *science*, a kind of superknowledge of the basic structure
of reality.

I can see only one way out of the dilemma which, while not identifying
philosophy with science, respects nonetheless the specificity of philosophical
discourse vis-à-vis both literal and metaphorical (poetic) discourse. The only
form of metaphysics possible would be an *indirect* or *negative* ontology which
does not claim to say anything directly about reality or being but which instead
points to a creative reality which is the always presupposed but never directly
known or intuited source of all creative, human discourse. It seems to me that
at times Ricoeur is actually tending toward such a position, as when in his
previous book, *Le conflit des interprétations*, he says: "ontology is indeed the
promised land for a philosophy that begins with language and with reflection;
but, like Moses, the speaking and reflecting subject can only glimpse this land
before dying." And yet here in this book Ricoeur does not fully follow up on
all the implications of such an assertion. For he says here that ontological
discourse is an independent mode of discourse which has its specific, conceptual
autonomy vis-à-vis poetic metaphor and, so to speak, its own specific field of
application and validity. He insists that an abstract, conceptual, i.e., philosophical, meaning can be produced through the very weakening or wearing
out (*usure*) of metaphor and that the conceptual meaning thus engendered
cannot be reduced to metaphorical meaning. The semantic aims of ontology
are quite different from those of poetry; there is a structure of reality which is
the proper referent of ontology. Ricoeur appears to want to say that philosophical discourse would not be possible if there were not a rigorously independent essence which is its "meaning" (see *MV*, p. 372; and *RM*, p. 293). But
is it really the case, I wonder, that a philosophical "concept" is something quite
independent of the metaphorical, analogical process of thinking whereby it is
engendered in the first place? This brings us back to Ricoeur's own "most
extreme hypothesis," namely, that the categories of reality that metaphor violates are themselves products of metaphor. A concept expresses the essence of
something, but what is it, really, to state the essence of something—*what* it
is—if it is not to draw a creative analogy and say what it is *like*? What is the
essence of something, if not a metaphor taken literally?

Thus it seems to me that this book concludes on what might be called a
hesitant or ambiguous note and betrays something like a nostalgia for the great
but bygone era of speculative, systematic metaphysics. This is not meant as a
criticism, simply as a reminder—by one devoted, but incorrigibly antiration-
alist, admirer of Ricoeur.

Note

This text was originally composed for presentation at a symposium sponsored by the Institute of Religious Studies at the University of California at Santa Barbara, April 29–May 1, 1976, honoring the work of Paul Ricoeur and entitled "On the Interpretation of a Text." It was subsequently published by Robert Lechner in *Philosophy Today*, supplement to vol. XXI, no. 4/4 (Winter 1977). In addition to other pieces on Ricoeur, this special supplement contains two of the responses that were made to my paper in Santa Barbara: Mary Gerhart, "The Extent and Limits of Metaphor: Reply to Gary Madison"; and David Pellauer, "A Response to Gary Madison's 'Reflections on Paul Ricoeur's Philosophy of Metaphor.' " The particular format of my text was dictated by the fact that the organizers of the symposium specifically requested that I write something "critical" and by the fact, as well, that Ricoeur was slated to be present for the reading of the text. A fuller development of the position underlying this critique can be found in G. B. Madison, *Understanding: A Phenomenological-Pragmatic Analysis* (Westport, Conn.: Greenwood Press, 1982), on which I was working at the time.

SIX

Ricoeur and the Hermeneutics
of the Subject

"Le symbole donne à penser; The symbol gives rise to thought," Paul Ricoeur wrote in the conclusion to his book *The Symbolism of Evil.* The hermeneutical reflections that he has pursued now for several decades on the various cultural signs, symbols, and texts that reveal and constitute the meaning of human existence themselves give rise to thought, are thought-provoking. It is the purpose of this essay to explore some of the more notable aspects of Ricoeur's hermeneutical attempt to elucidate the dimensions of human subjectivity.

To think, in the proper sense of the term, always means to think anew, to think afresh. One of Ricoeur's chief contributions to philosophy in our time is the way in which he had enabled us to think afresh that age-old and central question of philosophy which is ourselves, the question as to what it means to be a thinking, reflective subject. The existing individual, the human subject, has always been the focal point of Ricoeur's philosophical inquiries, coming as he does out of the tradition of French reflexive philosophy initiated by Descartes and represented in the twentieth century by his teacher, Jean Nabert. "When we say philosophy is reflection," he writes, "we mean, assuredly, self-reflection." Whence Ricoeur's guiding question: "Therefore, what does Reflection signify? What does the Self of self-reflection signify?"[1] Ricoeur's approach to subjectivity has been both *phenomenological* and *hermeneutical*—phenomenological, in that it seeks to clarify through reflective analysis that which is immediately and indubitably given to consciousness: the fact of the subject's own existence, the "mineness" characteristic of existence; hermeneutical, in that this reflective analysis is not descriptive in an intuitive or introspective sort of way but is indirect and interpretive and is, moveover, motivated by the basic goal of all hermeneutics: a heightened self-understanding. As Ricoeur wrote in the early 1980s in an account he gave of his philosophizing:

A reflexive philosophy considers the most radical philosophical problems to be those which concern the possibility of *self-understanding* as the subject of the operations of knowing, willing, evaluating, etc. Reflexion [*sic*] is that act of turning back upon itself by which a subject grasps, in a moment of intellectual clarity and moral responsibility, the unifying principle of the operations among which it is dispersed and forgets itself as subject.[2]

The two basic notions in Ricoeur's philosophizing could be said to be *meaning* and *existence*.[3] The goal he set himself is the very goal of philosophy as he sees it: "to clarify existence itself by use of concepts."[4] The operant presupposition or "central intution"[5] behind this endeavor is that existence is indeed meaningful, that, notwithstanding the very real existence of unmeaning, necessity (unfreedom), and evil, there is in existence a "super-abundance of meaning to the abundance of non-sense."[6] It is because it is guided throughout by the concept of meaning that Ricoeur's philosophy is in the most proper sense of the term phenomenological.

In light of the many penetrating criticisms that have been made in the last few decades of Husserlian phenomenology, one might well wonder, however, if Ricoeur's commitment to meaning does not lead him into an uncritical acceptance of the traditional idealist and metaphysical presuppositions that are still present in Husserl's thought. Falling into an "idealism of meaning" is perhaps the most serious danger which menaces any phenomenological philosophy. It is, nevertheless, one which Ricoeur is well aware of.

As was the case with French phenomenology in general, with Merleau-Ponty and Lévinas, for example, Ricoeur was distrustful from the outset of the "intellectualist" character of Husserl's philosophy, which is why in his first major work, *Le Volontaire et l'involontaire* (1950), he sought to expand the phenomenological, eidetic method in such a way as to enable it to deal with such noncognitive aspects of human being as volition, motivation, emotion, the body, and action. "The act of the Cogito," he said, "is not a pure act of self-positing; it lives on what it receives and in a dialouge with the conditions in which it is itself rooted."[7] But just as in his *Phenomenology of Perception*, Merleau-Ponty, "the greatest of French phenomenologists," as Ricoeur once described him, did not go so far as to bring into question the method itself of "intentional analysis" (with all of the idealist overtones that are present in it), so also it was only subsequently, after he had begun to emphasize the hermeneutical dimension of his work, that Ricoeur began to grapple in a serious way with the threat of idealism.[8]

In an interesting essay entitled "Phenomenology and Hermeneutics" dating from the mid-1970s, Ricoeur recognized that "phenomenology is always in danger of reducing itself to a transcendental subjectivism."[9] But is the situation any different in regard to hermeneutics? For, like phenomenology, hermeneutics, conceived of as the interpretive activity of a thinking subject which turns back and reflects on itself in the aim of achieving a heightened self-understanding, is guided by what could be called the "presupposition of meaning." As Ricoeur formulated it:

It must be supposed that experience in all its fullness . . . has an expressibility [*dicibilité*] in principle. Experience can be said, it demands to be said. To bring it to language is not to change it into something else, but, in articulating and developing it, to make it become itself.

Of course, as Ricoeur here recognized: "It is difficult, admittedly, to formulate this presupposition [of meaning] in a non-idealist language."[10]

Many today would no doubt regard this as a gross understatement. In what could fittingly be labeled the post–Merleau-Pontyian situation in French philosophy, an increasing number of writers have insisted that any commitment to "meaning" and the "subject" is hopelessly idealistic. The work of Lévi-Strauss (structuralism), Foucault, and Derrida (deconstruction) embodies an all-out attack on the very notion of the subject and of lived experience as the ultimate source of meaning. Those influenced by this work would likely view Ricoeur's hermeneutical inquiry into subjectivity as a remnant of the now discredited "metaphysics of presence" or of what they refer to as "humanism." Their goal is not to understand "man"—the reflecting subject—but, as Lévi-Strauss said, to dissolve him.

The structuralist and poststructuralist criticism of metaphysics, the philosophy of consciousness, subjectivism, anthropocentrism, logocentrism, and so on, in the post–Merleau-Pontyian period is something that it would be neither possible nor desirable to reject out of hand. Indeed, the work I have alluded to represents a valuable contribution to the working out of a genuine postmodern, post-Cartesian, postmetaphysical mode of philosophizing. What would be an error would be to reject the very notion of the subject—and Ricoeur's treatment of it—as being somehow "idealist" or "metaphysical." It would be a mistake to throw out the baby (subjectivity) with the bathwater (metaphysics). Ricoeur's vital contribution to current philosophy is to have shown that it is indeed possible to recover the former while at the same time to deconstruct the latter.

Ricoeur's contribution is, in effect, to have "desubjectivized" subjectivity. While it is true that he operates within the tradition of reflexive philosophy, it is also true that in his hands the program of such a philosophy has undergone a radical transformation. Traditional reflexive philosophy viewed the subject as something foundational, and its goal was ultimate, absolute self-transparency. As Ricoeur points out: "the [traditional] idea of reflexion carries with it the desire for absolute transparence, a perfect coincidence of the self with itself, which would make consciousness of self indubitable knowledge and, as such, more fundamental than all forms of positive knowledge."[11] It is precisely this foundational, metaphysical desire for ultimate transparency and certitude that Ricoeur has rejected, i.e, the Husserlian notion of "a thinking subject called 'transcendental,' a subject which is not bound up with the accidents of history, a kind of foundational subject which would be, in the awareness of itself, the source of all knowledge."[12] In doing so, in recognizing that "there is no self-understanding which is not *mediated* by signs, symbols and texts," he has effectively freed phenomenological hermeneutics from, as he himself says, "the idealism with which Husserl had tried to identify phenomenology."[13] Let us therefore attempt to explore in more detail Ricoeur's hermeneutical deconstruction and recovery of the subject.

Perhaps the most important lesson of Ricoeur's researches into the symbolism of evil was that meaning is not something constituted by a sovereign, transcendental Ego. Meaning does not originate in the conscious, reflecting subject but comes to it from the outside, from its encounter with certain throught-provoking symbols mediated by its culture. Meaning is the result, not of a work of constitution, but of an effort of appropriation. The thesis embodied in *Le Symbolique du mal* (1960) is that the conscious subject has access to itself and can know, achieve an understanding of itself, only by means of the mediation of symbols. As Ricoeur stated: " . . . the task of the philosopher guided by symbols would be to break out of the enchanted enclosure of consciousness of oneself, to end the prerogative of self-reflection."[14] The presence of the subject to itself, which is the very definition of subjectivity and self-consciousness, is an indirect, *mediated* presence. And thus were it not for its participation in the realm of culture, the subject would not exist as such. Moreover, the fact that the presence of the self to itself is irremediably indirect means that absolute knowledge (Hegel's *Wissenschaft*) is forever impossible; the ineradicable non-coincidence of the self is nothing other than an expression of the inscrutable presence of "evil" in our lives.[15]

At the time of *The Symbolism of Evil*, Ricoeur tended to equate hermeneutics with the interpretation of symbols, by which he understood those basic cultural expressions which contain a double meaning, such as the various cosmic "elements"—fire, water, earth, and so on—or, more particularly in his case, those double-sense expressions such as stain, fall, deviation, wandering, and captivity. The purpose of hermeneutics, as he then conceived of it, was to interpret, to explicate, to lay out the nonliteral, "symbolic" (or "sacred") meaning in these double-sense expressions. The subsequent development in his thought could perhaps best be described as a widening-out process whereby the focus of his interpretive concerns was extended from *symbols* to *texts*. He realized in effect that the phenomenon of multiple meaning is a characteristic, not of signs in themselves, but above all of the context in which they appear and are employed. His main concern became that of interpretation, textuality itself.

At the same time, Ricoeur realized that he had to take into serious account alternate interpretive strategies, particularly those which seek to *reduce* the second-level meaning of symbolic expressions to some hidden dimension totally foreign to the subject's own interpretation and understanding, such as unconscious drives or social determinants which supposedly operate "behind the back" of the subject. For the net effect of what he aptly termed the *hermeneutics of suspicion* would be to render illusory the goal of his own restorative hermeneutics which aims not "at demystifying a symbolism by unmasking the unavowed forces that are concealed within it" but, rather, at "a re-collection of meaning in its richest, its most elevated, most spiritual diversity."[16] In the hands of the "masters of suspicion," all consciousness tends to become mere false consciousness.

Ricoeur's strategy in dealing with reductive, demasking hermeneutics was typical of his approach in general, which eschews all forms of methodological short cuts: He argued that genuine self-understanding is an arduous, never-to-be-completed task that can be accomplished only in a roundabout way and that it must, in addition, incorporate a critical moment. A reflexive philosophy must not allow itself to be a philosophy of immediate consciousness. The reflecting subject has meaningful access to its own existence only through the *signs* in which gets expressed its effort to exist and its desire to be. Ricoeur made this point quite clearly in the 1960s:

> . . . the celebrated Cartesian *cogito*, which grasps itself directly in the experience of doubt, is a truth as vain as it is invincible . . . this truth is a vain truth; it is like a first step which cannot be followed by any other, so long as the *ego* of the *ego cogito* has not been recaptured in the mirror of its objects, of its works, and, finally, of its acts. Reflection is blind intuition if it is not mediated by what Dilthey called the expressions in which life objectifies itself. Or, to use the language of Jean Nabert, reflection is nothing other than the appropriation of our act of existing by means of a critique applied to the works and the acts which are the signs of this act of existing. Thus reflection is a critique . . . in the sense that the *cogito* can be recovered only by the detour of a decipherment of the documents of its life. Reflection is the appropriation of our effort to exist and of our desire to be by means of the works which testify to this effort and this desire.[17]

Reflection is a critique in another sense as well. Not only is consciousness not accessible to itself in immediate transparency such that it must seek to know itself through "a decipherment of the documents of its life," in addition, immediate self-consciousness is more often than not a *false consciousness*, as Ricoeur concedes to the hermeneuts of suspicion. The message of Freudianism is that "the subject is never the subject one thinks it is."[18] "Thus," as he says, "reflection must be doubly indirect: first, because existence is evinced only in the documents of life, but also because consciousness is first of all false consciousness, and it is always necessary to rise by means of a corrective critique from misunderstanding to understanding."[19] Yet while he fully recognizes the explanatory usefulness of the impersonal (or subpersonal) methodological, theoretical constructs of, for instance, Marxism, Ricoeur insists that these "abstractions" must not be taken for ultimate realities in such a way as to make us lose sight of concrete, individual subjects.[20] The fact remains that, for him, "the only reality, in the end, are individuals who do things."[21]

Ricoeur's reflexive philosophy is not a philosophy of consciousness, and the hermeneutical subject is not a metaphysical subject—neither a Cartesian coincidence of the self with itself in some inner retreat nor the soul-substance of traditional ontotheology. The subject *qua* metaphysical substrate or epistemological origin—this theoretical construct of traditional substantialistic and objectivistic philosophy—is in fact the great casualty of Ricoeur's phenomenological hermeneutics. The hermeneutical subject is a speaking/spoken subject; it exists only as the self-affirming object of effort and desire, and to the degree that it exists self-understandingly it does so only as the result of the constitutive and critical play of signs, symbols, and texts; it is not a natural (or metaphysical) given but the result of a process of semiosis.[22] There is, Ricoeur says, "no self-knowledge without some kind of detour through signs, symbols and cultural works, etc."[23] Our own existence, he goes on to say,

> cannot be separated from the account we can give of ourselves. It is in telling our
> own stories that we give ourselves an identity. We recognize ourselves in the stories
> we tell about ourselves. It makes little difference whether these stories are true
> or false, fiction as well as verifiable history provides us with an identity.[24]

Speaking of the result of emphasizing the semiotic makeup of self-identity, the mediating role of texts in the subject's own self-constitution, Ricoeur says:

> The most important consequence of all this is that an end is put once and for all
> to the Cartesian and Fictean—and to an extent Husserlian—ideal of the subject's
> transparence to itself. To understand oneself is to understand oneself as one con-
> fronts the text and to receive from it the conditions for a self other than that which
> first undertakes the reading.[25]

A "hermeneutical philosophy," he says, is precisely one which accepts the mediated nature of subjectivity and which "gives up the dream of a total mediation, at the end of which reflection would once again amount to intellectual intuition in the transparence to itself of an absolute subject."[26] Nothing could be further from Hegelianism and traditional metaphysics in general than this.

What Ricoeur has finally succeeded in doing, by means of his extensive researches into textuality and interpretation theory, is to have reformulated his long-standing presupposition of meaning in a nonidealist or nonmetaphysical language. The reflecting subject in search of meaning, self-understanding, is a linguistic subject, a subject which is given to and which knows itself by means of the language it inhabits. And language, when one goes beyond a merely structural approach and considers units of discourse of a sentence or longer in length, does not exist in a void. The characteristic of those autonomous linguistic entities called literary texts (whose meaning is not to be explained subjectivistically, in terms of authorial intention) is that they refer to a world, a world which they themselves project or bring into existence by means of their own literary devices. The task of interpretation or hermeneutics is to reconstruct the internal dynamic of a text so as to make manifest the world which it projects. This world is a possible world, one which I, as reader, could inhabit. In opening up worlds which express possibilities of being, literary texts generate meaning, allow for self-understanding. In revealing possibilities of being, texts further our self-understanding, for what we essentially are is what we can *become*, the being *otherwise* and being *more* that are the objects of effort and desire, the two basic characteristics of the act of existing.

Understanding, as Gadamer would say, is not so much an *activity* performed by a "subject" as it is the very being of the subject, something, therefore, which, as it were, the subject undergoes. Ricoeur makes much the same point when he says:

> To understand is not to project oneself into the text but to expose oneself to it; it is to receive a self enlarged by the appropriation of the proposed worlds which interpretation unfolds. In sum, it is the matter of the text which gives the reader his dimension of subjectivity; understanding is thus no longer a constitution of which the subject possesses the key. . . . if fiction is a fundamental dimension of the reference of the text, it is equally a fundamental dimension of the subjectivity of the reader: in reading, I 'unrealise myself.' Reading introduces me to imaginative variations of the *ego*. The metamorphosis of the world in play [in the text] is also the playful metamorphosis of the *ego*.[27]

The antimetaphysical thrust of Ricoeur's deconstruction and recovery of the subject is fully evident in his statement:

> In opposition to the idealist thesis of the ultimate self-responsibility of the mediating subject, hermeneutics proposes to make subjectivity the final, and not the first, category of a theory of understanding. Subjectivity must be lost as radical origin, if it is to be recovered in a more modest role.[28]

Given the hermeneutical, postmetaphysical way Ricoeur has redefined subjectivity, the "qualitative transformation of reflective consciousness"[29] he has instituted, it should be apparent that a poststructuralist criticism of Ricoeur's work on the grounds that it is still "metaphysical" or "idealist" would be hard to defend. Indeed, it could be argued that Ricoeur more decisively overcomes traditional philosophy than do either Foucault or Derrida, in that Ricoeur's overcoming of objectivism does not point in the direction of either relativism or nihilism.[30] A more pertinent criticism of Ricoeur has been made by Calvin O. Schrag, whose work greatly compliments that of Ricoeur.[31] Objecting to "a widespread misdirection in contemporary philosophy" having "to do with an excessive and self-limiting preoccupation with discourse and discursive practices," Schrag accuses Ricoeur of, if not reducing action to textuality (as he criticizes Derrida for doing), at least viewing it "through the metaphorics of textuality."[32]

This is an important criticism, for if "man," the human subject, is, as the Greeks said, the "speaking animal," it is equally true that he is the "acting animal," *animal agens*. If language is, as Heidegger would say, an *Existentiale*, an essential characteristic of human being, so likewise is action. Action is co-primordial with language; human existence is inconceivable apart from it. This is precisely Schrag's point; he wants to emphasize that action and discourse are equally primordial, "nonreducible twin halves of an undivided history."[33] Although Schrag recognizes that Ricoeur has made "an aggressive move into the domain of action," he feels that he has done so in such a way that action is subordinated to discourse, or considered simply from the point of discourse and textuality. While Ricoeur obviously does not maintain in a Derridian fashion that "il n'y a pas de hors-texte," he does not, Schrag suggests, consider action sufficiently in its own right.

In Schrag's defense, it must be admitted that when referring to action and history Ricoeur tends to speak of "quasi-texts." Does this mean that he downgrades action or subordinates it to discourse? It seems to me that it is rather an attempt to suggest a way of dealing meaningfully with human action that we find in one of Ricoeur's key articles (whose title is itself very revealing), "The Model of the Text: Meaningful Action Considered as a Text." It is significant, I think, that this article has had a wide impact on the practitioners of the social sciences, i.e., those whose prime concern is action.

To view action on the model of the text is, admittedly, to deal with it in what is apparently a marginal way. Is there, however, any other way of dealing meaningfully with action? Acting beings may be what we are, but how, as beings which have an insatiable desire to *understand* what we are and do, can we understand what we are and do other than by speaking and writing about it? It would be hard to deny, I think, that it is only by considering action as a text that we can hope to come to some understanding of it, and thus of that being which essentially we are. When we seek to understand human events, which is to say, action, to *account* for them, the giving of an account invariably assumes the form of telling a story. To understand an experience or an event is to make sense of it in the form of a story. As Hannah Arendt remarked: "The story reveals the meaning of what otherwise would remain an unbearable sequence of sheer happenings."[34]

One of the things we are concerned with when dealing with human action *in an attempt to understand it* is motive. How can motives, an essential ingredient of action, be understood? Ricoeur writes:

> . . . it seems that in order for a motive to have explanatory force, it must be given in the form of a kind of small autobiography. By that I mean that I must put my motive under the rules of story telling; and it is quite possible that this process of story telling might accompany the generation of intentions themselves, as if retrospection were always suffocating the prospective mood of action.

Emphasizing the inseparability of action from textuality, Ricoeur goes on to say:

> The intersection between the theory of texts and the theory of action becomes more obvious when the point of view of the onlooker is added to that of the agent,

because the onlooker will not only consider action in terms of its motive, but also in terms of its consequences, perhaps of its unintended consequences. A different way of making sense with actions occurs then, and also a different way of reading it as a quasi-text. Detached from its agent, a course of action acquires an autonomy similar to the semantic autonomy of a text. It leaves its mark on the course of events and eventually it becomes sedimented into social institutions. Human action has become archive and document. Thus it acquires potential meaning beyond its relevance to its initial situation.[35]

Text and action are quite simply inseparable; they are, as Schrag so aptly says, "twin halves of an undivided history." It is by means of literary-historical texts that we are able to understand what we are as acting beings, which is to say, as temporal beings. For time is the dimension of action, and is meaningful only in terms of action. A hermeneutical philosophy in search of the meaning of existence cannot avoid the methodological demand to reflect systematically on literary discourse and historical narrative and on their insuperable intertwining. It is thus understandable how Ricoeur should have come to be preoccupied with the dual theme: *Time and Narrative.*

Action and discourse are inseparable. One could in fact define action as that which naturally calls for, gives rise to, discourse as its teleological fulfillment. When all is said and done, action is nothing other than "un sujet de discours." What links the two inseparably together is manifested in that thing called *history*. Significantly, the word *history* signifies (in both French and English) both a certain form of *discourse* about action and the *action* itself which is talked about. *History* means *both* a particular discursive discipline ("historiography") *and* that which this discipline is about ("history," i.e., the actual happenings). It is significant also that in French "une histoire" can mean either a supposedly factual account of past events and actions or a mere fanciful tale. There is, as Ricoeur has convincingly argued in his latest work, no intrinsic, structural, or formal difference between "history" and "literature." In any event, it is significant that in his attempt to uncover the significance of human existence—which is both discourse and action—he should have been led into a thoroughgoing reflection on history.

And as he has shown, the central element in both history and fiction, which are simply two different forms of storytelling, is *emplotment*. The notion of plot is one which, he says, "I take as a guideline for my entire investigation, in the area of the history of historians (or historiography) as well as in that of fiction (from epics and folk tales to the modern novel)."[36] Emplotment, he says, consists mainly in the selection and arrangement of the events and the actions recounted, which make of the fable a story that is 'complete and entire' [Aristotle] with a beginning, middle and end.[37] No action, he goes on to say, "is a beginning except in a story that it inaugurates . . . no action constitutes a middle unless it instigates a change of fortune in the story told . . . no action, taken in itself, constitutes an end except insofar as it concludes a course of action in the story told." Emplotment is thus nothing other than the combinatory activity of the storyteller which makes bare events *into* a story. And this means that an event, as such, is what it is only to the degree that "it contributes to the progress of a story."[38] "An event is not only an occurrence, something that happens, but a narrative component." Plot is what makes action *intelligible* (it is what "holds together circumstances, ends and means, initiatives and unwanted consequences"). It is, in short, what makes for *understanding, meaning.*

It does not seem to me that Ricoeur's observations are in any way belied by the fact that some contemporary storytellers, such as the antinovelist Alain Robbe-Grillet, set out to compose stories in such a way as deliberately to frustrate the reader's desire for "emplotment." For the refusal of narrative emplotment and "closure" is understandable only in terms of that which it denies. A novel such as *Jalousie* does not, properly speaking, *lack* a plot (as if the writer were inept at his craft); it is the deliberate *refusal* of plot in the traditional sense. Moreover, it could be said that such a refusal of plot is actually meant as a means for better portraying the actual structure of lived experience. For it is a fact that in our actual lives there are no absolute beginings and endings, thus no absolutely decisive middles, either. Something is always beginning and something is always ending, and there is no single story line, but many overlapping and interlocking projects. The progression and unfolding of our lives is not continual and progressive but, so to speak, hesitant and episodic. And yet the fact remains that life itself has a teleological structure, which is simply confirmed and enriched in the narrator's art.[39] We read stories not in order to escape from life but in the hope of understanding it better.

In any event, what is central to narrative is, as Ricoeur has stressed, its temporal character:

> My basic hypothesis . . . is the following: the common feature of human experience, that which is marked, organized and clarified by the fact of storytelling in all its forms, is its *temporal character*. Everything that is recounted occurs in time, takes time, unfolds temporally; and what unfolds in time can be recounted. Perhaps, indeed, every temporal process is recognized as such only to the extent that it can, in one way or another, be recounted. This reciprocity which is assumed to exist between narrativity and temporality is the theme of my present research.[40]

To express the matter in another way: Experience is meaningful, precisely because it can be *recounted*, and it can be recounted precisely because it has a temporal structure which is essentially teleological ("emplotted"). One of the "major presuppositions," as Ricoeur says, of *Time and Narrative* is that "time becomes human time to the extent that it is organized after the manner of a narrative; narrative, in turn, is meaningful to the extent that it portrays the features of temporal experience."[41] The act of understanding and making intelligible—storytelling—is not a free-floating, groundless sort of aimless *play* (a "bottomless chessboard"), as certain poststructuralists would maintain, but is itself rooted in experience, in the temporality of existence, which is what

gets expressed and comes to light in the stories we compose about what
we do.

Of course, this is a thesis which many a poststructuralist would criticize.
Just as the antiphenomenological post–Merleau-Pontyians have sought to eliminate altogether the phenomenological notions of the "subject" and "meaning,"
so also have they attacked as "metaphysical" the very notion of *history*. One
of the dominant themes in recent philosophy has been the critique of the
teleological notion of history, of history as having a "beginning" (*archē*) and an
"end" (*telos*). What is proclaimed is the end of "the end of history." Again, to
the degree that these criticisms have undermined the traditional, metaphysical
conception of history, they are both justified and valuable. But again, as a
criticism of phenomenological hermeneutics as practiced by Ricoeur, they are
quite groundless.

In the first place, it would be absurd to deny that human action (as opposed
to purely natural processes or mere bodily, involuntary movements) has a
teleological structure. People act to achieve certain ends, and the very definition of action is that it is purposive behavior. This is a phenomenal fact and
is as undeniable as is the *cogito*, the fact of the reflective subject's own existence.
Just as "I-hood" is a necessary and undeniable *fact* of existence, just as, as
Emile Benveniste has shown,[42] there is no discourse which does not posit or
implicate a speaking subject (*le sujet du discours*), so also is action quite simply
unintelligible if it is not interpreted teleologically, with reference to purposeful
subjects. Ricoeur quite rightly observes:

> Directly or indirectly, history is always the history of men who are the bearers,
> the agents and the victims of the currents, institutions, functions and structures
> in which they find themselves placed. . . . action . . . implies agents, aims, cir-
> cumstances, interactions and results both intended and unintended.[43]

Of course, these phenomenal facts do not in any way justify or support a
metaphysical construction of them. They do not justify one in asserting that
history *has* an end, that it is going somewhere, or that in our lives meaning
will ultimately prevail over unmeaning, non-sense—just as the fact of "I-hood"
does not in any way justify one in positing a substantial self whose existence is
somehow inscribed in and guaranteed by the nature of things. Poststructuralism
is absolutely correct in deconstructing metaphysical mythmaking of this sort.

As we have seen, however, Ricoeur himself has decidedly forsworn traditional metaphysics. Moreover, his hermeneutical reading of action and temporality can appeal for support to the actual practice of the social sciences. This
is emminently fitting, since, unlike Gadamer, Ricoeur has always been at pains
to address himself to the methodological concerns of the various human disciplines and has energetically sought to maintain a dialogue with them. This
dialogue has borne fruit. One of the areas in which it has most recently proven
productive is economics.[44] Not only have economists begun to look to Ricoeur's
work for support in ridding their discipline of positivistic objectivism, but cer-

tain positions that they themselves have long maintained lend, as it were, support to Ricoeur's own hermeneutical theses. A case in point is what is referred to as Austrian economics.

In his major treatise, *Human Action*, a systematic presentation of the economic theory which he labels "praxeology," Ludwig von Mises (1881–1973), an acute observer, as indeed most economists are, of human affairs, observed that the two basic, indeed, as he would say, aprioristic, characteristics of action are "to remove uneasiness" and to make ourselves "better off." The very meaning of action is that it is purposeful; it is the deliberate attempt on the part of human beings to improve their position, to make their lives more livable, more meaningful. The nature of action is, as we have said, teleological. As Mises observed in another work:

> In fact, nothing is more certain for the human mind than what the category of human action brings into relief. There is no human being to whom the intent is foreign to substitute by appropriate conduct one state of affairs for another state of affairs that would prevail if he did not interfere. Only where there is action are there men.
>
> What we know about our own actions and about those of other people is conditioned by our familiarity with the category of action that we owe to a process of self-examination and introspection as well as of understanding of other people's conduct. To question this insight is no less impossible than to question the fact that we are alive.[45]

The phenomenological hermeneutics of human existence cannot but agree. The phenomenological fact—confirmed by economic observation—is that existence is meaningful in that it is unintelligible except in terms of meaningful action. No discourse, therefore, is possible which rejects the "postulate of meaningfulness." It is logically impossible to deny meaning, just as it is logically impossible to deny one's own existence as a subject.[46]

It must be remembered, however, that this assertion is phenomenological, and not metaphysical. Those who would seek to pass from phenomenological facts to metaphysical essences and spell out the "ultimate meaning of being" are engaged, as we now know after the death of metaphysics, in a hopeless pursuit. There is nothing to be regretted here, however, for the notion of "being in itself" is phenomenological non-sense anyway. The loss of illusions, consoling though they may be, is not something we should regret, as Ricoeur has been at ample pains to point out.[47]

Thus the recognition that, phenomenologically or hermeneutically speaking, existence is meaningful is in no way a denial of contingency, ambiguity, uncertainty, unmeaning. The latter are equally undeniable facts of experience. But if, from the point of view of action, metaphysical gnosis—the presumption on the part of reason (as Merleau-Ponty would have said) to grasp the ultimate meaning of being—is without warrant, so likewise are all forms of fatalism or nihilism. Ricoeur's wager for meaningfulness is itself fully warranted when it

is extricated from all metaphysical contexts, as indeed it is when it is grounded
in the hermeneutical implications of human action and narrative discursivity.

To conclude this examination of Ricoeur's philosophy of the subject it might
be instructive to contrast him with one of his earlier contemporaries, Albert
Camus. The problem that Camus posed in his book *Le Mythe de Sisyphe*,
subtitled "Essai sur l'absurde," was essentially this: In the absence of any access
on our part to transcendent values (or what today people might refer to as
"transcendental signifieds"), what, if any, are our "grounds" for asserting the
priority of meaning over meaninglessness? Camus, of course, concluded that
there are none and proceeded accordingly to elaborate a philosophy of the
absurd whose purpose was to banish hope as a form of escapism. This conclusion
was logical and consistent, given Camus's approach to the question of meaning;
it was dictated by his method, which was basically that of a philosophy of
consciousness.

In this book, Camus, in a quasi-Cartesian fashion, undertook to do an inventory of consciousness, asking in effect: What exactly do I know with certainty? *That* I am is certain, but *who* or *what* I am most certainly is not. All
statements as to the "what" or "who" of existence, its meaning, are mere *interpretations*, and thus do not qualify as *knowledge*. Whence Camus's conclusion:
Existence is basically meaningless, absurd. The point to note, however, is this:
Camus's demand for epistemological and metaphysical certainty, *knowledge*,
for a stable Archimedean point, was itself thoroughly foundationalist and ra-
tionalistic, thus quite unreasonable. Above all, it ignored that most basic characteristic of human existence: action. As we have seen, it is the very nature of
action that it commits us to meaning, purposiveness. As acting subjects, we
always go beyond what we know, and quite rightly so. Camus was never able
to give a convincing rebuttal to the suicide option—which is what he wanted
to do—because he considered human beings merely in their quality of knowing
subjects and completely ignored the fact that they are also acting beings. Thus
the conclusion that Ricoeur draws in regard to the question as to the meaningfulness of existence is actually much more in line with the phenomenological-
hermeneutical facts of existence.

In the last analysis, we have no epistemological or metaphysical grounds
for *knowing* that existence is meaningful; there is no possible way in which the
"postulate of meaningfulness" could be "verified." Yet the desire for meaning,
the hope for the ultimate triumph of sense over non-sense in our lives, the
triumph of reconciliation, as Arendt would say, over, as Merleau-Ponty so aptly
called it, adversity, is not delusory. Reiterating a conviction he had stated in
his early collection of essays, *History and Truth*, where he spoke of the "rational
feeling of hope,"[48] Ricoeur says in his latest work: "For my part, I hold that
the search for concordance is part of the unavoidable assumptions of discourse
and of communication."[49] His ontological commitment to meaning is firmly
grounded in the phenomenological makeup of human existence, in undeniable
facts of experience, which are, after all, the one and only ultimate grounding
to which we, as acting beings, have access. The fact that we are inescapably

acting and narrating beings is sufficient justification for what is no doubt the ultimate underlying category in Ricoeur's philosophy: *hope*. In his hermeneutics of the subject, Paul Ricoeur has succeeded in outlining a true *poétique du possible*.

Notes

This essay was written for inclusion in *The Philosophy of Paul Ricoeur*, Library of Living Philosophers, ed. Lewis E. Hahn (Peru, Ill.: Open Court, forthcoming).

1. Paul Ricoeur, *Freud and Philosophy: An Essay on Interpretation*, trans. Denis Savage (New Haven, Conn.: Yale University Press, 1970), pp. 42–43.

2. Ricoeur, "On Interpretation," in *Philosophy in France Today*, ed. Alan Montefiore (Cambridge, Eng.: Cambridge University Press, 1983), p. 188.

3. *Sens et existence* was the title which, on Ricoeur's own suggestion, I gave to the anthology in Ricoeur's honor that I published on the occasion of his sixtieth birthday (Paris: Éditions du Seuil, 1975).

4. Ricoeur, *Freedom and Nature: The Voluntary and the Involuntary*, trans. Erazim V. Kohak (Evanston, Ill.: Northwestern University Press, 1966), p. 17.

5. See T. M. Van Leeuwen, *The Surplus of Meaning: Ontology and Eschatology in the Philosophy of Paul Ricoeur* (Amsterdam: Editions Rodopi, 1981), p. 1.

6. Ricoeur, *The Conflict of Interpretations*, ed. Don Ihde (Evanston, Ill.: Northwestern University Press, 1974), p. 411.

7. *Freedom and Nature*, p. 18.

8. In *Freud and Philosophy* (French edition, 1965) Ricoeur says, speaking of his earlier *Freedom and Nature*: "A hermeneutic method, coupled with reflection, goes much farther than an eidetic method I was then practicing. . . . The rootedness of reflection in life is itself understood in reflective consciousness only in the form of a hermeneutic [deciphered, interpreted, not descriptive] truth" (p. 458).

9. Ricoeur, "Phenomenology and Hermeneutics" in *Hermeneutics and the Human Sciences*, ed. John B. Thompson (Cambridge, Eng.: Cambridge University Press, 1981), p. 112.

10. Ibid., p. 115.

11. "On Interpretation," p. 188.

12. "History as Narrative and Practice," interview with Paul Ricoeur by Peter Kemp, *Philosophy Today*, Fall 1985, p. 219.

13. "On Interpretation," p. 191.

14. Ricoeur, *The Symbolism of Evil*, trans. Emerson Buchanan (Boston: Beacon Press, 1969), p. 356.

15. "All symbols give rise to thought, but the symbols of evil show in an exemplary way that there is always more in myths and symbols than in all of our philosophy, and that a philosophical interpretation of symbols will never become absolute knowledge. . . . Thus the symbols of evil attest to the unsurpassable character of all symbolism; while telling us of the failure of our existence and of our power of existing, they also declare the failure of systems of thought that would swallow up symbols in an absolute knowledge" (*Freud and Philosophy*, p. 527).

16. "On Interpretation," pp. 192–93.

17. *The Conflict of Interpretations*, pp. 17–18. See also *Freud and Philosophy*, pp. 42–47.

18. *Freud and Philosophy*, p. 420.

19. *The Conflict of Interpretations*, p. 18.

20. See "History as Narrative and Practice," p. 217.

21. Ibid., p. 216.

22. " . . . a philosophy of reflection is not a philosophy of consciousness, if by consciousness we mean immediate self-consciousness. Consciousness . . . is a task, but it is a task because it is not a given" (*Freud and Philosophy*, pp. 43–44).

23. "History as Narrative and Practice," p. 213.

24. Ibid., p. 214.

25. "On Interpretation," p. 193.

26. Ibid., p. 194.

27. Ricoeur, "Hermeneutics and the Critique of Ideology" in *Hermeneutics and the Human Sciences*, ed. Thompson, p. 94.

28. "Phenomenology and Hermeneutics," pp. 112–13.

29. *The Symbolism of Evil*, p. 356.

30. I am using the terms "objectivism" and "relativism" in the sense in which Richard Bernstein uses them in his book, *Beyond Objectivism and Relativism: Science, Hermeneutics, and Praxis* (Philadelphia: University of Pennsylvania Press, 1983).

31. Calvin O. Schrag, *Communicative Praxis and the Space of Subjectivity* (Bloomington: Indiana University Press, 1986). That Schrag's project is fully complementary to that of Ricoeur is evidenced by his remark: "The disassemblage of the classical substance-attribute categorial scheme and the modern empirico-transcendental doublet does not entail a displacement of the subject in every sense you please. We wish to show, quite to the contrary, that the proper charge of such a disassemblage is to provide a clearing for a restoration of the subject. It opens the path to a transvalued subjectivity within a new space, making it possible to speak of a new humanism at the end of philosophy" (Schrag, "Subjectivity and Praxis at the End of Philosophy," in *Hermeneutics and Deconstruction*, ed. H. Silverman and D. Ihde [Albany: State University of New York Press 1985], p. 25).

32. *Communicative Praxis and the Space of Subjectivity*, pp. 11, 170.

33. Ibid., pp. 170–71.

34. Hannah Arendt, *Men in Dark Times* (New York: Harcourt Brace Jovanovich, 1968), p. 104.

35. Hans-Georg Gadamer and Paul Ricoeur, "The Conflict of Interpretations," in *Phenomenology: Dialogues and Bridges*, ed. R. Bruzina and B. Wilshire (Albany: State University of New York Press, 1982), p. 308.

36. "On Interpretation," p. 178.

37. Ibid., p. 177.

38. Ibid., p. 178.

39. For an excellent treatment of this issue, see David Carr, "Life and the Narrator's Art," in *Hermeneutics and Deconstruction*, ed. Silverman and Ihde; as well as David Carr, *Time, Narrative, and History* (Bloomington: Indiana University Press, 1986).

40. "On Interpretation," p. 170.

41. Ricoeur, *Time and Narrative*, vol. 1, trans. K. McLaughlin and D. Pellauer (Chicago: University of Chicago Press, 1984), p. 3.

42. See, for instance, Emile Benveniste, "Subjectivity in Language," in *Problems in General Linguistics* (Coral Gables, Fla.: University of Miami Press, 1971).

43. "On Interpretation," p. 180.

44. In this regard, special reference should be made to the Society for Interpretive Economics, Department of Economics, George Mason University. Representative of the interest shown by this group in hermeneutics in general and Ricoeur in particular is the publication of Don Lavoie, *The Interpretive Dimension of Economics: Science, Hermeneutics, and Praxeology*, Working Paper No. 15 (1985), Center for the Study of Market Processes, George Mason University.

45. Ludwig von Mises, *The Ultimate Foundation of Economic Science: An Essay on Method* (Kansas City: Sheed Andres and McMeel, 1978), p. 71.

46. Schrag makes the following pertinent remark: "One can doubt and think away the reality of everything save the reality that one is doubting, that one is thinking. Thus the strategy of systematic doubt allegedly delivers an indubitable cogito intuitively grasped in every performance of thought reflectively directed to itself. Thought presupposes a 'who' that is thinking; doubt presupposes a 'who' that is doubting. "There is, we suggest, a similar play operative in the strategy of deconstruction, yielding not the truth of Cartesian subjectivity, the 'I think, therefore I am,' but rather a deconstructionalist modification—'I deconstruct, therefore I am.' In dismantling subjectivity as a positional center and a zero-point consciousness, peeling away the sedimented layers of philosophical construction, some species of claim upon the subject remain in force. The very strategy of deconstruction serendipitously reinvents the subject and instructs us that no complete deconstruction is possible" ("Subjectivity and Praxis at the End of Philosophy," p. 26; see also *Communicative Praxis and the Space of Subjectivity*, pp. 10–11).

47. See, for instance, Ricoeur, "Religion, Atheism, and Faith," in *The Conflict of Interpretations*.

48. See Ricoeur, *History and Truth*, trans. C. A. Kelbley (Evanston, Ill.: Northwestern University Press, 1965), p. 12.

49. Ricoeur, *Time and Narrative*, vol. 2, trans. K. McLaughlin and D. Pellauer (Chicago: University of Chicago Press 1985) p. 28.

SEVEN

Beyond Seriousness and Frivolity: A Gadamerian Response to Deconstruction

1. IN SEARCH OF A STRATEGY.

In the preface to his grandiose *Phänomenologie des Geistes*, in which, like some hired ghostwriter, he narrates the autobiography of the Absolute itself, the archmetaphysician Hegel asserted that philosophy is "serious business." Unlike the artist or the craftsman who merely toys around with things, the philosopher is a *scientist* who penetrates to the very heart of *die Sachen selbst*. In saying this, G. W. F. Hegel was merely reasserting what mainline, serious-minded philosophers—whom I shall simply call "metaphysicians"—have always maintained, from Plato through Descartes and Kant to Husserl and beyond. Philosophy's claim to the status of Science is, however, one which has always been contested by those thinkers who go to make up what I call the Counter-Tradition: the Greek sophists and rhetoricians, the Pyrrhonian skeptics, Montaigne, Kierkegaard, Nietzsche. . . . [1] And the metaphysicians have always retaliated by accusing the counter-traditionalists of "not being serious," of, in fact, being frivolous. It certainly cannot be denied that many of them have indeed delighted in being intellectually playful: Think, for instance, of Gorgias's tongue-in-cheek anti-Parmenedian treatise, *On Non-Being*, Kierkegaardian irony, Nietzschean wit . . . The principal target of the dialectical fireworks of writers such as these has been precisely what Sartre would call "l'esprit du sérieux" of orthodox philosophy. [2] However, does being an antimetaphysician, an antifoundationalist, necessarily entail being frivolous? This is in effect the background question I would like to raise in this paper by way of comparing the intellectual endeavors of Hans-Georg Gadamer and Jacques Derrida. When Gadamerian hermeneutics is compared to Derridian deconstruction, the answer to the question appears to be a "No": One can quite well reject metaphysical seriousness without courting frivolity.

A comparative analysis of these two key figures of our postmodernity is by no means an easy undertaking. While, as a result of many years of close personal association, I feel I understand Gadamer fairly well and have a pretty good idea of what he is up to and of the significance and import of his philosophical project, I cannot say the same for Derrida, even though I first encountered both the man and his work back in the late 1960s when I was teaching as an assistant to Paul Ricoeur at the University of Paris (at that time Derrida was interested among other things in finding out more about Peirce). In fact, directly contrary to my experience with Gadamer, I almost feel I have progressively understood Derrida less and less as the years go by, in the sense that each new work of his has been less and less intelligible to me. It may be because (and I do not mean this frivolously) there is less and less to understand in each new work of his. So I do not pretend to know what Derrida means, wants to say, and am not surprised when he intimates that there is nothing he wants to say, that the *vouloir-dire* is a hopelessly metaphysical notion.[3] Not only is Derrida not a "serious" philosopher, his irony is so extreme that in his case it is not, or so it would seem, a matter of saying one thing and meaning something else thereby but, rather, of saying this and that and the other thing and not really meaning anything at all. In any event, I can only say of him what Gadamer himself has said: "I will not say that I was extremely successful in understanding him."[4]

To be more precise, I believe I understand fairly well the negative or critical significance of Derrida's deconstructive attack on the "metaphysics of presence." This is in fact something I sympathize with wholeheartedly. But this aspect of his undertaking is as fully characteristic, as I shall be arguing, of Gadamer's hermeneutics as it is of Derrida's own deconstruction. What I fail to understand in Derrida is precisely what I fail to understand in Richard Rorty as well: the positive, *philosophical* significance of the critique of metaphysics and epistemology. Where does it all get us? What future, if any, is there for philosophy after the end of Philosophy (in Rorty's sense of the term, which is also that of Derrida, i.e., Platonism)? Is there nothing left for the philosopher to do, after the demise of metaphysical seriousness, but to be an intellectual "kibitzer," a concern-free creator of "abnormal" discourse, an insouciant player of deconstructive and fanciful word games, an agile figure skater on the thin ice of a "bottomless chessboard"?[5]

According to Rorty, the new breed of "intellectuals" who are to displace the traditional "metaphysicians" should not, it appears, have any fixed views on anything. Although Derrida does not quite say this, it often seems to me to be what he implies by his intellectual practice and his approach to texts, as well as by his near-total silence on the ethical and political dimensions of the philosophical enterprise.[6] Rorty's distinction between metaphysicians and intellectuals ("intellectual dilettantes") furnishes me in fact with the interpretive strategy (and the *tertium comparationis*) I need if I am to make some meaningful comparison between Gadamer and Derrida, which otherwise could be as difficult as comparing apples and oranges. Accepting this distinction, I wish to argue the following: While Derrida embodies the traits of Rorty's carefree "intellectual," Gadamer, equally as antimetaphysical as Derrida, does not; he transcends the distinction and in fact provides us with an alternative to it. Whence the title of this paper: "Beyond Seriousness and Frivolity."

The intertextual allusions (or "parasitism") of this title will not fail to be noted, and they in fact provide the reader at the outset with the substance of my argument (which is indeed a Gadamerian *response* to deconstruction).[7] With Richard Bernstein's *Beyond Objectivism and Relativism* in mind, I wish to argue that while Gadamer successfully leads us beyond both objectivism (metaphysics, epistemology) and relativism, Derrida's critique of metaphysics lands us, for all practical purposes, in a debilitating relativism, a kind of philosophical nihilism. I would like to say of Derrida what Bernstein says of Rorty, that from a Gadamerian perspective Derrida's hermeneutics, his handling of texts, is "mutilated or castrated, for it is a hermeneutics without the claim to knowledge or truth."[8] It seems to provide only for autoaffectional "supplements," not the kind of "knowledge" which is achieved through genuine intersubjective intercourse. It is, to use Derrida's words, the "adventurous excess of a writing that is no longer directed by any knowledge."[9] In contrast, what Gadamer's work shows is that it is not at all necessary to abandon the notions of knowledge and truth, that it is in fact fully possible to extricate them from any and all metaphysical-epistemological contexts. To so extricate them is to point the way beyond both objectivism and relativism, beyond both "seriousness" and "frivolity"[10]

2. HERMENEUTICS.

One of the major motivations of Gadamer's hermeneutical project is to overcome or displace what he has called "l'ère de la théorie de la connaissance," the age of epistemology.[11] His critique of classical hermeneutics in the person of Dilthey is directed primarily at the fact that it remains caught up in the modern epistemological, foundationalist project.[12] Phenomenological hermeneutics is thus a thoroughly postmodern form of thought which understandably appeals to an antifoundationalist such as Rorty. What is surprising is that Derrida appears unwilling to recognize the postepistemological and postmetaphysical significance of Gadamer's enterprise.

In *Spurs/Éperons* Derrida does, however, make a number of pejorative references to "hermeneutics." It seems that by "hermeneutics" ("le projet herméneutique") he understands the attempt to get at "the true meaning of the text."[13] The implication seems to be that "hermeneutics" presupposes that a text has a definite, in-itself sort of meaning that it would be the business of interpretation to *reproduce* in as accurate a form as possible, this meaning being the author's intended meaning.[14] In opposition to hermeneutical naiveté of this sort, "la question de la femme" (as Derrida calls it) reveals that there is no "decidable opposition of true and not true"; "philosophical decidability" falls by the wayside (*S/E*, p. 106). Just as it cannot be decided what Nietzsche meant when he scribbled on a scrap of paper " 'I have forgotten my umbrella,' " so it cannot be denied that, "in some monstrous way," the meaning of the totality of Nietzsche's text might be undecidable. "The hermeneut cannot but be provoked and disconcerted," Derrida tells us, by the freeplay (*jeu*) of the text (see *S/E*, pp. 132–33), the endless play of signifiers devoid of decidable meaning which makes of reading itelf not interpretation aiming at truth but free, parodying play.

What actually provokes the "hermeneut" and what he finds disconcerting in all this is Derrida's failure to say what *he* means by "hermeneutics," i.e., exactly who or what he is referring to. The text itself leaves the issue undecided. If by hermeneutics Derrida means the classical hermeneutical tradition stemming from Schleiermacher (whom he alludes to) up to Betti and Hirsh, then Derrida is, whether he likes it or not, stating something "true" when he characterizes it as the attempt to reproduce objective, determinate meanings. If, however, the term is a blanket one meant also to cover Gadamer, and phenomenological hermeneutics in general (the various references to Heidegger and "phenomenology" in the text seem to indicate as much), it is manifestly false. Any meaningful confrontation between Gadamerian hermeneutics and Derridian deconstruction would require that this matter be set straight.

For the sake of the record (or to set it straight), let us simply take note of some of the central theses of Gadamer's hermeneutics. For the sake of the present discussion I shall single out three: (1) *To understand is in fact to interpret* ("All understanding is interpretation . . . " [*TM*, p. 350]). Understanding must not, therefore, be conceived of "epistemologically," as the "correct" *representation* of some "objective" state of affairs. It is not so much reproductive as it is productive, transformative (" . . . understanding is not merely a reproductive, but always productive attitude as well" [*TM*, p. 264]). (2) *All understanding is essentially bound up with language* ("Being that can be understood is language" [*TM*, p. xxii]; " . . . language is the universal medium in which understanding itself is realised" [*TM*, p. 350]). (3) *The understanding of the meaning of text is inseparable from its application* (" . . . understanding always involves something like the application of the text to be understood to the present situation of the interpreter" [*TM*, p. 274]).

These main theses[15] have some important implications, especially in regard to the notions of meaning and truth, as we shall see in the remainder of this paper. Suffice it for the moment to remark on how they entail a decisive break with the logocentric metaphysics of presence in that they render meaningless the metaphysical notion of meanings that would be timeless and invariant, free from the unsettling play of language, and which would simply have to be intuited or otherwise directly reproduced in order to be grasped (for there to be "truth").

One thing which makes a comparison between Gadamer and Derrida difficult is that they are not out to do the same kind of thing. Whereas Gadamer outlines a general philosophical theory, Derrida mainly presents us with a technique for reading.[16] Derrida's interpretive tactic or reading strategy consists in showing how what an author actually does in his text tends to subvert in one way or another what he says, what he *intends*. A deconstructive reading seeks to discover "blind spots" in a text around which it organizes itself (such as the usage of the word "supplement" in Rousseau) with the aim of discrediting the metaphysical and epistemological assumptions held by the author (in particular the assumption that philosophy is a form of pure reason—and not just another form of "writing"—free from the metaphorical and rhetorical play of language), of discrediting, ultimately, the entire metaphysical or ontotheological project. Derrida's work pretty much exhausts itself in this sort of activity (it is, borrowing his own words, "a strategy without finality" [see *Dis*, p. 7]). That it should not be able to do any more is understandable, given the fact that Derrida appears to equate philosophy with metaphysics ("Philosophy" in Rorty's sense), and thus is led to say that deconstruction seeks to determine "from a certain exterior that is unqualifiable or unnameable by philosophy" that which philosophy has dissimulated or forbidden (see *Pos*, p. 6). It is not too much to speak of nihilism if that on the basis of which or in terms of which we criticize the tradition and seek to overcome it is "unqualifiable or unnameable" by us. It is hard to know where we stand and what we are left with when the deconstructive enterprise turns around and, as we are told it must, deconstructs ("erases") itself.[17] Deconstruction, as Derrida rightly observes, is essentially a *critique*. Unlike ordinary, run-of-the-mill critiques (for example, Marxism), it is, however, a critique from, so to speak, nowhere. But because it is from nowhere, it leads us nowhere, and this is precisely why it is basically nihilistic. If there is not a good philosophical *reason* for deconstructing metaphysics that can be stated and argued for, if, for instance, there is not some justifying theoretical-practical point to it (such as arriving at a less mythical conception of *truth* or furthering the cause of *emancipation*), the activity itself becomes purely and simply *destructive*, a kind of theoretical vandalism.

Although it too is critical (as Gadamer's *Auseinandersetzung* with Habermas makes clear), Gadamerian hermeneutics, on the other hand, is not primarily a method or technique for reading and interpreting texts. This, of course, is where it differs from classical hermeneutics as well. As Gadamer is at pains to point out in the foreword to the second edition of *Truth and Method*, what he is proposing is not (unlike Hirsch, for instance) a new and better method for determining the correct meaning of texts. His phenomenological hermeneutics does not propose a method of understanding to be used in order to avoid misunderstanding or to make the unfamiliar familiar, as Schleiermacher would have said. It is not, indeed, concerned with the epistemological questions of method and methodology at all. Rather, its goal is properly philosophical (whence the term "philosophical hermeneutics") in that it seeks to determine what is involved in the understanding process itself, what it is that has actually happened whenever we claim to have arrived at an understanding of things, the world, ourselves.[18] Since Gadamer is building on Heidegger's insight that understanding is not something we "have" but, rather, is what as existing beings we *are* (an *Existentiale*), the scope of hermeneutics conceived of in this way is indeed *universal*. This claim to universal scope is reflected in Gadamer's literary style, as when he says typically that *all* understanding is of such-and-such a sort. The purpose of his investigations has been, quite simply, "to discover what is common to all modes of understanding"; it is concerned with "all human experience of the world and human living" (*TM*, pp. xix, xviii).

Because of its claim to universality, Gadamerian hermeneutics is properly *philosophical* in its intent, and in this regard it contrasts sharply with the equivocal position in regard to philosophy taken by deconstruction, which does not seem to know quite where it stands (inside still, outside already, or, like Derrida's own signature, only "on the edge"?). Because it makes universal claims, ones, moreover, which are completely at odds with traditional logocentrism (as we shall see in more detail in what follows), it amounts in fact to a displacement or overcoming of the metaphysics of presence. Precisely because it so displaces traditional foundationalist thinking, it is in its results at least as "deconstructive" as deconstruction.[19] A consideration of the way Gadamer approaches the subjects of "meaning" and "truth" should confirm all of this.

3. MEANING.

Deconstructive freeplay (*le jeu*), Derrida tells us, "is the disruption of presence."[20] This is to say that it discredits meaning in the traditional metaphysical sense, for metaphysics "considers in a way meaning as a presence (*vorhanden*) to be exhumed,"[21] as, in other words, an objective state of affairs of one sort or another that it would be the function of epistemological "knowing" to reproduce, mirror. But for Derrida meaning is nothing other than the ephemeral play of language itself. Language does not refer to anything outside itself; it refers only to itself, in an endless, disseminating deferral of any definite referent.

Derrida arrives at this view by capitalizing on the structuralist notion that the "value" (i.e., meaning) of any given linguistic unit is (like that of a piece in a chess set) determined solely by its differences from all the other units in the language (*la langue*, the linguistic code). What any given sign "means" or "signifies" (its meaning, the "signified") is a function solely of its diacritical oppositions to other signs or "signifiers." Meaning is thus a wholly intralinguistic sort of affair; there is no "transcendental signified," something outside the play of signifiers themselves whose function it would be to confer on them their meaning, be this an empirical or ideal state of affairs or a psychological meaning-intention. We can never step outside language, and since, moreover, any present linguistic meaning is a function of absent signifiers, meaning itself can never be fully present, determined.[22] To Saussure, who said that in language "there is nothing but differences,"[23] Derrida adds: There is nothing but *différance* (a term which, if it refers to anything at all, must remain without meaning).[24] Derrida draws from the semiological view of language[25] the conclusion that language is nothing but a differential system of slippage and dissemination and that meaning (as something decidable) is something that is forever deferred: Meaning "is infinite implication, the indefinite referral of signifier to signifier" (*WD*, p. 25).

Thus for Derrida there is no exit from the labyrinth of a text, no finished, decidable meaning, merely an endless play of signifiers. There is, quite simply, nothing outside the text: *Il n'y a pas de hors-texte* (*G*, p. 158). What are the results of all this for the business of textual interpretation, which is, one would think, the attempt to articulate the meaning of a text? What, in this view of things, is there to interpret? Not much it seems.[26] Because for Derrida a writer does not dominate his language but can use it only by letting himself be used by it, the aim of reading cannot or should not be that of recapturing, reproducing the author's signifying intention, of "doubling the text" (see *G*, p. 158).[27] We seem to be faced here with a kind of either-or: Either we are constrained in our interpretations by a preexistent meaning which we seek merely to double ("hermeneutics" in Derrida's sense) or we are set free to engage in an "active interpretation" (*WD*, p. 292), one which is, so to speak, *déchaînée*.[28] Freeplay does away with all decidable meaning; the interpretive game engenders an endless series of proliferating interpretations. In our interpretive efforts (our attempt to understand the text, to get at its meaning), we are condemned to an "abyss," a perpetual oscillation between conflicting interpretations with the impossibility of making a decisive choice.

Just as language is not about anything, so it would appear neither is interpretation. "For Derrida," Rorty says, "writing always leads to more writing, and more, and still more."[29] Derrida is one of Rorty's heroes because he is what Rorty would call a "strong textualist," who is in the interpretation business "for what he can get out of it, not for the satisfaction of getting something right."[30] Derrida himself is not quite so cavalier about the matter. He does recognize that there must be constraints on reading (one must recognize and respect the "classical exigencies"—although, he adds, these have always only *protected*, never *opened* a reading [*G*, p. 158]), and he does say that although "reading is transformation," "this transformation cannot be executed however one wishes" and that it requires "protocols of reading" (*Pos*, p. 63). He does not, however, tell us what these protocols should be ("Why not say it bluntly: I have not yet found any that satisfy me"). Given the way he has misrepresented hermeneutics, and given also his misreading of Peirce (to which I shall turn in what immediately follows), one wonders what usefulness these unspecified "protocols" might have (unless it be that of helping to engender what Harold Bloom would call "strong misreadings").

Let us consider for a moment Derrida's handling of Peirce, as this particular "blind spot" in his text can light up for us the way hermeneutics escapes the deconstructionist either-or. Peirce appeals greatly to Derrida ("Peirce goes very far in the direction that I have called the de-construction of the transcendental signified, which, at one time or another, would place a reassuring end to the reference from sign to sign" [*G*, p. 49]), but Derrida ignores about as many important things in Peirce as Rorty does in Gadamer. What appeals to Derrida is Peirce's "semiotic," as he called it, specifically his notion of the "interpretant," i.e., Peirce's theory that the meaning of one sign is simply another sign that can be substituted for it.[31] It all sounds like Derrida's endless play of signifiers in which meaning is forever deferred ("every signified is also in the position of a signifer" [*Pos*, p. 20]). But there is, nonetheless, a *différence* (*avec-un-e*).

Peirce maintains, as Derrida says he does, that we think only in signs. But he does not maintain, as Derrida says he does, that "there are nothing but signs" (*G*, p. 50). Derrida has no grounds for enlisting Peirce's support for his notion of freeplay. The fact of the matter is that in texts that Derrida passes over in silence Peirce speaks of a *final* interpretant. At first glance this might seem to contradict his theory that the meaning of one sign is another sign (its "interpretant") and that this interpretive process is without end. But it does not. When Peirce says that the process of interpretation is endless he means that it is potentially endless; no given interpretant can ever be final in the sense that it is not open to further interpretation. This is why Peirce says that the meaning of a sign is something "altogether virtual." If this were all Peirce had to say, we could no doubt view him as a protodeconstructionist. But he fully realized that to leave things at this point would land us in a form of nihilism; it would mean that *at no time* do we ever have access to decidable meanings. Peirce realized the need for something which, here and now, at any given moment, will provide meaning, even though this meaning will not be immune to futher change. He called this "the living definition, the veritable and final logical interpretant." The important thing for us to note is that Peirce locates this "final logical interpretant," not in the order of language or textuality, but in the order of *praxis*. He writes: "Consequently, the most perfect account of a concept that words can convey will consist in a description of the habit which that concept is calculated to produce." This, of course, fully reflects Peirce's pragmatic bent: his linking of belief to habit, and habit to action. Meaning is not something which is free-floating; if we wish to determine the meaning of a particular belief or concept, and do not wish to get caught up in endless word games, we must take into consideration the kind of action to which it gives rise. It is in habit and action that we discover the true meaning of beliefs (our own as well as those of others).[32]

If I have taken the time to recall a crucial element in Peirce's semiotic, it is because there is a striking parallel between it and a crucial element in Gadamer's hermeneutic: the latter's notion of *application*. While both Peirce and Gadamer reject any notion of a transcendental signified, they do not conclude from this that we have to do only with an endless play of signifiers. They realize quite well that although we are always in the process of producing texts, and that although there can never be any final text, there is nevertheless always something outside the text and the order of textuality, and that it is this which allows for decidable meanings. Let us focus on this crucial difference, on the real difference between deconstruction and hermeneutics.

Deconstruction maintains that because writing exceeds the signifying intention of the author, the object of reading should not be that of rediscovering and reduplicating this meaning. This, it says, is what "hermeneutics" seeks to do. Consider, however, some of the things Gadamer has to say: " . . . the sense of a text in general reaches far beyond what its author originally intended" (*TM*, p. 335). "The mens auctoris is not admissible as a yardstick for the meaning of a work of art" (*TM*, p. xix). "Does an author really know so exactly and in every sentence what he means?" (*TM*, p. 489). "Not occasionally only, but always, the meaning of a text goes beyond its author" (*TM*, p. 264).

For Gadamer, understanding is not only thoroughly *linguistic* in character, it is also *transformative, productive* of new meanings ("It is enough to say that we understand in a different way if we understand at all" [*TM*, p. 264]), and in insisting on these two characteristics of understanding, his hermeneutics overlaps with deconstruction. However, the act of reading is not for him a form of free-floating play. It is always tied to a concrete situation. This is why, unlike Derrida, he also maintains that understanding is inseparable from *appplication*, i.e., from the reading subject's reaction to and appropriation of the text. While all understanding is ultimately linguistic in character, yet in a very important sense writing does not simply give rise to more writing (" . . . there will never be anything but texts" [*G*, p. 29, n. 38]) but has its fulfillment (end) outside itself, in the realm of the existential-practical, in the transformation it produces in the reading subject (in his or her world orientation). The task that phenomenological hermeneutics sets itself is not, contrary to what Derrida would have us believe, that of reconstituting a past, originating meaning but is, instead, that of explicating the possible senses that a text has for us today, what it says to us, here and now.

Gadamer's central thesis that meaning is inseparable from application is thoroughly postmodern and is *at least* as anti- or nonmetaphysical as anything to be found in deconstruction (it is one of Hirsch's main targets for criticism), for it is one of the central tenets of the metaphysics or epistemology of language (one that Derrida has sought expressly to deconstruct) that there is a radical distinction between sense and reference, between meaning (what words invariably mean) and application (how they are applied in particular situations). However, we do not find in Gadamer the blind spot which is so salient in Derrida's work. Derrida quite simply omits to take into account in his theorizing (if it can be called that) the fact that texts have *readers*.[33] And these readers are always *particular individuals* existing in *particular situations*, in the light of which and by application to which the text assumes, by means of what Gadamer calls a "fusion of horizons," a particular, decidable meaning. Given his animus toward the "subject," it really is no wonder that Derrida can find no decidable meanings in texts, for it makes no sense to speak about the meaning of a text apart from our reading of it. No reading, however, is context-free, and it is precisely this *phenomenological fact* that there is always a context that serves to anchor the text in our actual living and to allow it to have a decidable meaning.[34]

Deconstruction tends to issue in relativism, interpretive arbitrariness, because while it maintains (as Gadamer himself does) that there is no meaning *present* in the text, one that it would be the task of interpretation simply to re-present (there is no original, fixed, hidden meaning to be uncovered), it maintains, at the same time, in accordance with its structuralist inspiration, that there is nothing but texts, that meaning is nothing but the interplay of signs which are themselves without instrinsic meaning. The deconstructionist project is a hopeless venture because it cannot, in accordance with its anti-phenomenological bias against "subjectivity," allow for the moment of appropriation (to use the term favored by Paul Ricoeur)—no doubt because it links this to the supposedly metaphysical notion of the *proper*, i.e., that which is "absolutely *proximate* to itself" (*G*, p. 50).[35] There is no reason, however, why subjectivity should be viewed, metaphysically, as pure self-presence (and accordingly rejected *en bloc*), and, indeed, it is one of the positive accomplishments of phenomenological hermeneutics to have decentered the subject, to have, so to speak, desubjectivized subjectivity.[36]

To the deconstructionist notion of undecidability should be opposed the quite different hermeneutical notion of *inexhaustibility* (see *TM*, p. 336). In contrast to deconstruction, hermeneutics maintains that there is always the possibility of meaning, but, in contrast to logocentrism, it maintains that it is never possible to arrive at a final meaning: "the discovery of the true meaning of a text or a work of art is never finished; it is in fact an infinite process" (*TM*, p. 265). Unlike "undecidability," "inexhaustibility" points not to the eternal vanity of all human endeavor but, rather, to the limitless possibility of interrogation, expression, and understanding.[37] "Inexhaustibility" means that in the already acquired we can always find that which can serve to renew our lives and to break the metaphysical circle of the eternal repetition of the Same.[38] Nor does the fact that we never have access to a transcendental signified mean that our interpretations are free-floating and "groundless"; they are anchored in our effective history, which they also serve to reshape and which, although it is a ground without a ground (i.e., not a foundation in the metaphysical sense, a Cartesian *fundamentum inconcussum*), is yet sure and stable enough to allow for a viable and enduring *human* community.

If "knowledge," once deconstructed, is reconstructed in a nonfoundational way to mean "understanding" in the hermeneutical sense (the generation and possession of viable meaning), then hermeneutics gives us what deconstruction cannot give us and does not even claim to give us ("we know something here which is no longer anything, with a knowledge whose form can no longer be recognized under the old name" [*Dis*, p. 21]), namely, knowlege. That is, it leaves us with something more than the cacophony of everyone's parodying, fanciful interpretations of things, and it allows us to contruct a society which is something more than a deconstructed Tower of Babel.

4. TRUTH.

As philosophy has always maintained, the notions of meaning and truth are intimately related. In Gadamer's case, if interpretation does not work with the expectation of encountering both meaning and truth in that which is to be interpreted, understanding is quite simply impossible (see *TM*, pp. 261–62). Thus what was said above about Gadamer and Derrida in regard to the subject of meaning contains implicitly most of what needs to be said about them in regard to the subject of truth. Here, too, the crucial difference, "the difference that makes a difference," as Bernstein would say,[39] has to do with Gadamer's notion of application. Just as the meaning of the text is realized in the reader, in the history of its effects, so also is its truth.

Although the notion of truth is perhaps the least explicated of Gadamer's key concepts, it is nevertheless one of, if not the most, central of them, as is instanced by the appearance of the term in the very title of his *magnum opus* and by the fact also that it forms the very last word of the book (there is a parallel here with Proust's monumental *À la recherche du temps perdu*, which, in a similar fashion, posts its key term in its title and which ends with the words "dans le temps"). We can say of it, however, what we said of meaning. Just as it is meaningless to speak of meaning if there is nothing outside the play of signs (Derrida is, like Lévi-Strauss, quite right on this score),[40] so also is it utterly vacuous to speak of truth *if*, as Gadamer indeed has, one has abandoned the metaphysical-epistemological conception of truth as the representation of an "objective" state of affairs *and* if one maintains that all there is is the freeplay of signs. Then, indeed, we enter into "the epochal regime of quotation marks" (*S/E*, p. 107), in which everything, being without "reference," is also without truth, and philosophy, seen now to be a form of fiction, reaches its end. There can be truth only if there is something *outside* the linguistic code and outside "quotation marks," and only if there is something more than just "a play of traces or differance that has no sense" (*Dif*, p. 154). And indeed, as we have seen, there is, in a sense, an "outside" for Gadamer, although this is in no way a Derridean, metaphysical Origin. Language, for Gadamer, is not, as it is for the (post)structuralists, a kind of self-enclosed, self-subsisting entity, even if this entity which has no outside has, as it is said, no internal self-centeredness, either (see *Dis*, pp. 35–36). While it is all-encompassing and, as he says, "ubiquitous," language nonetheless is not a prison (however much an internally decentered and Kafkaesque hall of mirrors this may be).[41] It is nothing other than the universal medium of our *experience* of the world, the form in which the *play of experience* realizes itself.[42]

The notion of play (*Spiel, jeu*), which is as central to Gadamer as it is to Derrida, is one of the more notable instances of the overlap between hermeneutics and deconstruction. And yet, as is to be expected, it is one in which is revealed most clearly the crucial difference between these two instances of postmodern thought. Derrida joyfully embraces a "Nietzschean" notion of play, a groundless and aimless play in which all standards and distinctions are meaningless, a form of play which rules out in advance any notion of "progress" (progression) and in which meaning is forever deferred in an endless supplementarity.[43] Derridas's "jeu" is "the Nietzschean *affirmation*, that is the joyous affirmation of the play of the world and of the innocence of becoming, the affirmation of a world of signs without fault, without truth, and without origin which is offered to an active interpretation" (*WD*, p. 292). It is a form of play which is both pointless, i.e., without goal, and meaningless. For Gadamer, however, the play of linguistic experience is, to borrow a phrase from Huizinga, *zwecklos aber doch sinnvoll.*[44] It is "goal-less" in that, unlike metaphysical progression, it does not aim at a final, ultimate meaning or understanding in which would be revealed the ultimate truth of things. It is not, however, without meaning, this meaning lying in the enhanced self-understanding the player receives as a result of the play of understanding.

Gadamer's concentration on play as a metaphor for the understanding process is not meant as a Nietzschean rejection of rules or of the subject; its purpose is, rather, to enable us to conceive of subjectivity anew, in a postmodern, postepistemological fashion. Differing in a salutary way from his mentor, Heidegger, in this regard, Gadamer does not direct his deconstructive critique against subjectivity and traditional humanism as such. His purpose (certain ill-chosen remarks of his notwithstanding) is not to abandon subjectivity, as if it were some dreadful metaphysical construct which gets in the way of the advent of Being (*Ereignis*), but to arrive at a less "subjectivistic," less Cartesian conception of it. Play for Gadamer, whose thinking is fully a part of the classical tradition of *humanitas*, is not, as it is for Derrida and other such contemporary antihumanists, an attempt to "pass beyond man and humanism" (*WD*, p. 292). Play for Gadamer is most definitely not *eine Spiel ohne Spieler.*[45] The very meaning of Gadamer's notion of the fusion of horizons is that what we have to do with in the play of understanding is the transformation of one subject in his or her encounter with another. We have to do with a self which, in and by means of the dialogical encounter with the other, comes to a greater realization (in the concrete sense of the term) of itself, becomes, as Kierkegaard would say, who or what he or she is. In this context, truth does not mean correspondence with reality (truth as presence)—what possible meaning could that have?—but refers rather to the disclosure of possibilities for being and acting that emerge in and by means of the playful encounter. Truth refers not to a static, mirroring relation between a subject and an object but to the transformation process which occurs in all instances of genuine understanding. Truth refers to the self-enrichment and self-realization that occurs as a result of the play of meaning.

This process of "realization" must not, however, be understood in a Hegelian, i.e., metaphysical, sense. Metaphysical *parousia*, the final possession of the truth (Derrida's "full presence"), is not even an ideal for Gadamer, not even in the mode of nostalgia. There is absolutely no place for the metaphysical notion of "totality" (or totalization) in his thinking ("the idea of the whole is itself to be understood only relatively" [*TM*, p. xxiii]). He deliberately seeks to avoid "a metaphysics of infinity in the Hegelian manner" (*TM*, p. 433). Instead, he resolutely insists on "the constitutional incompletion (*Unvollendbarkeit*) of experience."[46] Gadamerian self-realization is not a Hegelian *Bildung*. If there is a teleology of truth and becoming for Gadamer, it is, as Merleau-Ponty would have said, a teleology without a telos.[47] "The dialectic of experience," he writes, "has its own fulfillment not in definitive knowledge, but in that openness to experience that is encouraged by experience itself" (*TM*, p. 319).

I could perhaps sum this all up by saying that for Gadamer play is not just "mere" play. In contrast to Derrida's *jeu* (his "pure play"), it must, in Gadamer's case, be said: *Il y a quelque chose qui est en jeu dans le jeu; il y a un enjeu au jeu.* There is something that is at stake, at issue (*en jeu*), in the play of understanding, something, as in the Pascalian wager, that is to be won or lost, and this is nothing other than our *being* itself, the never-to-be-completed realization of our own utmost possibilities of being.[48] This is why, of course, there is no trace of Nietzschean fatalism in Gadamer's hermeneutics, a kind of nihilism that would have to be masked by a heavy dose (*pharmakon*) of Dionysian gleeful exuberance over the "innocence of becoming" ("*amor fati*").

Unlike Derrida, who is (through no fault of his own) unable to specify what a postmetaphysical culture might look like, Gadamer can and does.[49] His *Ueberwindung der Metaphysik*, his overcoming of the tradition, does not exhaust itself in a vain and sterile (i.e., "disseminating") protest against its untenable, idealist presuppositions. This is because Gadamer finds in the tradition itself the wherewithal productively to overcome it.[50]

Notes

This text was written at the invitation of Hugh J. Silverman for inclusion in a forthcoming volume in the Continental Philosophy series edited by Silverman and published by Routledge and Kegan Paul.

1. See G. B. Madison, *Understanding: A Phenomenological-Pragmatic Analysis* (Westport, Conn.: Greenwood Press, 1982); as well as "Merleau-Ponty and the Counter-Tradition," appendix I, in G. B. Madison, *The Phenomenology of Merleau-Ponty* (Athens, Ohio: Ohio University Press, 1981).

2. Richard Bernstein accurately describes the playfulness characteristic of postmodern thought when he says: "What characterizes so much of what is sometimes called post-modernity is a new playful spirit of negativity, deconstruction, suspicion, unmasking. Satire, ridicule, jokes and punning become the rhetorical devices for undermining 'puritanical seriousness.' This *esprit* pervades the writings of Rorty, Feyerabend, and Derrida" (*Philosophical Profiles* [Philadelphia: University of Pennsylvania Press, 1986], p. 59).

3. See Derrida, *Positions*, trans. Alan Bass (Chicago: University of Chicago Press, 1981), pp. 12, 14 (henceforth cited as *Pos*).

4. Hans-Georg Gadamer, "Destruction and Deconstruction," talk given at McMaster University, November 14, 1985.

5. For "bottomless chessboard," see Derrida, "Difference," in *Speech and Phenomena*, trans. David Allison (Evanston, Ill.: Northwestern University Press, 1973), p. 154 (henceforth cited as *Dif*).

6. And yet Derrida *says* that he recognizes the need for ethical reflections: " . . . je crois qu'une théorie de l'éthique, de la spécificité des actes éthiques, des intentions éthiques, des lois morales, etc., est indispensable, qu'elle est à constituer" ("Table ronde: Philosophie et Communication," in *La communication*, Actes du XXᵉ congrès de l'Association des Sociétés de philosophie de langue française, Montréal 1971 [Montréal: Éditions Montmorency, 1973], vol. II, p. 426).

7. In much the same way that my paper, "Eine Kritik an Hirschs Begriff der 'Richtigkeit,' " in *Seminar: Die Hermeneutik und die Wissenschaften*, ed. H.-G. Gadamer and G. Boehm (Frankfurt: Suhrkamp Verlag, 1978), was a Gadamerian response to E. D. Hirsch.

8. Bernstein, *Philosophical Profiles*, p.61.

9. Derrida, *Dissemination*, trans. B. Johnson (Chicago: University of Chicago Press, 1981), p. 54 (henceforth cited as *Dis*).

10. I think the following words of Richard Rorty in praise of Derrida amount in fact to a devastating criticism of him: "Lack of seriousness, in the sense in which I just attributed it to Derrida, is simply this refusal to take the standard rules seriously, conjoined with the refusal to give a clear answer to the question, 'Is it the old game played differently, or rather a new game?' " (*Consequences of Pragmatism* [Minneapolis: University of Minnesota Press, 1982], p. 98).

11. Gadamer, "Le défi herméneutique," *Revue internationale de philosophie*, no. 151, 1984, p. 334.

12. See, for instance, Gadamer, *Truth and Method* (New York: Seabury Press, 1975), p. 460 (henceforth cited as *TM*). See also Gadamer's discussion of Dilthey in his essay, "The Problem of Historical Consciousness," in *Interpretive Social Science: A Reader*, ed. P. Rabinow and W. M. Sullivan (Berkeley: University of California Press, 1979).

13. Jacques Derrida, *Spurs/Éperons*, trans. Barbara Harlow (Chicago: University of Chicago Press, 1979), p. 106 (henceforth cited as S/E).

14. See S/E, p. 130, where Derrida speaks of the assumption of the "herméneute ontologiste" that a text "doit vouloir dire quelque chose" and "doit venir du plus intime de la pensée de l'auteur".

15. The three themes of interpretation, language, and application are most forcefully linked together in *TM*, pp. 274–75.

16. Deconstruction, Irene Harvey tells us, is not a theory; rather, "it can be called, tentatively of course, a 'textual strategy' and more precisely a 'practice' instead of a theory" ("Hermeneutics and Deconstruction: Ricoeur and Derrida," paper presented at the Penn State Conference on Interpretation Theory, April 5, 1984). I wish to thank Professor Harvey for graciously providing me with a copy of her manuscript. A summary of some of the points she makes in this paper can be found in Richard Palmer, "The Scope of Hermeneutics and the Problem of Critique and the Crisis of Modernity," in *Texte* (University of Toronto), 1984 (3).

17. " . . . the enterprise of deconstruction always in a certain way falls prey to its own work" (Derrida, *Of Grammatology*, trans. G. Spivak (Baltimore: Johns Hopkins University Press, 1976), p. 24 (henceforth cited as G).

18. The work of hermeneutics, Gadamer says, "is not to develop a procedure of understanding, but to clarify the conditions in which understanding takes place. But these conditions are not of the nature of a 'procedure' or a method, which the interpreter must of himself bring to bear on the text . . . " (*TM*, p. 263).

19. Richard Palmer is, in my opinion, absolutely right when he portrays hermeneutics as itself including a deconstructive moment. He speaks, for instance, of "the importance of seeing the unfolding of the hermeneutical problematic in terms of the philosophical critique of the metaphysics of modernity" and says: "The demands of the critique of modernity generate the need for the hermeneutical strategy of deconstruction. In this context, deconstruction appears not as some incommensurable strategy that emerges from the blue but as the latest stage in the development of hermeneutics. . . . The relation of deconstruction to hermeneutics is, I think, more like that of child and parent, parasite and host, member and tradition to which that member relates. . . . Derrida offers us in deconstruction what is intrinsically a hermeneutical approach. . . . deconstruction is essentially a hermeneutical strategy . . . " ("The Scope of Hermeneutics . . . ," pp. 233–34).

20. Derrida, *Writing and Difference*, trans. Alan Bass (Chicago: University of Chicago Press, 1978), p. 292 (henceforth cited as *WD*).

21. Derrida, "Bonnes volontés de puissance (Une réponse à Hans-Georg Gadamer," *Revue internationale de philosophie*, no. 151, 1984, p. 337.

22. "The play of differences supposes, in effect, syntheses and referrals which forbid at any moment, or in any sense, that a simple element be *present* in and of itself, referring only to itself. Whether in the order of spoken or written discourse, no element can function as a sign without referring to another element which itself is not simply present. This interweaving (*enchaînement*) results in each 'element'—phoneme or grapheme—being constituted on the basis of the trace within it of the other elements of the chain or system. This interweaving, this textile, is the *text* produced only in the transformation of another text. Nothing, neither among the elements nor within the system, is anywhere ever simply present or absent. There are only, everywhere, differences and traces of traces" (*Pos*, p. 26). See also *Dif*, pp. 142–43.

23. Ferdinand de Saussure *Course in General Linguistics* trans. W. Barkin (New York: Philosophical Library, 1959), p. 120.

24. " . . . *différance* is . . . the production, if it can still be put this way, of these differences, of the diacriticity that the linguistics generated by Saussure, and all the structural sciences modelled upon it, have recalled is the condition for any signification and any structure" (*Pos*, p. 9).

25. "The concept of *différance* . . . develops the most legitimate principled exigencies of 'structuralism' " (*Pos*, p. 28). See also *Dif*, pp. 140–41. The structuralist origins of deconstruction are attested to by Derrida's remarks in ibid., p. 146.

26. The logic of Derrida's position leads him to maintain that there is not even such a "thing" as *a* text. Speaking of "what used to be called a text," he says: " . . . a 'text' . . . is henceforth no longer a finished corpus of writing, some content enclosed in a book or its margins, but a differential network, a fabric of traces referring endlessly to something other than itself, to other differential traces" ("Living On," in Harold Bloom et al., *Deconstruction and Criticism* [New York: Continuum, 1984], pp. 83–84).

27. Reading "cannot legitimately transgress the text toward something other than it, toward a referent (a reality that is metaphysical, historical, psychobiographical, etc.) or toward a signified outside the text whose content could take place, could have taken place outside of language . . . " (*G*, p. 158).

28. "Reading is freed from the horizon of the meaning or truth of being. . . . Whereupon the question of style is immediately unloosed (*se déchaîne*) as a question of writing. The question posed by the spurring-operation is more powerful than any content, thesis or meaning" (*S/E*, p. 107).

29. Rorty, *Consequences of Pragmatism*, p. 94.

30. Ibid., p. 152.

31. For a succinct account of Peirce's semiotic and for references to the following Peirce quotations, see my *Understanding*, pp. 20–22.

32. For a good account of Peirce's theory of signs which emphasizes the difference between his "semiotic" (which incorporates the elements of habit and action) and Saussurian or structuralist "semiology" (which takes into account nothing more than the diacritical play of signifiers), see Milton Singer, *Man's Glassy Essence: Explorations in Semiotic Anthropology* (Bloomington: Indiana University Press, 1984).

33. I fully expect that Derrida would protest this assertion. In answer to Paul Ricoeur, who said to him, " . . . si on fait une théorie de l'écriture, il fait faire une théorie de la lecture. Vous ne pouvez pas faire une théorie abstraite de l'écriture, vous ne pouvez faire qu'une théorie du couple écriture-lecture. . . . c'est dans la lecture que s'achève l'écriture . . . ," Derrida responded, " . . . je pense tout à fait comme vous qu'une théorie de l'écriture est inséparable d'une théorie de la lecture" ("Table ronde," in *La communication*, vol. II, pp. 413–14). I simply do not see Derrida taking his own assertion

seriously; to do so he would have to take seriously the hermeneutical notion of *application*, with all that that entails, in regard, notably, to the question of "decidability." Derrida's "reader" simply is not "un individu singulier et irremplaçable" (see ibid., p. 407), which is what, as a matter of phenomenological fact, all readers are.

34. For what is in effect a Gadamerian or hermeneutical response to deconstruction which seeks to emphasize the importance of context, see Stanley Fish, "Normal Circumstances and Other Special Cases," in *Is There a Text in This Class? The Authority of Interpretive Communities* (Cambridge, Mass.: Harvard University Press, 1980). Fish writes: "In the view I put forward, determinacy and decidability are always available, not, however, because of the constraints imposed by the language or the world—that is, by entities independent of context—but because of the constraints built into the context or contexts in which we find ourselves operating . . . language does not have a shape independent of context, but since language is only encountered in contexts and never in the abstract, it always has a shape, although it is not always the same one. The problem with this formulation is that for many people determinacy is inseparable from stability: the reason that we can specify the meaning of a text is because a text and its meanings never change. What I am suggesting is that change is continually occurring but that its consequence is *never* the absence of the norms, standards, and certainties we desire, because they will be features of any situation we happen to be in" (*ibid.*, pp. 268–69).

The matter could be put the other way around by saying that where there is no "context," that is, where we do not already have some kind of *preunderstanding* (in Gadamer's sense of the term) in terms of which we can approach that which is to be understood ("prejudices" which are constitutive of *our* personal-cultural being at any given time), then what we are confronted with in a text is indeed nothing but a collection of signifiers which refer to nothing other than themselves and thus which mean, can mean, for us, nothing at all. This sort of situation is rare, for normally we are not lacking in some kind of preunderstanding of even the very foreign and remote. But it does happen. This is precisely why the meaning of Mayan "writing" remains completely undecidable (that we even have to do with "signifiers" here is itself a "prejudice"—dare I say a "grammatological" one?). As the teacher–tour guide in Italo Calvino's *Mr. Palomar* says of a pre-Columbian relief-frieze to a group of schoolchildren, contradicting the interpretation offered by a self-appointed expert: "*No se sabe lo que quiere decir*; We don't know what it means."

35. Regarding the "proper," see also Derrida, "*Ousia* and *Gramme*," in Derrida, *Margins of Philosophy*, trans. A. Bass (Chicago: University of Chicago Press, 1982), p. 64, n. 39. Mario Valdés of the Centre for Comparative Literature at the University of Toronto is putting it mildly when he says: ". . . the process of appropriation through which the reader engages the text remains to be considered by Derrida" ("Paul Ricoeur's Hermeneutics as a Basis for Literary Criticism," *Revue de l'Université de l'Ottawa/Ottawa Quarterly*, vol. 55, no. 4, Oct.-Dec., 1985, p. 126).

36. See, for instance, my article, "Ricoeur and the Hermeneutics of the Subject," in *The Philosophy of Paul Ricoeur*, Library of Living Philosophers, ed. Lewis E. Hahn (Peru, Ill.: Open Court, forthcoming) (included here as essay 6).

37. Derrida's critique of totality and enclosure is, as he himself says, primarily *not* one which "opens an inexhaustible wealth of meaning on the transcendence of a semantic excess" (*Pos*, p. 46).

38. "Inasmuch as the tradition is newly experienced in language, something comes into being and exists from now on that had not existed before" (*TM*, p. 419).

39. See Bernstein, "What is the Difference that Makes a Difference? Gadamer, Habermas, and Rorty," in *Philosophical Profiles*.

40. As Lévi-Strauss once said to Ricoeur in the course of a famous discussion: " . . . dans ma perspective, le sens n'est jamais un phénomène premier: le sens est

toujours réductible. Autrement dit, derrière tout sens il y a un non-sens, et le contraire n'est pas vrai" ("Reponses à quelques questions," *Esprit*, XXXI, Nov. 1963, pp. 636–37.

41. "[T]he linguistic world in which we live is not a barrier that prevents knowledge of being in itself, but fundamentally embraces everything in which our insight can be enlarged and deepened" (*TM*, p. 405).

42. I am not using the word *experience* in a metaphysical, i.e., Derridian, sense (see, for instance, *G*, p. 60).

43. ". . . from the first texts I published, I have attempted to systematize a deconstructive critique precisely against . . . history determined in the last analysis as the history of meaning . . ." (*Pos*, p. 49). For Derrida, to think of history as the history of meaning is hopelessly metaphysical. See ibid., p. 56.

44. Johan Huizinga, *Homo Ludens* (Boston: Beacon Press, 1955), p. 19.

45. We are, it is evident, in disagreement with the interpretation offered by Richard Detsch, which presents Gadamer's use of "play" as an attempt "to banish subjectivity." See Detsch's article, "A Non-subjectivist Concept of Play—Gadamer and Heidegger versus Rilke and Nietzsche," *Philosophy Today*, vol. 29, Summer 1985, p. 159.

46. Gadamer, "Le défi herméneutique," p. 336.

47. See Madison, *The Phenomenology of Merleau-Ponty*, pp. 252, 263.

48. In the Derridian *jeu de différance*, on the other hand, there are no winners and no losers; eveyone is a winner and everyone is a loser: ". . . we must admit a game where whoever loses wins and where one wins and loses each time" (*Dif*, p. 151). A kind of perpetual zero-sum game, in effect, a genuine merry-go-round.

49. It would be the task of another paper to spell out in detail the specifics of the Gadamerian alternative to "metaphysics." The reader will understand, I hope, that no attempt can be made to do so here.

50. Gadamer's "retrieval" thus contrasts with Heidegger's *Wiederholung* in that it does not seek to overcome the tradition by going back *beyond* the tradition to a mythical age of metaphysical innocence in the presocratics so as to effect a *totally new beginning.* He is not reduced, therefore, to saying that "only a god can save us now." "What man needs," he says instead, "is not only a persistent asking of ultimate questions, but the sense of what is feasible, what is possible, what is correct, here and now" (*TM*, p. xxv). It is his practical concern with the "here and now" which sets Gadamer apart (in different ways) from both Heidegger (whose "problem of Being" is one which, as he says, he has bypassed [see "The Problem of Historical Consciousness," p. 106]) and Derrida. A good example of Gadamer's creative, appropriative rereading of tradition is his recently published study, *The Idea of the Good in Platonic and Aristotelian Philosophy*, trans. P. Christopher Smith (New Haven, Conn.: Yale University Press, 1986).

Part Two
Themes

EIGHT

Metaphysics as Myth

Metaphysics, from one point of view at least, is the art of asking fascinating questions. Like, "Why is there something rather than not simply nothing at all?" Or, "Why is everything what it is and not rather something else?" Or, "Where does everything come from, and why does it come from there rather than from somewhere else?" Metaphysicians love to ponder over imponderables such as these. They are professionals at the business (much as some people are professional game players). Besides liking to ask *Why* questions of this sort, they also like to ask *What* questions. "What is this?" and "What is that?" and, above all, "What is the *what* that this or this is, and which makes this be this rather than that?" In other words, "What is *whatness*?" (*quidditas, ousia, essentia*). One *What Is* question metaphysicians invariably ask is "What is metaphysics?" After all, how can you claim to account for anything and everything—*ta panta, das Seiende im Ganzen*—which is what metaphysicians claim to do, if you can't give an account of your own accounting?

"What is metaphysics?" is in effect the question I am raising in this paper, whose title should nevertheless be enough to indicate that the answer I shall be giving to the question is not of the sort metaphysicians are accustomed to giving. I should hope, indeed, that it will have nothing metaphysical about it—which is mainly why I have condensed my answer into the formula: Metaphysics is myth. This should serve at once to set me on the antimetaphysical side of the debate where, in any event, I was asked to be. For myth, as metaphysicians understand it (this being also the reason why they abhor it), is mere fanciful storytelling of dubious epistemic value. Metaphysics, in contrast, is not merely a likely story, a *fabula*, but is the actual truth about things; it is, as Hegel said, "serious business," i.e., *Wissenschaft*.[1]

That metaphysics is a serious business I do not doubt. But then, too, so is myth. Thus, to compare metaphysical theorizing with mythical storytelling is not to degrade the former. The title of this paper is not meant to harbor pejorative connotations. Both myth and metaphysics perform, by different yet related means, a very useful function in that, by conferring some semblance of intelligibility on the chaotic reality of our lived experience, the blooming, buzzing confusion of things William James spoke of, by enabling us to have the feeling that we understand the Why, What, and Wherefore of things, they help us to feel at home in the world and thereby serve to allay the cosmic anxiety, the ontological *Angst* to which the human being is particularly prone. They thereby enable people to feel, as Camus said, that "*la vie vaut la peine d'être vécue*," that life is worth living.[2]

Because they serve to transform chaos into a cosmos, both myth and metaphysics are world-constructive activities. While the much-vaunted shift from *mythos* to *logos* does represent a change in stylistic form, it does not amount to one in epistemic substance—or in existential purpose. For, like the *mythos*, the *logos*—reason—is an activity of the mind which consists, on the one hand, in dividing up the kaleidoscopic flux of living experience into distinct particulars or "kinds" (as Plato would say) and, on the other hand, in combining these basic elements into orderly patterns. The path of reason is that of analysis and synthesis (as Plato also said). To name and to order is the soul of both mythical and metaphysical thinking, which, at different times, have both laid claim to the title of "wisdom." *Sapientia est ordinare*: the *philo-sophos* is the lover of cosmic law and order,[3] and metaphysics is the conceptual realization of the fabulous dreams and the profoundest aspirations of the primitive mythmaker.

Like the mythmaker, the metaphysician is also a consummate artisan. Working in the medium not of greater-than-life, superhuman personages but of abstract, incorporeal ideas and bloodless "principles," metaphysicians fabricate worlds, to which they attach the name "reality." *Homo sapiens* is also *homo faber*, and what the *animal rationale* is best at making is *entia rationis*, or what Occam appropriately termed *ficta*, mental artifacts (from which he concluded that being does not exist as a metaphysical entity and that, therefore, there is no such thing as metaphysical knowledge).

The theorizing of the metaphysican is thus a kind of doing. From this point of view, metaphysics is like myth in that it too is basically poetry, a *poiesis*. The metaphysician could in fact be called the "poet of ideas." Unlike what is today called "art," however, myth and metaphysics involve no willing suspension of belief. The metaphysician may be every bit as imaginative as the poet, but he actually believes that the products of his fertile imagination are the literal truth. This is why he calls what he is doing "science," since the object of science is What Is.

I realize that these propositions are not such as to be readily believed by an audience of metaphysicians. Let me, therefore, attempt to present my case in greater detail.

The best place to begin is no doubt at the beginning and (to follow the example of the metaphysicans themselves) with the most general of generalities. Metaphysics, then, is a function of the human intelligence. On this, we can all agree. Let us look at this intelligence in action.

As instanced in early Greek mathematics, the form of intelligence in question amounts to a passage from the concrete to the abstract—theoretical, metaphysical intelligence could be defined as the transcendence of experience by means of ideas[4]—and is an attempt to extract an intelligible and universally valid essence from a mass of particular, observable details. The function of intellection, as we see it at work with the Greeks—contrasting markedly with the way it worked with the Egyptians and the Babylonians—is that of discovering a unity, a constancy of relations and a permanency of structure amid the diversity of the empirically given. As exemplified in mathematics, that most Greek of all Greek inventions, the task of theoretical reason is that of discovering the reason which (it is supposed) is innate in things and which, as Anaxagoaras said, "rules the world." The function of theory here is not limited to practical objectives, such as reassigning to people their plots of land whose boundaries have been effaced by the annual flooding of the Nile or determining the right time for holding a New Year's festival. It is the unlimited one of laying bare the overriding unity in all multiplicity, the cosmic harmony in the ever-present diversity, the nonappearing reality which (it is supposed) underlies all that which appears, in its mutiple and deceitful guises. Speaking of Heraclitus, Kirk and Raven say: "Men should try to comprehend the underlying coherence of things: it is expressed in the Logos, the formula or element of arrangement common to all things."[5]

Many fail to comprehend the Logos, Heraclitus complained, because they allow themselves to be absorbed in the multiplicity of appearances. Indeed, the Logos does not appear and cannot be seen but, like a mathematical formula, must be thought. Like the music of the celestial spheres, it speaks only to the ears of the soul, and what it proclaims, for those who have the ears to hear (and whose souls are dry—Heraclitus, incidentally, died while attempting to dry out his soul, after an overconsumption of alcohol, no doubt, by burying himself in a dung heap), is that, though apparently plural and discrete, "all things are one."[6]

Greek rationalism not only transformed Egyptian surveying, Babylonian stargazing, and Phoenician calculation into the theoretical disciplines of geometry, astronomy, and arithmetic, it further combined all three disciplines, creating thereby a formidable tool for disengaging the underlying unity of nature (which to a great extent could be said to be as much a function of the tool as of anything else).

As the "reason"—the *logos*—for what appears, its *ratio* and proportion, the intelligible, mathematical essence is *reality* in the supreme instance. As the intelligible *reason* for everything which appears, it is the true *cause* of all that which exists. And being first in the order of causation, it is necessarily first in the order of being. This is metaphysics, for metaphysics has traditionally defined itself as "knowledge by causes," *aitia*,[7] whose object is that of the first principles of all things, the *archai* which are the substrate of all things.

In its beginning, then, mathematics and metaphysics are inseparable. Mathematics stands as the paradigm of metaphysical thought which has always sought reality beyond that which is merely apparent and is subject to so many varying interpretations. Where appearances reign, there is to be found only a conflict of interpretations. To speak of conflict is to speak of irrationality, for, as Heraclitus said, the Logos is that which is *common* to all, such that he who does not speak that which is common does not know that whereof he speaks.

That which has to do with disparate and multiple realities is that which traffics in irrationality and speaks only of nonentity. True being is and must be truly *One*, for this is all that it can be thought to be, and is, therefore, all it can be. For Thought and Being are themselves one—unquestionably so, since, from the point of view of thought, they cannot be thought apart, as Parmenides said: *to gar auto noein estin te kai einai.*[8]

The discovery by the Greeks of *the mathematical* was a heady experience. As could have been expected (supposing that there were any phenomenological observers of human doings around at the time who were aware of what Sextus Empiricus was later to call "the trickery of reason"), this discovery was immediately misinterpreted, given the natural credulity of the human mind which invariably confers on its offspring the title of "reality" (a title it readily confers, even though, or perhaps especially because, it has always had the most serious, nocturnal doubts about its own self-substantial reality). To the cultivated intellects of the time, these mathematicals were far more fascinating than the old gods and demons of man's primitive prehistory, and, accordingly, they rapidly, though only by stages, displaced the former, while (as is normal in any such *prise de pouvoir*) at the same time inheriting their divine attributes (the disciples of Pythagoras, who themselves were called "prophets to declare the voice of god," claimed that Pythagoras was Apollo come down from the north).[9] Mathematics became the religion of the educated, who banded together in quasi-monastic communities whose members abstained from taking baths (or so Aristophon says) and from eating beans.

Overcome by their discovery that the principal musical consonances result from the sounding of proportionate lengths of a stretched string, the Pythagoreans set out to expound the laws of cosmic harmony which, they supposed, regulate the relationships between all natural phenomena. "Care for your soul," Pythagoras exhorted his disciples, "and endeavor to penetrate the mysteries of the universe by observing numerical correspondences." Accordingly, as Xenophanes said of them:

> They are wont,
> If haply they a foreigner do find,
> To hold a cross-examination
> Of doctrines' worth, to trouble and confound him
> With terms, equations, and antitheses
> Brain-bung'd with magnitudes and periphrases.[10]

The nature of the universe, as these aboriginal metaphysicians confidently proclaimed, is number. Numbers that are things. Not, as most of us view the matter nowadays, abstractions, idealizations, or even useful fictions, but entities endowed with real, spatial existence. Occult entities, one might say, which, in interacting and intercoursing (in their own numerical way), give rise to the sensible world as we know it. As Aristotle relays their position, from Limit and the Unlimited there proceeds a One, and from the One proceeds somehow the numbers that are things.[11]

The metaphysical imagination, pursuing the course thus opened up to it, sought to reconcile the newly discovered realm of the intelligible with the old, down-to-earth realm of the sensible. In being contrasted, as it had to be, with the newly discovered intelligible, the sensible became something problematic in its own right, to be accounted for by means of intelligible essences, or simply denied, as the case might be (even the philosopher's own sensible being had to be "intelligiblized," as when Empedocles, a reputed pupil of Pythagoras who was thrown out of the school for having stolen the discourses of the master, in order to rationalize, i.e., immortalize, himself, jumped into Mount Etna and roasted himself alive, thinking no one would find out about it but would instead conclude that he had ascended into heaven under his own power, but forgetting his sandal on the rim, which gave the game away and only served to prove that he was as sensible and, indeed, as senseless as any of his fellow mortals).[12]

The old tripartite mythical universe consisting of a celestial world, a terrestrial world, and an infernal world is rejected. The world becomes a closed and unitary system in which nothing is created and nothing is destroyed, but what we call entities are but the visible and superficial expressions of the combinations and separations of that which already exists, but is nowhere to be seen but has to be thought. The logic of the ratio dictates that what is is and what isn't isn't, and that what is, whatever it be, *is* more truly than what simply appears to be which, strictly speaking, *is* not at all, or, at the very least, is not really *real*. Whether the appearances are painstakingly saved or whether they are unceremoniously thrown overboard, they are now, in any event, only appearances whose reality lies elsewhere, in the realm of the rationally, theoretically intelligible, which, it goes without saying, is preeminently that which does not appear—since, if it did, people would not, as Heraclitus said, have such divergent opinions on what in fact it is.

With Plato the metaphysical inversion of things is complete, and has remained so ever since. The real world has become the shadowy world of mere appearence and *doxa*, and the imperceptible, nonappearing world of theoretical ratiocination has become the really real world. Not the real, but the ideal is that which is most real or most "being," "the beingly being and the true *ousia*," as Plotinus was later to say. The sensible, which is the realm of flux and imprecision, is knowable, thus real, only in the light of theoretical reason. The real, as we ordinary people say, is thus real only to the degree that it embodies or participates in the mathematical, which is to say, only to the degree that it can be theorized.[13]

The history of metaphysics down through the ages is mostly the history of Platonism, with occasional Aristotelian footnotes (as when Saint Thomas widened out the notion of essence to include matter and tacked onto Platonic essentialism thus extended an ontology of existence [*esse*]). Metaphysics finds its ultimate expression in modern, mathematical physics. To be sure, modern physics does not believe in separated substance (the philosophical distillate of the gods of old), but it does believe in the separateness of the intelligible. Despite the fact that it calls itself "empirical," modern science places no more faith in the senses than did that of the Eleatics and deals as much with "insensible substance" as did the metaphysics of Aristotle.[14] The real table, Eddington said and scientists continue to this very day to say, is not what I see, or rest upon, but a mass of insubstantial, swarming atoms which I cannot see and cannot rest upon, for if I attempted to, I would be engulfed in the void of their immense interstices. Solidity vanishes into the ethereal realm of the purely intelligible which has as little to do with the sensible as did Plato's ideal Forms. For modern science, the substance or reality of things consists, as it did for the Pythagoreans, in the numerical and the theoretical. One of the great founders of twentieth-century physics, Werner Heisenberg, relates the strong impression that a reading of that great Pythagorean work, Plato's *Timaeus*, had on him as a young man (reading it while lying on the roof of a building in the midst of street fighting in Munich). "I was enthralled," he writes, "by the idea that the smallest particles of matter must reduce to some mathematical form."[15] Metaphysics is alive and well and lives on in modern physics. There is no reason not to agree with Whitehead when he says: "Let us grant that the pursuit of mathematics is a divine madness of the human spirit."[16]

It is not my intention here to undertake a survey of the history of metaphysics. I am not qualified to do so, nor is there any reason why I should even make the attempt. This is something that over the years Professor Ivor Leclerc has done in a truly masterful way. I for one have been deeply impressed by his painstaking, historical analyses of the metaphysical search for "being" and am convinced that his contributions to this subject rank among the most valuable at our disposal. What strikes me as being of the greatest significance in Leclerc's work is the realization it embodies to the effect that metaphysics is simply not posssible today (assuming that it's possible at all) except on the basis and indeed in the form of the history of metaphysics. "Adequate philosophy," he has said, "is inseparable from the history of philosophy."[17] The very word *being* (or its functional equivalents) must remain empty and devoid of any real meaning to us moderns so long as we remain oblivious to the way it came to be and since then has become. It is a term we constantly use, but only because it is one we have inherited from a long and largely overlooked tradition of thought. Its apparent meaningfulness is simply the result of long acquaintance. If metaphysics is to surmount the crisis in which, as Leclerc believes, it currently finds itself, it is necessary to undertake a fundamental inquiry into the history of the concept of being, an archaeology of being, so to speak, for, as Hegel would say, what something is is what it has been: *Wesen ist was gewesen ist.*

Though he might not express it in quite this way, it seems to me that this is pretty much the sense of Leclerc's undertaking. Now the history of metaphysics as he has unraveled it has some very important lessons to teach us. I shall focus briefly on the two most significant features of the metaphysical enterprise that Leclerc's work—which is guided by the dual theme of history and language—serves to emphasize, although the ultimate lesson I shall draw from them is most definitely not the one he himself would draw. In short, whereas I am led thereby to the conclusion that metaphysics is myth (in, as I say, a nonpejorative sense of the term), Leclerc is encouraged thereby to redouble his efforts to make of metaphysics a genuine science which would be capable of disclosing the objective truth of things.

The two features I have alluded to and which are revealed by a reflective, descriptive (i.e., hermeneutical) analysis of the way in which metaphysicians have come to put forward their theories I shall label (1) *intertextuality* and (2) *metaphorical transsubstantiation*.

(1) The first feature is one which becomes apparent when we abstract from what metaphysicians say they are doing and focus instead on what it is evident that, at the very least, they are in fact doing. Metaphysicians say they are speaking about the nature of things, *de rerum natura*, and so entitle their books. Perhaps they are, but if they are, their discourse is only indirectly about things. What in the first instance metaphysicians talk about, the immediate referent of their discourse, is other metaphysicians and *their* theories. That unrivaled observer of human affairs, Michel de Montaigne, said:

> Il y a plus affaire à interpréter les interprétations qu'à interpréter les choses, et plus de livres que sur autre suject: nous ne faisons que nous entregloser.[18]

This is eminently true of that body of writing called metaphysics. Ever since its inception, metaphysics has existed as the critique of metaphysics. A new, upstart metaphysician such as a Plato, an Aristotle, or a Descartes, invariably advances his theories as that which alone is capable of filling in the lacunae and remedying the deficiencies in the theories of his predecessors. These "deficiencies" are, of course, ones which the new metaphysician is the first to proclaim, and which, indeed, it is a mark of his genius to have perceived. Think, for instance, of how Aristotle sets the stage for his own ingenious system when in the first book of the *Metaphysics* he carefully enumerates the shortcomings of his predecessors. This sort of thing was already part of a long-established tradition. Parmenides, a dissident disciple of Pythagoras (as we are told), launched his career by picking up on a perceived contradiction in the Pythagorean system, the resolution of which he proclaimed (not in his own voice, to be sure, but, in accordance with a standard metaphysical conceit, in that of a goddess). Plotinus, who founded perhaps the most influential metaphysical system of all (and one which is most typically metaphysical in that it generalizes thinking to include everything that is being), viewed his work as making Plato more consistent and coherent. He who makes a place for himself in the history of metaphysics is often he who pushes the logic of a particular position to the extreme. (Much later in the unfolding of this particular tradition, Descartes arrived at his metaphysical system by setting forth a solution to the internal difficulties in the Neoplatonic atomistic materialism of the postmedieval period.)

Of course, all such resolutions of contradictions or conceptual tensions generate contradictions or tensions of their own, the existence and resolution of which another generation will proclaim. And so proceeds the history and glory of metaphysics. "Nos opinions s'entent les unes sur les autres," Montaigne said. "La première sert de tige à la seconde, la seconde à la tierce. Nous eschellons ainsi de degré en degré."[19] As to the manner in which it unfolds, metaphysics is nothing other than an immensely long-drawn-out and never-ending conversation—or confabulation—between metaphysicians.

Let us, therefore, not deceive ourselves. Although metaphysicians are given to saying that they are talking about the nature of things, "being" or what-have-you, they are in fact talking about other metaphysicians. It is the same in all human endeavors. The metaphysician can no more describe being in the nude—can express the "naked truth" about things—than a painter can paint nature as it "really is in itself." There never has existed any such thing as a painting d'après nature. Renaissance painters thought that nature was composed of straight lines organized according to the laws of Euclidian geometry. The Impressionists thought that nature was composed of a mass of sense data impinging on the retina. Cézanne, whose style was the result of his confrontation with Pissarro and the Impressionists, wanted to get back to the things themselves. But when we look at one of Cézanne's paintings, it is Cézanne we see, with all his stylistic peculiarities, not nature itself—although, if we look at Cézanne long enough, all of Provence will begin to look like a painting of his. There surely is no purer vision than that of the painter, and yet what the painter sees is a function not of his unobstructed and unclouded biological eyesight but of the vision of other painters, from whom he has learned how to see.

Similarly, what a writer writes—and metaphysicians are, at the very least, writers—is a function of what other writers have written. What for any given person the things are is a function of what other people have said they are. Only mystics claim that what they say about things is what the things themselves told them—but one can always find that what they say is pretty much in tune with what other mystics have already said; mysticism is indeed one thing of which there is a very long tradition. Contrary to what Leonardo thought when he disparaged the book learning of the humanists and asserted that his works met the test of experience and not just the dicta of other men (typifying thereby the attitude of modern science), experience in itself does not have much to say. It must be made to speak, and, when it does, it is not in a language properly its own. It does not even give clear-cut, unambiguous yes-and-no answers to straightforward questions. As we know now, the experimentum crucis is but a myth.[20] As Heraclitus said of the lord whose oracle is at Delphi, nature neither speaks out nor conceals, but merely gives a sign,[21] a sign whose meaning is elusive and can be interpreted only by means of a whole host of other signs. The meaning of one sign is another sign,[22] just as the meaning of one text is what another text says it is. The Great Book of Nature—whose alphabet, Galileo proclaimed in a letter to Fortuno Luceti, consists of "triangles, squares, circles, spheres, cones, pyramids and other mathematical figures"—exists only in a reconstructed version; it is, in fact, a collage of bits and pieces from books about other books about "nature." And, much to the chagrin of the physicists, the Book of Nature (as Whitehead once remarked) is today, more so than at any other time, in tatters. To the degree that it exists for us, the world is not a direct *explicatio Dei*, as Nicholas of Cusa said, but is, rather, like the cleverly reassembled shards of the anthropologist, the indirect resultant of an *explication de textes*.

Thus, to reflect on the history of metaphysics, no less than that of modern science, is to reflect on the significant effect of texts, which is other texts. As one text has for its significant effect another text which it calls forth and which in its turn will call forth another and so in this way is essentialy oriented toward an indefinite future with no foreseeable end, each text opening up unlimited possibilites of new texts, so likewise one text refers back to another text which refers back to another, this constant referring-back being that which ensures the continued existence of each text as part of an ongoing speaking and writing community. Like the future which texts project, this retro-reference is without discernible end. Just as no metaphysician can hope to have the last word (no matter how much, like Hegel, he might like to), so nowhere in our archives do we find any Ur-text, any primal utterance devoid of glosses, any primeval parchment which is not in fact a worn-out palimpsest, whose meaning and reference would be the things themselves in their pristine and unsullied extralinguistic reality. If there ever was one, it was lost a long time ago, as likewise were any records of it. The archaeology of being has so far failed to turn up any genuine *archē*.

(2) As Leclerc's work demonstrates superbly, in this ongoing conversation between texts there is a kind of momentous logic, a logic with a momentum all its own, which forces thinkers along in certain directions. In the development of thought, nothing is predetermined (except, in a sense, within a given system of thought), but nothing is accidental, either. Leclerc's work shows us how metaphysical, conceptual systems come to be and are generated out of previous systems. The logic of metaphysical innovation is none other than that of the creative process itself.

Creative insight never arises out of nothing but builds on what came before and always involves the perception of something like a contradiction in a system that had previously gone unnoticed. As I have described it in my book *Understanding: A Phenomenological-Pragmatic Analysis*, creativity lies not in what one sees (as if it consisted in the "discovery" of new "facts") but in how one sees. Creative work is, to use the expression of Lévi-Strauss, a kind of *bricolage*—a tinkering around with the inner arrangement of a system. Meaning is nothing other than pattern or arrangement, and new meanings are generated by rearranging the elements of a system. Pushed to its limits, this repatterning can produce an altogether new system. When Pascal was accused of a lack of originality, he replied: "Let no one say that I have said nothing new; the arrangement of the material is new."[23]

In order to overcome perceived difficulties or contradictions, metaphysicians invariably end up by creating new concepts. The heart of this creative process is none other than metaphorical analogy, which is why I have labeled this aspect *metaphorical transsubstantiation*.[24] It is the process whereby, through an appropriately creative misuse of words, one thing is changed into another and new entities—such as "mind" or "substance" or, even, "being"— are called into being. "On eschange un mot pour un autre mot, et souvent plus incogneu," as Montaigne said.[25] This is no doubt the feature of metaphysical discourse that moved Gorgias to remark on how in the succession of metaphysical theories he had already witnessed each one was more incredible than the other and placed ever-greater demands on the imagination.[26]

Leclerc has provided us with a wealth of concrete analyses of the way metaphysicians arrive at new concepts through the creative misuse of inherited terms. One need think only of the treatment to which Parmenides subjected the term *esti* or Plato the term *ousia* or Aristotle the term *energeia*. Whatever else it might be, from a purely descriptive point of view it must be said that metaphysics is a marvelous *jeu de mots*.

Is it anything more than this? I have been attempting to indicate, in an extremely and no doubt over condensed way, what is going on in metaphysical thinking. The question which now forces itself upon us is: What is the upshot of all this? What are we to conclude from it regarding the nature of metaphysics itself?

The first thing that is obvious and not to be denied—and which Leclerc would surely not deny—is that metaphysical thinking is as creative an endeavor as any. This fact is often overlooked, precisely because metaphysics calls itself a science, and people tend to oppose science to art and to look upon science as the straightforward description of what things are in themselves without any assistance from the imagination. This was more or less the view of science taken by the positivists, but it is a view which much recent work in the philosophy of science has completely discredited. It is now recognized that the mechanism of scientific thinking is truly creative.[27] As the scientist and writer on science Jacob Bronowski remarks:

> There exists a single creative activity, which is displayed alike in the arts and in the sciences. It is wrong to think of science as a mechanical record of facts, and it is wrong to think of the arts as remote and private fancies. What makes each human, what makes them universal, is the stamp of the creative mind.[28]

This very realization has, however, generated a new problem for believers in the metaphysical ideal of science (in either the metaphysical or physical sense of the term): How can it be that one ends up by "discovering" something "objectively true" about "reality itself" when the process of thinking in question is one that is genuinely imaginative and creative? We seem to have a paradox on our hands.

When in the course of human thinking (to paraphrase Thomas Jefferson) a serious problem arises, it is usually a result of a clash between old presuppositions and new insights. In the present instance, the insight has to do with the creative aspect of metaphysical thinking, and the inherited presupposition is that metaphysics is a quasi-literal statement of the way things really are in themselves. In a case like this, the best tactic always is to put into abeyance, or to suspend, as best one can, one's presuppositions and to describe, to the degree that it is possible, the way things appear to be, making no reference to the way we think they ought to be, which, unfortunately, is generally what we tend to do.

So let us adopt this approach and see what comes of it. We suspend, then, our metaphysical belief in a reality somehow transcending the realm of appearance and which is supposed to be its reason and cause, neither denying nor affirming its existence. We shall make no "positive assertion regarding the external realities,"[29] those said by the metaphysicians to underlie and be the reason or cause for "appearences," for what we do experience. We shall hold "to phenomena alone."[30] Restricting ourselves to what does appear and is evident and which, as such, is the object of truthful statements about it, we focus our attention on the evident means—the creative, metaphorical transmutation of concepts—whereby metaphysicians are led to say what they do and are led to posit as the reason for what is that which they so posit. Can we, in this way, give a fully adequate account of the "objects" of metaphysical thinking—in terms, that is, of the mechanism of this thinking itself? I believe we can.

As I have argued in my book, and shall here simply state as a conclusion, *to describe the act of understanding is to account for the constitution of what is understood.*[31] When one suspends metaphysical presuppositions about human understanding and language and how they are related to what is called "reality" and simply describes the way in which, as a matter of fact, they operate—an approach I have called *transcendental pragmatics*—it becomes apparent that an account of the way creative understanding functions is fully sufficient to account for the "what" that understanding comes to understand in this way. For what is now apparent is that, as James said: "The way in which the ideas are combined is a part of the inner constitution of the thought's object or content."[32]

Thus, once one has accounted for the act of understanding, it is no longer necessary to give an account for what, in the traditional view of these matters, is and must remain highly mysterious: the fact, pointed out above, that by means of *creativity* one "*discovers*" something "objectively true" about "reality itself." For it is now apparent that to use language creatively, which is what all great metaphysicians do, is, *eo ipso*, to engender a new semantic construct, which is to say, a new object of belief, a new "reality."

Indeed, what above all is revealed by a reflective, hermeneutical analysis of the way in which human understanding functions in point of fact is that understanding is basically of a doxic nature. That is, to say that one "knows" something is, as Peirce pointed out, simply a shorthand way of saying that one *believes* it to be true.[33] "Knowledge *is* belief. Or, as James expressed the matter: "Belief is thus the mental state or function of cognizing reality."[34] From a reflective point of view, knowing and believing are functional or pragmatic equivalents. What our suspension of metaphysical belief enables us to see is that, as Husserl said, "consciousness of the world is consciousness in the mode of certainty of belief."[35] This is something Pascal already knew. "The mind naturally believes" he said.[36]

Were we to follow up on these realizations, we would see that the so-called *referent* of metaphysical discourse can be fully accounted for—that is, we can can account for how it comes to be as an object for understanding—in terms of the way in which human understanding invariably works. As soon as, through a metaphorical use of words, a concept has been generated, that of which the concept is said to be a concept is simultaneously generated, which amounts to saying that the referent of language is a functional equivalent of its *sense*. As Husserl would say in regard to noesis and noema, "thought" and "object," the two are strictly correlative. Moreover, sense is itself a function of intertextuality and metaphorical transsubstantiation. Thus, what is called the objective referent of language is but, in the words of the literary critic George Steiner, "the surplus-value of the labour performed by language." Which is what leads him to say: "Language is a constant creation of alternative worlds."[37]

This is something that Leclerc himself in effect realizes. For, as he has said, "The Greek philosophy was determined, shaped by the Greek language." And more particularly: "The Greek philosophy was determined by the accident of the verb 'be' being static and excluding becoming."[38] In stressing the importance of language and the need to study philosophy in different languages, Leclerc gives weight and substance to Gadamer's assertion: "Being that can be thought is language."[39]

Where does this leave us? If we can do without the knowledge-belief distinction, as I have been suggesting we can, we can also do without the reality-appearance distinction, since the latter is but the ontological counterpart of the former. Note, however, that the individual terms of a distinction have meaning only in terms of the distinction itself, so that if the distinction is abolished, so also are its terms. We are thus left without "reality" and without "knowledge," in the metaphysical sense of the term (*epistemē*, science). We are thus left without metaphysics, which is the supposed "science" of "reality." "Reality" or "being," we are compelled to say, is the product of the creative imagination, and metaphysics is myth.

In unearthing the subterranean means whereby metaphysical concepts/entities come into being and develop, Leclerc's historical investigations amount to the "destruction of the history of metaphysics," to use a Heideggerian expression, or to what we might today call the deconstruction of metaphysics. Why, one wonders, does he not view his own work in this light? Why does he nevertheless continue to believe that metaphysics might someday come up with what it calls "the truth"?

Perhaps one reason is that he sees that modern metaphysics has constructed a world in which human beings, if they are to remain human, simply cannot live. The modern materialistic, mechanistic world view is incompatible with the ideal of human dignity. This metaphysical theory must be overcome. But how? It must be deconstructed, but what then? By what criterion could one argue that an alternate metaphysics is more "true"? Is it merely a matter of substituting a more humane myth for one which is less humane? Does it suffice, to combat the overextension of the metaphor of the machine, that we should interpret everything in terms of organism, for instance? This metaphor has at times guided metaphysical thinking in the past, often with ludicrous results. Why should we look to metaphysics for an answer to the cosmic riddle anyhow? Why should we even suppose that there is an answer?

Rather than defending one myth in the place of another, thereby exposing ourselves to the "trickery of reason" and to the natural tendency of human understanding to misunderstand itself by reifying its creative products and interpreting itself in the light of them, it seems far more prudent to follow Occam's advice and not multiply entities beyond necessity. Why should we attempt to substitute another metaphysics for the metaphysics of the machine, the myth of the machine, as Lewis Mumford called it, [40] if there is no need to do so, in order to combat the insidious effects that are attendant upon a belief in that metaphor?

And, indeed, there is no need to do so. In order to combat the human evils of the metaphysics of materialistic mechanism, it suffices to deconstruct this particular metaphysics while at the same time abstaining from metaphysics altogether. (To be sure, the work of metaphysical deconstruction is a never-ending task, since man is, after all, the "metaphysical animal" who, it can safely be predicted, will continue to fabricate metaphysical entities and, like the indefatigable spider, spin metaphysical tales.) It suffices that, by means of the suspension of metaphysical belief, belief in the "non-evident objects of scientific inquiry,"[41] we should realize that man, the creator of belief-objects, such as the object "l'homme-machine," is of infinitely more worth and possesses greater ontological status than any of his sundry ideational creations. We must resist the temptation to explain understanding ("What is man?") in terms of something that itself is a product of a particular system of understanding. In a word, we must avoid what James called "the stock rationalist trick of treating the *name* of a concrete phenomenal reality as an independent prior entity, and placing it behind the reality as its explanation."[42] As a manifestation of human creativity and inventiveness, metaphysics is unquestionably a testimony to the *grandeur* of man, but, as a prime instance of the natural tendency on the part of human understanding to misunderstand itself, it also undoubtedly accounts for much of his *misère*.

Let us frankly admit that all being is interpreted being, that what appears to someone is what is for that person, that there is no being in itself to which, by theorizing, we could have access and, as that which is more real than what appears to be, is of greater ontological worth than it. What does it matter if, like all the other of the "highest concepts," the being *qua* being metaphysicians have spoken of is, as Nietzsche said, "the last fumes of evaporating reality"?[43]

During the Renaissance people wondered about what would happen if you could get to the edge of the universe and stick your arm through it. Where would your arm be? Nowhere, obviously. Similarly, what would metaphysicians find if they really could get to the limit of the realm of appearance, of that which as a matter of fact is, and probe beyond it? Nothing, obviously. In reaction to what Nietzsche was later to call "the error of being as it was formulated by the Eleatics,"[44] Gorgias wrote an antimetaphysical treatise entitled *On Non-Being*, which has long since been lost or destroyed (a highly likely possibility) in which he maintained that being is not. His argument was threefold: (1) Nothing is, or being is not; (2) even if being did exist, it could not be known to human beings; (3) even if it did exist and were knowable, it could not be expressed and communicated to one's neighbor.[45]

Let us assume, simply for the sake of the argument, that in his own sophistic way Gorgias had a point. What then? Then it would follow that metaphysics, which attempts to utter the meaning of being in, as Heraclitus said of the Oracle at Delphi, a "mirthless, unadorned, and unperfumed" way, is myth. But what about philosophy? What becomes of philosophy when first philosophy becomes myth? One thing philosophy must be if it is to be philosophy and not myth is science. And yet it cannot be science, in the traditional metaphysical sense of the term, if the traditional object of this science, "being," reality in itself, is, *qua* concept, facticious (*facticius*), a *fictum*. The question we end up with is one Gadamer has stated in the following way: "So the question arises as to how it [philosophy] can possess the binding character of science without itself being science."[46]

I submit that philosophy can have the binding character of science without itself being science when, under the suspension of metaphysical belief, it sets itself the task of elucidating the way in which theories about reality come into being and gain credence. The proper study of philosophy would then be the various ways in which human beings strive to achieve an understanding of reality, foremost among these being metaphysics. To a considerable extent, Leclerc's work falls into just this category.

Perhaps Leclerc is reluctant to let go of metaphysics because he thinks that to abandon the metaphysical belief in "the truth" is to disqualify oneself from making truthful statements of any sort, and thus of combatting metaphysical "errors." Apart from the fact that metaphysical "errors" cannot be eliminated by substituting for them metaphysical "truths," the fact is that even when one does not subscribe to the metaphysical postulates of Reality and Truth, one can still say many truthful things. If we suspend our ungrounded belief in reality in itself, we can still make statements about that which is apparent and self-evident. What, in the suspension of metaphysical belief, becomes apparent to us is human understanding in its actual workings: human understanding as it posits theoretical entities in order to account for its own basic self-awareness. Because the statements of people and the various rhetorical means by which they defend them are or can be made apparent, *truthful statements can be made about them.*[47]

Nor must it be thought that in rejecting what metaphysicians call reality, we are condemning ourselves to the realm of *mere* appearance, i.e., appearance as metaphysicians understand it, this being the realm of illusion and error. What was said about "reality" in the reality-appearance distinction applies to "appearance" as well. It ceases to exist at the same time as does reality. As Nietzsche said in a passage from *Twilight of the Idols* entitled "How the 'Real World' at Last Became a Myth": "We have abolished the real world: what world is left? the apparent world perhaps? . . . But no! *with the real world we have also abolished the apparent world.*"[48]

I put it to you that, in this remark of Nietzsche's, there is something worth thinking about.

In any event, as Pascal once said: "If man studied himself first, he would see how incapable he is of going beyond."[49] Perhaps he should not even attempt to "go beyond," beyond the great divide, *meta ta physica*; perhaps the proper and fitting concern of man is not Being in itself, being as such, *ens qua ens*, but that particular being which he himself is. "Know thyself!"—that is surely as worthy a task as any imaginable. Perhaps, in reflecting on his own cosmic-constitutive activities and in gaining a better understanding of how it is that those things he calls by the name of "reality" come to be for him, the human being might actually succeed in better understanding what it means for him to be. Philosophy could then with some legitimacy claim the title of science or knowledge, for as Montaigne's disciple, Pierre Charron, observed: "*la vraye science et le vray estude de l'homme, c'est l'homme.*"[50]

Notes

This paper was originally composed for presentation (before a live audience) at the Guelph-McMaster Philosophy Colloquium, "Metaphysical Thinking: Foundational or Empty?" May 7–9, 1984. When I was asked if I would care to speak on the antimetaphysics side of the issue, I gladly accepted the invitation.

1. See G. W. F. Hegel, *La Phénoménologie de l'esprit*, trans. J. Hyppolite (Paris: Aubier, 1961), vol. I, p. 57.
2. See Albert Camus, *Le mythe de Sisyphe* (Paris: Gallimard, collection "Idées," 1970), p. 15: "Juger que la vie vaut ou ne vaut pas la peine d'être vécue, c'est répondre à la question fondamentale de la philosophie."
3. According to C. G. Jung, if man is such a "reason-monger," it is because he sees in theoretical reason the only line of defense between himself and the horrors of the great unknown. "He protects himself with the shield of science and the armour of reason. His enlightenment is born of fear; in the day-time he believes in an ordered cosmos, and he tries to maintain this faith against the fear of chaos that besets him by night." He strives "to construct a conscious world that is safe and manageable in that natural law holds in it the place of statute law in a commonwealth" ("Psychology and Literature," in *Modern Man in Search of a Soul*, trans. W. S. Dell and C. F. Baynes [London: Routledge and Kegan Paul, 1966], pp. 187–88).

4. To borrow an expression from Jules Vuillemin, who speaks of "la raison comme la faculté de transcender l'expérience par les idées." See J. Vuillemin, "La raison au regard de l'instauration et du développement scientifiques," in *Rationality Today/La rationalité aujourd'hui*, ed. T. Geraets (Ottawa: Éditions de l'Université d'Ottawa, 1979), p. 68.

5. G. S. Kirk and J. E. Raven, *The Presocratic Philosophers* (Cambridge, Eng.: Cambridge University Press, 1966), p. 187.

6. "Listening not to me but to the Logos it is wise to agree that all things are one" (Fr. 50, Kirk and Raven, p. 188).

7. Understanding "cause" in the traditional sense as that by which and in terms of which a thing has its being. In this sense, the mathematical can readily be viewed as a cause.

8. Fr. 3, Kirk and Raven, p. 269.

9. Diogenes Laertius, *Lives of Eminent Philosophers (Vitae philosophorum)*, trans. R. D. Hicks (Cambridge, Mass: Harvard University Press, 1972), VIII, 19.

10. Ibid., p. 37.

11. Aristotle, *Metaphysics*, 986 a 15–21. Diogenes writes: "The principle of all things is the monad or unit; arising from this monad the undefined dyad or two serves as material substratum to the monad, which is cause; from the monad and the undefined dyad spring numbers; from numbers, points; from points, lines, from lines, plane figures; from plane figures, solid figures, from solid figures, sensible bodies, the elements of which are four, fire, water, earth and air; these elements interchange and turn into one another completely, and combine to produce a universe animate, intelligent, spherical, with the earth at its centre, the earth itself too being spherical and inhabited round about" (*Vitae philosophorum*, VIII, 22).

In his book *Mathematics: The Loss of Certainty* (New York: Oxford University Press, 1980), Morris Kline writes: "The decisive step in dispelling the mystery, mysticism, and seeming chaos in the workings of nature and in replacing them by an understandable pattern was the application of mathematics. Here the Greeks displayed an insight almost as pregnant and as original as the discovery of the power of reason. The universe is mathematically designed, and through mathematics man can penetrate to that design. The first major group to offer a mathematical plan of nature was the Pythagoreans, a school led by Pythagoras (*c.* 585–*c.* 500 B.C.) and rooted in southern Italy. . . . The Pythagoreans were struck by the fact that phenomena most diverse from a qualitative point of view exhibit identical mathematical properties. Hence mathematical properties must be the essence of these phenomena. More specifically, the Pythagoreans found this essence in number and in numerical relationships. Number was the first principle in their explanation of nature. All objects were made up of elementary particles of matter of 'units of existence' in combinations corresponding to the various geometrical figures. The total number of units represented, in fact, the material object. Number was the matter and form of the universe. Hence the Pythagorean doctrine, 'All things are numbers.' Since number is the 'essence' of all objects, the explanation of natural phenomena could be achieved only through number" (pp. 11–12).

12. Like Porphyry, and in the spirit of Plato's puritanism, a great many metaphysicians have been motivated by a positive distaste for the body and have, as Nietzsche pointed out, sought to wreak *revenge* on it. It is thus not surprising if for them the sensible has value only to the degree that it is *aufgehoben* into the intelligible.

13. Kline writes: "The later Pythagoreans and the Platonists distinguished sharply between the world of things and the world of ideas. Objects and relationships in the material world were subject to imperfections, change, and decay and hence did not represent the ultimate truth, but there was an ideal world in which there were absolute and unchanging truths. These truths were the proper concern of the philosopher. About the physical world we can only have opinions. The visible and sensuous world is just a vague, dim, and imperfect realization of the ideal world. 'Things are the shadows of

ideas thrown on the screen of experience.' Reality then was to be found in the ideas of sensuous, physical objects. Thus Plato would say that there is nothing real in a horse, a house, or a beautiful woman. The reality is in the universal type or idea of a horse, a house, or a woman. Infallible knowledge can be obtained only about pure ideal forms. These ideas are in fact constant and invariable, and knowledge concerning them is firm and indestructible.

"Plato insisted that the reality and intelligibility of the physical world could be comprehended only through the mathematics of the ideal world. There was no question that this world was mathematically structured. Plutarch reports Plato's famous, 'God eternally geometrizes.' In the *Republic*, Plato said 'the knowledge at which geometry aims is knowledge of the eternal, and not of aught perishing and transient.' Mathematical laws were not only the essence of reality but eternal and unchanging. Number relations too, were part of reality, and collections of things were mere imitations of numbers. Whereas with the earlier Pythagoreans numbers were immanent in things, with Plato they transcended things.

"Plato went further than the Pythagoreans in that he wished not merely to understand nature through mathematics but to substitute mathematics for nature herself. He believed that a few penetrating glances at the physical world would suggest basic truths with which reason could then carry on unaided. From that point on there would be just mathematics. Mathematics would substitute for physical investigation" (*Mathematics*, pp. 16–17).

14. Modern science is founded upon a denial of what Merleau-Ponty in his later writings referred to as "la foi perceptive." "La science manipule les choses et renonce à les habiter" (*L'oeil et l'esprit* [Paris: Gallimard, 1964], p. 9). Scientific thinking is an instance of what in *Le visible et l'invisible* Merleau-Ponty termed "la pensée du survol." For a study of Merleau-Ponty's philosophy, see G. B. Madison, *The Phenomenology of Merleau-Ponty* (Athens, Ohio: Ohio University Press, 1981).

Morris Kline writes: "Modern science has been praised for eliminating humors, devils, angels, demons, mystic forces, and animism by providing rational explanations of natural phenomena. We must now add that modern science is gradually removing the intuitive and physical content, both of which appeal to the senses; it is eliminating matter; it is utilizing purely synthetic and ideal concepts such as fields and electrons about which all we know are mathematical laws. Science retains only a small but nevertheless vital contact with sense perceptions after long chains of mathematical deduction. Science is rationalized fiction, rationalized by mathematics" (*Mathematics*, pp. 337–38).

15. Werner Heisenberg, *Physics and Beyond* (New York: Harper Torchbooks, 1972), p. 8. Etienne Gilson penetratingly remarked: "If there were such a thing as a phenomenology of metaphysics [there is, indeed!], Platonism would no doubt appear as the normal philosophy of mathematicians and of physico-mathematicians. Living as they do in a world of abstract, intelligible relations, they naturally consider number as an adequate expression of reality. In this sense, modern science is a continually self-revising version of the *Timaeus*, and this is why, when they philosophize, modern scientists usually fall into some sort of loose Platonism. Plato's world precisely is the very world they live in, at least *qua* scientists. (*Being and Some Philosophers* [Toronto: Pontifical Institute of Mediaeval Studies, 1961], p. 41).

16. Cited by Kline, *Mathematics*, p. 354.

17. In the discussion following his lecture, "The Ontological Background: Classical Neoplatonism," McMaster University, March, 15, 1984.

18. Montaigne, *Essais*, livre III, ch. XIII ("De l'expérience"), in *Oeuvres complètes* (Paris: Gallimard, Bibliothèque de la Pléiade, 1962), p. 1045.

19. Ibid., p. 1046.

20. See, for instance, Gerald Holton, "Einstein, Michelson, and the 'Crucial' Experiment," in *Thematic Origins of Scientific Thought* (Cambridge Mass.: Harvard University Press, 1973).

21. Fr. 93 Kirk and Raven, p. 211.

22. For Peirce, thought is essentially bound up with language and the manipulation of signs, and the meaning of a proposition is another proposition. For a discussion of Peirce's theory of signs, or his "semiotic," as he called it, see G. B. Madison, *Understanding: A Phenomenological-Pragmatic Analysis* (Westport, Conn.: Greenwood Press, 1982), pp. 20–22.

23. B. Pascal, *Pensees*, trans. A. J. Krailsheimer (Harmondsworth, Eng.: Penguin Books, 1966), no. 696 (Lafuma), no. 22 (Brunschvicg). Pascal goes on to say: "I would just as soon be told that I have used old words. As if the same thoughts did not form a different argument by being differently arranged, just as the same words make different thoughts when arranged differently!"

A good example of creative *bricolage* is furnished by Einstein (see Madison, *Understanding*, pp. 215–16). By rearranging elements within the system of physics and by combining in an imaginative way elements of different subsystems, Einstein was able to perceive inconsistencies in contemporary physics that were nonexistent for others and, once having done so, was able to reconcile them through a restructuring of the entire system of physics. As the physicist and historian of science Gerald Holton remarks: "A . . . creative use of apparent opposites can be found in Einstein's contribution to quantum physics, centering on the wave-particle duality. It really is the hallmark of Einstein's most famous contribution that he could deal with, use, illuminate, transform the existence of apparent contradictories or opposites, sometimes in concepts that had not been widely perceived to have polar character. One need only think of his bridging of mechanics and electrodynamics, energy and mass, space coordinates and time coordinates, inertial mass and gravitational mass" (*Thematic Origins of Scientific Thought* [Cambridge, Mass.: Harvard University Press, 1963], pp. 368–69).

Arthur Koestler has coined the term *"bisociation"* to refer to this fundamental characteristic of the creative act, the merging of disparate contexts, and the seeing of a likeness or affinity where before only insignificant difference was perceived. Referring to Einstein as well, he writes: "From Pythagoras, who combined arithmetic and geometry, to Newton, who combined Galileo's studies of the motion of projectiles with Kepler's equations of planetary orbits, to Einstein, who unified energy and matter in a single sinsiter equation, the pattern is always the same. The creative act does not create something out of nothing, like the God of the Old Testament; it combines, reshuffles and relates already existing but hitherto separate ideas, facts, frames of perception, associative contexts. This act of cross-fertilization—or self-fertilization within a single brain—seems to be the essence of creativity, and to justify the term 'bisociation' (*The Ghost in the Machine* [London: Pan Books, 1970], p. 214).

24. For a detailed analysis of metaphor, see Madison, *Understanding*, pp. 198–213.

25. *Essais*, p. 1046.

26. While theory—the transcendence of experience by means of ideas—begins its ascent into the meta-empirical by, in the words of the anthropologist Robin Horton, "the drawing of an analogy between the unfamiliar and the familiar [which] is followed by the making of a model in which something akin to the familiar is postulated as the reality underlying the unfamiliar," the theoretical model is afterward "developed in ways which sometimes obscure the analogy on which it was formed" ("African Traditional Thought and Western Science," in *Rationality*, ed. B. R. Wilson [New York: Harper Torchbooks, 1971], p. 148). Once formed, a theoretical model (of a mathematical or any other sort) has a life of its own. As a result of continued mental "tinkering" (*bricolage*), as Lévi-Strauss would say, a new, extended, higher-level understanding emerges as the basis for further theoretical constructions, more remote still from the original, usually common-sense analogy of the beginning (cf. Madison, *Understanding*, p. 262, n.26). This is why, as Gorgias said, newer metaphysical theories place ever greater demands on the imagination.

27. An extensive and usefully organized bibliography of works dealing with analogical-metaphorical thinking in science—with creative thinking in science—can be found in W. H. Leatherdale, *The Role of Analogy, Model and Metaphor in Science* (Amsterdam: North-Holland Pub. Co., 1974).

28. Jacob Bronowski, *Science and Human Values* (New York: Harper Torchbooks, 1965), p. 27.

29. Sextus Empiricus, *Outlines of Pyrrhonism*, I, 15.

30. Diogenes Laertius, *Vitae Philosophorum*, IX, 107.

31. See Madison, *Understanding*, p. 218.

32. W. James, *The Principles of Psychology* (New York: Dover Publications, 1956), vol. II, p. 286.

33. In his famous article of 1872, "The Fixation of Belief," Peirce wrote: "Hence, the sole object of inquiry is the settlement of opinion. We may fancy that this is not enough for us, and that we seek, not merely an opinion, but a true opinion. But put this fancy to the test, and it proves groundless; for as soon as a firm belief is reached we are entirely satisfied, whether the belief be true or false. . . . The most that can be maintained is, that we seek for a belief that we shall *think* to be true. But we think each one of our beliefs to be true, and, indeed, it is a mere tautology to say so.

34. James, *Principles of Psychology*, vol. II, p. 283.

35. Husserl, *Experience and Judgment* (Evanston, Ill.: Northwestern University Press, 1973), § 7, p.30.

36. Pascal, *Pensées*, no. 661 (Lafuma), no. 81 (Brunschvicg).

37. George Steiner, *After Babel* (New York: Oxford University Press, 1975), p. 280.

38. In a discussion following his lecture, "The Ontological Background: Greek Ontology," McMaster University, March 9, 1984.

39. H.-G. Gadamer, *Truth and Method* (New York: Seabury Press, 1975), p. xxii.

40. See Lewis Mumford, *The Myth of the Machine: Technics and Human Development* (New York: Harcourt, Brace, and World, 1967).

41. Sextus Empiricus, *Outlines of Pyrrhonism*, I, 13.

42. James, "Pragmatism's Conception of Truth," in *Pragmatism and Other Essays* (New York: Washington Square Press, 1963), p. 101.

43. F. Nietzsche, *Twilight of the Idols/The Anti-Christ*, trans. R. J. Hollingdale (Harmondsworth, Eng.: Penguin Books, 1968), p. 37.

44. Ibid., p. 38.

45. For a summary of Gorgias's argument, see Sextus Empiricus, *Against the Logicians*, I, 65ff.

46. H.-G. Gadamer, *Reason in the Age of Science*, trans. F. Lawrence (Cambridge, Mass.: MIT Press, 1981), p. 9.

47. See Madison, *Understanding*, p. 281.

48. Nietzsche, *Twilight of the Idols*, p. 41.

49. Pascal, *Pensées*, no. 199 (Lafuma), no. 72 (Brunschvicg). "Si l'homme s'étudiait le premier, il verrait combien il est incapable de passer outre."

50. P. Charron, *De la Sagesse* (Geneva: Slatkine Reprints, 1968), vol. 1, p. 2.

NINE

Dialogue on Metaphor

MADISON ON METAPHOR, BY DONALD STEWART

In his book *Understanding: A Phenomenological-Pragmatic Analysis*, Gary Madison, true to his title, offers us a phenomenological-pragmatic account of metaphor. "The 'meaning' of metaphorical discourse," he says, "is nothing other than the practical transformation it brings about in the listening and speaking subject, the orientation it communicates to understanding."[1] According to him, "a metaphor does not say what it means, for what it says, its literal meaning, is precisely what it does not mean."[2] Rather, its true "meaning" is said to lie "entirely in its 'perlocutionary force,' in the effect the words have on us."[3]

This view of the matter, though I believe incorrect, has the salutary merit of taking the now generally accepted view of metaphor initiated by I. A. Richards and developed in one form or another by such authors as Wheelwright, Beardsley, Black, Khatchadourian, Goodman, and Ricoeur to its logical and extreme conclusion—that metaphor is, speaking strictly, meaningless. His analysis, which sets itself against what he calls the "rationalist" view that metaphor is a figure of speech based on simile or "essential similarities" (Aristotle), contends that since metaphor is meaningless literally, it creates an entirely new (type of) meaning which is original, unparaphraseable without cognitive loss and quite literally unspecifiable. What Madison's analysis achieves is a way out of the paradox so succinctly captured by Alston in the claim that "it is an extremely important fact about language that it is possible to use a word intelligibly without using it in any of its senses."[4] For Madison, the intelligibility of metaphor does not lie in its meaning at all, for it has none, but in its power to effect a change of attitude, direction, and, ultimately, understanding on the part of the listener. The power of metaphor is performative, not semantic. It changes the subject, directs the subject to a new way of looking at something, effects a new opening into the world.

The problem with this phenomenological-pragmatic view of metaphor, like that of the tradition from which it stems, is that it has no measure whatever of the appropriateness of the metaphorical attribution. It is all very well to say with Wheelwright, Black, and Madison that, far from discovering preexistent similarities, "the likenesses that metaphor articulates are actually, in a very important sense, created by metaphor,"[5] but it is quite another to show that they are then *really* likenesses rather than merely distorting or idiosyncratic images. Even if we want to maintain that the primary function of metaphor is to create insight, we still want to be able to say that not all metaphor reduces to the wild diaphor of *dada*, and on this theory we cannot.

Let me take one of Madison's most important examples, that of Saint Thomas's account of the analogical predication of properties to God. Madison rejects Thomas's "rationalist" account of analogical predication and maintains that "there is more to Thomas' practice than filters through his rationalist theories."[6] The important thing about (metaphorically) calling God good is, according to Madison, that we turn ourselves to God, not the question whether God *is* good. But unless there is meaning to the phrase, then it is hard to see how this statement, rather than *any* other, turns us to God. Perlocutionary force is dependent, in almost every case, upon semantic meaning. "God is good" may turn us toward him, but it can do so only where there is meaning, and we can see that the attribution of goodness to him is, at least initially, not simply absurd, even if not wholly literal. Unless Madison is willing to admit either that similarities do inform metaphor antecedently, or that metaphors gain meaning in some other way, he is unable to deal with the problem of just how the understanding is changed.

Fortunately, there is more to Madison's practice than filters through his phenomenological-pragmatic theory. In an earlier chapter entitled "Analogy and Being," he gave an account of analogy as midway between the rationalism of those who hold that the meanings of terms are essences and the relativism of those who hold that words mean whatever you want them to. "Only analogy of proper proportionality," he says, "constitutes a true analogy; only it provides a genuine alternative to both univocity and equivocity."[7] It is this insight which I would like to follow up, for it can, as Madison says, mediate between the essentialist view of meaning, which relegates metaphor to a merely figurative way of saying something literal, and Madison's phenomenological-pragmatic view, which claims that metaphor has meaning only in what it does rather than in what it says.

Madison, if I read him correctly, seems, in fact, to have accepted the dichotomy between essentialism and relativism in accepting the distinction between metaphorical meaning (relativism) and literal meaning (essentialism). It is hard to see why he did not follow up the lead of analogy in this connection, though he seems to have been sidetracked into thinking of analogy merely as a way of speaking rather than as a basis for both metaphorical and literal speech.

If, as he claims, "metaphorical 'likeness' is prior to and more basic to the life of understanding than logical 'identity,' "[8] then it would seem reasonable to claim that such likeness is prior in reality as well as in metaphor. This is to say that two or more instances denoted univocally by a term are qualitatively, as well as numerically, distinct. The relation between them is one of likeness rather than identity. On this view, no two things, properties or events univocally called by the same name need be qualitatively or substantively identical, though they may turn out to be so. They are *similar* with respect to the univocal use of a given term to denote or describe them. Essences, in other words, are nominal. Further, we may choose to classify objects and properties according to different similarities than those we have in fact chosen.

When we do this with the intent of permanent reclassification, we attempt to redefine the terms we use. When we do so for specific purposes in specific contexts, we speak metaphorically. Thus, when Sir Walter Raleigh writes, "The hardest steel eaten with softest rust / The firm and solid tree rent and rotten," we immediately pick out the similarity between the action of rust on steel and animals eating. Moreover, the similarity is such that we could redefine the animal kingdom so that rust would be included. It would be puerile to do so since we would miss important differences between animate and inanimate objects, but this does not mean that it is theoretically impossible. Indeed, philosophical understanding is often achieved in just this way, as when Berkeley defined being in terms of perception, or Hegel, substance in terms of subjectivity.

That is not what is at issue here, however. The point I want to make here is that the term "eaten" is meaningful in the normal way—on the basis of a perceived similarity—and that this is true of literal language as well. Look at the second line of the Raleigh verse. Is "rent" used metaphorically or not? Cloth is normally rent but trees seldom, yet it is much less metaphorical than the use of the term "eaten" in the previous line. "Rent" is used in its normal sense and the whole sentence makes perfectly good, if not *quite* literal, sense. So too, "eaten" is used in its normal sense, though it is used metaphorically. Further, both sentences are meaningful because both are based on a clear similarity. It is in this similarity that the appropriateness, even the truth, of metaphor resides.

There is, in principle, no difference in the way in which metaphor carries its meaning and the way literal language carries its. Both are founded upon similarities which can seldom, if ever, be reduced to univocal reference to essences. Just as the action of rust eating steel is only similar to that of, say, a man eating flesh, so the action of the man is only similar to that of a horse, both of those to the action of a fish eating flies, and all of these to, let us say, moths eating holes in sweaters. Similarity is not reducible to identity except nominally, and this is crucially important for it shows that it is a matter of decision what we call literal and what metaphorical. We fix our language in certain, by and large, consistent configurations of univocal uses. But these configurations could be otherwise, and it is this fact that both allows for and encourages metaphor.

Metaphor can pick out the similarities which our literal language must, perforce, overlook or relegate to mere accidental features of our experience. In calling a man a wolf, for example, we gain the immediacy which literal language must pass over in, let us say, calling him fierce. To do the job we should have to call him "wolf-fierce," and while this, too, is not impossible it remains metaphorical precisely because men are "man-fierce," not "wolf-fierce," though both presumably are part of what is intended by the literal and univocal uses of the term "fierce" over men, wolves, lions, and so on. Metaphor gains the specificity, which to a large degree literal language overlooks and *must* overlook. In principle, however, there is no difference between the two types of language since, were we to accept the metaphorical classification of men as wolves on the basis of the similarities between them, we should be faced with a new literal structure which would require a new metaphor to (re)establish the difference specific to each.[9]

This also explains why writers such as Black and Madison want to say that metaphor creates similarity rather than discovers it. We "create" similarities when we see that dissimilars are yet similar, when we see that, though God's goodness is different from our goodness, both are comparable. Aristotle said that the greatest thing of all is to be the master of metaphor, for then one "saw" the similarity among dissimilars, and he was right. The act of comparison is an essential element in discovering similarities.

Madison seems perfectly aware of this when he writes:

> To see something as something else (my loved one as a rose, man as a wolf) requires at the same time a realization that one thing is not the other thing (if this is not realized, the metaphor ceases to be a metaphor). To say that something is like something else is to say that it both is and is not that other thing.[10]

The problem with this analysis is that it implicitly accepts the "rationalist" hypothesis that there really are natural kinds or essences which define both literal language and, derivatively, metaphorical language. It is to pass over the fact which he himself maintains, that the world is, in its relations between particulars, analogical and open to any reasonably sensible choice among all the possible language systems which can describe it. Literal language is just the one we have hit upon; it has no special theoretical status over any other possible system even though it has very considerable practical advantages over most such "metaphorical" systems. To put it in terms of Saussure's distinction betwen *la langue* and *la parole, la parole métaphorique* invokes a different *langue* than that which we now accept.

Madison is absolutely right in saying that reality is analogical. When he says that "to say that something is like something else is to say that it both is and is not that other thing," he is fundamentally right. What it seems to me he fails to see is that this is true whether or not we speak in analogies, speak literally or speak metaphorically. It is not the fact that we use an analogy which creates the difference in unity which he characterizes by saying something is and is not something else; all speech rests upon this basic truth, for univocity is nothing other than the cancellation of the differences in the similarities upon which it is based.

When we say, then, that the statement that God is good is metaphorical, we are not consigning it to the class of speech whose meaning is merely performative. Rather, we are recognizing the vast difference between God's goodness and our own while maintaining that the term is univocal over the two cases. This is not Thomas's rationalist view. Neither is it Madison's phenomenological-pragmatic view. Rather, it is a view which I hope does some justice to the insights of both sides.

ON STEWART ON MADISON ON METAPHOR, BY G. B. MADISON

In a letter to me Don Stewart said: "I *think* I have understood your position— I hope I haven't mangled it." Well, I don't think he has understood what he calls the Madisonian theory, and I do think that he's mangled it. On the other hand, he may have understood it all too well and simply not liked what he saw there. Many people, rationalists especially, haven't—not that I'm accusing Stewart of being a member of that dreadful bunch of people. On yet another hand (there's always another hand!), I may not have understood his critique of me. That's quite possible. With these caveats, *respondeo*:

Stewart's main point is that there is no real difference in kind between metaphor and literal speech. He does not like my saying that there is. But there is, like it or not. (Why should we have two different terms, "metaphorical" and "literal," anyway, if there were not two different things to be referred to here?) Let me try to say, with sufficient clarity, I hope, just what it is that I meant.

First of all, as regards generalities, the difference between metaphorical and literal discourse is a free-floating and ever-changing one. That is, new, living metaphors are ever degenerating into stale, dead metaphors, clichés, literalities (if I may be allowed to coin a word). Moreover, like newly minted coins, they rapidly lose their luster as they circulate throughout a speaking and writing community. Because of linguistic inflation also, they lose whatever intrinsic value they might have had, becoming the near-worthless (in that they no longer give rise to new, insightful understanding) medium for the exchange of hackneyed, trite, and trivial ways of understanding and talking about things. Then, if I may be allowed to play with the metaphor (talking about metaphor metaphorically is no doubt the best way of saying what it in fact is; let us not forget that the word *metaphor* is itself a metaphor for what it is, albeit a dead one), they, like paper currency, have absolutely no intrinsic value. They are rapidly worn out as they are passed from hand to hand, thoughtlessly. Fortunately, however, human inventiveness being what it is, crisp, new metaphors are constantly being printed and put into circulation.

It is a basic tenet of phenomenological hermeneutics (of the variety I represent, in any event) that it is precisely this wearing-out process which is the source of literal meanings, of "concepts" which are taken to be the straightforward description of what things as a matter of prosaic fact are. All literal, pedestrianly descriptive meanings are nothing more than the fossilized remains of living, creative, playful metaphors. Univocal concepts, expressing the unadorned, literal truth of things, are nothing more than dead metaphors. The end, banal result of this degenerative process is the formal, frozen, mummified language of symbolic logic. Here words are reduced to mere *signs*, mere signifiers devoid of transcendent signifieds, meaningless signs, therefore, in that they point to nothing beyond themselves and, in their pure diacriticality, are expressive of nothing other than themselves.

Thus, although the difference between the metaphorical and the literal is a shifting and sliding one, it is nevertheless as deep and momentous a difference as the difference between what in my book I referred to as active (creative, insightful) understanding and passive (habitual, routinized) understanding. There is as great and significant a difference between the two as there is between (using these words in a purely metaphorical sense) wakefulness and sleep, poetry and prose.

With regard to more linguistically specific matters, what I want to maintain is that the logic (or illogic) of metaphorical predication is not at all the same as that of nonmetaphorical, "literal" predication. This is what I was trying to get at in my book by talking about the is/is-not character of metaphorical statements. Unlike straightforward constative utterances, a metaphor says, at one and the same time, that something both is and is not (like) something else. If we read or understand metaphors as straightforward, literal statements ("This is that"), we totally misread and misunderstand them. Thus, although metaphors *look* like constative utterances, they most definitely are not constative utterances. Looks, as everyone knows, can be deceiving. Products of a playful, ironic turn of mind, metaphors are deliberately deceptive and misleading. They do not really mean what they merely seem to mean, so that if we take them literally, we are quite simply taken in by them. Or as I said in my book (and it is important to note that I was there speaking from a semiological or grammatical point of view, most definitely not from a phenomenological point of view, i.e., the way in which we actually experience metaphor):

A metaphor does not "say" what it means, for what it actually says, its literal meaning, is precisely what it does not mean. The mode of metaphorical communication is indirect; there is no direct transmission of "information" here, in the way in which computers exchange information. When one truly means what one metaphorically says, one never wants to be understood by those by whom one wants to be understood (which is not always everybody) as meaning what one merely seems to mean. What one says metaphorically is not to be taken literally, at its accustomed face value, for when this happens one's true meaning has not been grasped. The meaning of a metaphor is not like the meaning of a straightforward referential proposition or a constative utterance; it is not what is apparently said but is, rather, what the utterance shows in transcending itself toward what is not said in the saying, and it is what the utterance does when it leads another person to recreate for himself a meaning analogous to the intended by the maker of the metaphor. (p. 308)

One of the most striking differences between metaphors and literal statements lies precisely in the metaphor's deceitfulness. Linguistic analysts such as Searle and others have pointed out that an essential feature of normal, constative utterances is that they carry with them an implicit claim that the utterers are sincere and *mean* what they *say*. This, from a grammatical point of view, is obviously not the case in regard to metaphorical utterances, and so it should be equally obvious that, linguistically speaking, metaphors are in a different class altogether from literal statements.

I said above, in quoting myself, that the real "meaning" of a metaphor lies not in what it "says" but in what it "shows." The real meaning of a metaphor is something extralinguistic. I do not mean by that that its meaning is its "reference," an extralinguistic state of affairs in the "real" world to which it is commonly said it is the business of language to "refer." Such a state of affairs is, as I have argued in my book, nothing more than a rationalist's fiction.[1] I mean, rather, that the meaning of a metaphor is not what it says but what it does, the perlocutionary effect it has on us, this being the change it brings about in our customary way of viewing things, of *seeing* them (all seeing is a seeing-as, and metaphor enables us to see things in new ways). Metaphors are really not constatives at all but *performatives*. All language says something, but when metaphors say something they turn around and cancel out what they say. They are (to use a metaphor that Wittgenstein plagiarized from Sextus Empiricus) like ladders that one kicks away after one has, by their means, ascended to a higher place, a heightened understanding.

To assert, as Stewart does, that this amounts to saying that metaphors are meaningless is to assert something that one has no right to assert—unless it be the case that meaning is a purely theoretical, linguistic, semiotic affair and that our lived experience and the realm of praxis is itself meaningless. Being an unrepentant and unabashed phenomenologist, I refuse to accept that, to believe that our lived-through, preverbalized experience is not meaningful in some meaningful sense of the term. Being that can be thought is language, as Gadamer says, but that does not mean that being is nothing but words, that, as Derrida has wildly and nihilisticaly proclaimed, there is no "hors-texte." What that means is that "in the mirror of language everything that exists is reflected."[2] But, of course, that does not mean that language is but a mirror whose function is merely to mirror a reality which is what it is outside of the mirror. After Rorty, it is perhaps best not to speak of mirrors at all.

I am *not* saying that metaphors have no meaning. I am saying that their meaning *is* their power to effect a change of attitudes, direction, and, ultimately, understanding of the part of the listener or reader. I am thus saying that the meaning of a metaphor is not *merely* linguistic, semantic, that it is indeed something much more than this. Metaphor is more than just an odd way of saying things with words, it is a superbly effective way of *doing* things with words, of altering our way of being-in-the-world. As Bachelard says, the poetic image, i.e., true metaphor, "becomes a new being in our language, expressing us by making us what it expressses . . . it is at once a becoming of expression and a becoming of our being. Here expression creates being."[3]

Now for some specific rebuttals. Stewart feels that the big problem with my "phenomenological-pragmatic" theory of metaphor is that it has no way of dealing with the "appropriateness" of metaphorical attribution. Well, that's no big problem for me. I feel quite happy with saying that metaphor does not discover preexistent similarities and that "the likenesses that metaphor articulates are actually, in a very important sense, created by metaphor." Of course, Stewart is right: that means that I cannot show that these likenesses are "*really* likenesses rather than merely distorting or idiosyncratic images." I could only show that if I believed that the characteristics things are said to have belong properly to them. Only if I subscribed to what I. A. Richards so nicely called The Proper Meaning Superstition. Only if, in a word, I believed in essences. But I most emphatically do not believe in essences, and my whole book was a sustained attempt to get rid of them once and for all. I view it as a kind of Essay on Liberation—liberation from the false consciousness inculcated in us by traditional metaphysics and its insidious idea-products, that of "essence" in particular. I simply do not believe in "essences," those figments of the metaphysician's metaphorical imagination that no man, woman, or child has ever actually seen. Plato never was able to respond unsophistically to Antisthenes's question: Does the "essence" horse look anything like a real horse?

I am opposed to essences for the same reason that my forerunner in what I call the Counter-Tradition, William of Occam, was: They limit my freedom, and being a being who is essentially free, I don't like that. I don't want to be constrained by essences. I am opposed to them because they restrict the freeplay of my imagination. I don't want to be limited in my talk about things to merely "factual" statements about what they supposedly are, or about what I am. Why do things have to be what they merely are? Why do I have to be what I merely am? Why can't things be other than they are? Why can't I be other and more than what I am? Essences represent the repression of desire, and a being of desire is again what I essentially am. I don't want to be repressed. I don't want to live in a world pinned down by essences any more than I would want to live in the ideal Republic of that person who first invented essences, Plato. Nietzsche said:

> A thing would be defined once all creatures had asked "what is that?" and had answered their question. Supposing one single creature, with its own relationships and perspectives for all things, were missing, then the thing would not yet be "defined."
>
> In short: the essence of a thing is only an *opinion* about the "thing."[4]

I for one hope that the day will never come when everything is defined, and we are stuck with things that are nothing more than what they are, which is to say, have been said to be. Being a hermeneuticist, I would like, as Rorty might say, to keep the conversation of mankind going. Besides, what is wrong with Dada or Surrealism? What is wrong with, as Max Ernst said, an umbrella making love to a sewing machine on a dissecting table? Or, in other words, "the pairing of two realities which apparently cannot be paired on a place apparently not suited to them"? Do I detect, in Stewart's reservations, a trace of the metaphysician's unspoken fear of that horrific prospect that things might not really be what they're thought to be, that being and thinking might not overlap, his *Angst* in the face of the cosmic abyss, of the wild being (*l'être sauvage*) which transpires through the cracks in the cosmic egg produced by playful metaphors?

I do not deny that there are similarities that inform metaphor antecedently— indeed, I said as much in my book in talking about metaphor *qua* epiphor— but I maintain that these "similarities" are themselves simply the rigidified remains of previous metaphors which first *created* them.

While it is true that I reject essentialism, as Stewart recognizes, it is most definitely not true, as he nonetheless says, that I accept the dichotomy between essentialism and relativism and accordingly view metaphorical meaning in a merely relativist way. The essentialism-relativism dichotomy is the great either-or, as Richard Bernstein would say (*Beyond Objectivism and Relativism*), of modern objectivistic-subjectivistic philosophy which it is the goal of phenomenological hermeneutics, and the goal of my book, to overcome.

Stewart is adding insult to injury when he says that my analysis "implicitly accepts the 'rationalist' hypothesis that there really are natural kinds or essences which define both literal language and, derivatively, metaphorical language." If dealing with a certain conceptuality in the attempt to explode or deconstruct it is to "accept" it, then I must plead guilty. Maybe, like Cratylus, I should not have said anything at all. It is not easy, as I said in my book, to avoid completely the double bind which menaces any critique of rationalism. So I am not surprised if I have been misunderstood or misrepresented. I did say, after all, that "the critique of rationalism is almost universally misunderstood, for it is taken in terms of precisely that which it rejects"(p.39).

Stewart makes a number of points with which I fully concur, and for which I in fact congratulate him. For instance: "We fix our language in certain, by and large, consistent configurations of univocal uses. But these configurations could be otherwise, and it is this fact that both allows for and encourages metaphor." The fact that Stewart can say this, and, when he does so, think that he is saying something different from what I said in my book just goes to show, however, how much he has mangled my position.

Stewart says that univocity "is nothing else than the cancellation of the differences in the similarities upon which it is based." That is one thing I can agree with him on. But what does that mean? I am not sure Stewart would be prepared to accept what it implies: that purely univocal concepts are intrinsically meaningless, for where there are no differences there is nothing but pure Identity, which is as unthinkable and thus as unintelligible a concept as any dreamed up by metaphysicians, being on a par with other such unthinkables as Infinity and Eternity. All of these pure positivities are nothing but empty sounds. When we think them we are, like the yogi in trance, no longer thinking anything in particular at all.

Stewart says that when the term or "name" (as Saint Thomas would say) "good" is predicated both of God and man, the term "is univocal over the two cases." He recognizes that this is not Thomas's view, and that it most definitely is not mine. But it is a view which he hopes "does some justice to the insights of both sides." Maybe someday he will tell me how. I am sure it must be in a very subtle way that it does so. As subtle as the way in which Duns Scotus, the *doctor subtilis*, argued for the univocity of "being"—so subtly in fact that hardly anyone but a Scotian has ever claimed to have understood exactly what it was he meant.

Notes

This "dialogue" was the result of an initiative taken by Donald Stewart of the University of Guelph. He was sufficiently provoked by the discussion of metaphor in my book *Understanding: A Phenomenological-Pragmatic Analysis* to want to write a critical piece on it and wondered if I would be interested in drafting a reply. I readily accepted the challenge and applied myself to the task with all the seriousness called for by a meaningful discussion of metaphor. It was subsequently published in *Dialogue*, vol. XXIV, no. 4, 1985, over the objections of one of the initial referees (a modernistic philosopher, no doubt), who (speaking obviously of my response) expressed the view that it would be more appropriate "for a literary journal of a modish Gallic sort." The reader will find a further discussion of metaphor in essay 11, "The Philosophic Centrality of the Imagination: A Postmodern Approach."

MADISON ON METAPHOR, BY DONALD STEWART

1. G. B. Madison, *Understanding: A Phenomenological-Pragmatic Analysis* (Westport, Conn.: Greenwood Press, 1982), p. 212.
2. Ibid., p. 308.
3. Ibid.
4. W. Alston, *The Philosophy of Language* (Englewood Cliffs, N.J.: Prentice Hall, 1965), p. 96.
5. Madison, *Understanding*, p. 206.
6. Ibid., p. 212.
7. Ibid., p. 125.
8. Ibid., p. 209.
9. For a fuller account of this view, see Donald Stewart, "Metaphor, Truth and Definition," *Journal of Aesthetics and Art Criticism*, vol. 32, no. 2 (1973), pp. 205–18. Nelson Goodman has a similar account in his *Languages of Art* (Indianapolis, Ind.: Bobbs-Merrill, 1968), though, unaccountably, he ends with a hard and fast distinction between what he calls "intrinsic" properties and "metaphorical" properties.
10. Madison, *Understanding*, p. 211.

ON STEWART ON MADISON ON METAPHOR, BY G. B. MADISON

1. I have also argued the point in my article, "Reflections on Paul Ricoeur's Philosophy of Metaphor," *Philosophy Today*, supplement to vol. XXI, no. 4/4 (Winter 1977), pp. 424–30 (reprinted in this volume as essay 5).

2. H.-G. Gadamer, "Rhetorik, Hermeneutik und Ideologiekritik," in *Kleine Schriften*, vol. 1 (Tübingen: J. C. B. Mohr, 1967), p. 123.

3. G. Bachelard, *Poetics of Space* (Boston: Beacon Press, 1969), p. xix.

4. F. W. Nietzsche, *The Will to Power*, trans. W. Kaufmann (New York: Vintage Books, 1968), § 556.

TEN

The Hermeneutics of (Inter)Subjectivity, or: The Mind-Body Problem Deconstructed

> "Mr. Palomar thinks that every translation requires another translation, and so on. . . . Yet he knows he could never suppress in himself the need to translate, to move from one language to another, from concrete figures to abstract words, to weave and reweave a network of analogies. Not to interpret is impossible, as refraining from thinking is impossible."
>
> —Italo Calvino, *Mr. Palomar*

Some thirteen years ago I flew down to Rio to present a paper entitled, "Mind and Body Revisited: A New Look at an Old Problem."[1] It is time, I think, to take yet another look, a fresher one, at this old problem. If I revisit it yet again, it is, quite frankly, in the hope that the problem may be relegated to the ash heap of history once and for all. It is time that it be simply deconstructed, along with the whole tradition of metaphysics of which it is so inseparably a part.

What makes humans human is that they have an overriding *concern* for their being (the essence of subjectivity is, as Kierkegaard said, "interestedness") and thus an insatiable *desire* to know who they are, to be themselves, truly, understandingly. (This is why, ever since humans have been humans, they have sat around the fire telling and listening to stories about themselves and other selves—many of which were fictional selves, gods, demons, demigods, heroes, and other deified humans.) It is only natural, therefore, that philosophy, that supremely human undertaking, should from its inception have concerned itself with the question of what constitutes the humanness of human beings. Traditionally and for the most part, it dealt with this question in the way in which it dealt with the others it raised—metaphysically, in terms of natures and essences. That is, it proceeded to translate the existential question, "Who am I?" into the metaphysical question, "What is 'man'?" ("*Was ist der Mensch?*"). The hermeneutical question, "How does it stand with us?" became the epistemological question, "What is man's place in nature?" ("*Qu'est-ce que l'homme dans la nature?*").

To ask *what* something is, is to seek out its essence.[2] Does man have an essence then? Obviously he must, since he is not nothing (one who knows anything, knows that one is[3]), must therefore be something, something different from the other things that are. What then is that particular substance that we call "man"? What is it that is particular to it and differentiates it from other substances (for everything that exists is, according to metaphysics, either substance or modification of substance)? Since it is a basic and, to all appeareances, unique, characteristic of human existence that humans exist reflectively in the consciousness of their own existence (a reed exists but doesn't know that it exists), philosophy located the *differentia*, or specific difference, of man in precisely this consciousness, this awareness of self. Man is a body, but unlike other bodies a body endowed with consciousness. For metaphysics, which, as I say, thinks in terms of categories, accidents, things, substance, this meant: man is an intelligence, a soul, a spirit, a mind, a psyche, a nous, an immaterial something or other somehow united, more or less, accidentally or essentially, with a material body. The overriding problem for that branch of metaphysics (*metaphysica specialis*) called anthropology or psychology (*psychologia rationalis*) became that of determining the relation that obtains between "mind" and "body."

Like so many age-old metaphysical problems, this one is still being debated,[4] and philosophers, on the whole, are no closer to arriving at a universally agreed upon solution to the problem today than they were when in their newly invented metaphysical language games they first started tossing it around in the schools of Athens. Like any good metaphysical problem, it continues to generate a good deal of confused discussion, if not heated debate. Privileging, as they are wont to do, seeing (*theorein*), thinking, consciousness, metaphysicians seek to determine exactly what it is that we are conscious of when we exist self-consciously. Is it ideas in our own mind? Or is it movements in our body? And how can we be certain that we are really conscious of what we think we are conscious of, not merely oneirically imagining the whole thing?

In this despiritualized age of ours from which the gods have flown, the suspicion seems to be growing, however, that the ongoing lack of an answer to the mind-body problem may be due to the fact that there is no real problem here at all. The problem, it is increasingly said, is a pseudoproblem. While everyone agrees that there are bodies (even though there are in fact radically different ways of conceiving of body—"body" is one of the most equivocal of terms), more and more people seem prepared to think that the terms "mind" or "psyche" (hardly anybody, apart from unrepentant Thomists, uses the word "soul" anymore) don't refer to anything at all or, as those Antipodians who go by the name of Identity Theorists maintain, are simply roundabout ways of refering to the material body.

This is generally the view of working scientists, of hard-core behavioral psychologists, neurophysiologists, sociobiologists, and such like. The notion of mind plays no more role in their actual work than it does in that of mechanics and bridge builders, and so if they do not outrightly deny the very existence of mind, they accord it at the most some kind of vague epiphenomenal status, relegating it to the outskirts of serious discussion, a subject to be publicly discussed only when they are invited over to the other side of campus to give talks to philosophy students. This is only natural, since science seeks to provide a total explanation for observed phenomena, and the notion of a mind having some kind of existence irreducible to material body and the laws of brute physics is a notion which in this context is devoid of any explanatory usefulness. It is thus natural that science, in accordance with its innate reductionist, totalizing bent, should effectively deny the existence of mind by reducing it to something which is scientifically meaningful, such as neural activity.

But is the human person, the self, the subject, am I, are you nothing but, nothing more than a bundle of conditioned reflexes, a flow of neural impulses, a self-programming computer, a haphazard colony of selfish genes? Any decent, self-respecting human being would protest this dehumanizing reduction of the self, but even if we desire to be nothing more than good scientists, the wholesale denial of "mind" confronts us with serious problems of an epistemological sort.

In their widely read book, *The Mind's I*, Hofstadter and Dennett include an article by H. Morowitz entitled "Rediscovering the Mind." Morowitz starts his piece by observing how the trend in those sciences dealing with the human being has been decidedly reductionistic; human behavior is to be made intelligble by being reduced to its biological basis. (The very notion of a *basis* is, as we shall see shortly, a thoroughly metaphysical concept.) While psychologists of various persuasions have sought to reduce their science to biology, biologists have sought to reduce biology to chemistry and physics, looking to the atomic level for ultimate explanations, the net result being "a sequence of explanation going from mind to anatomy and physiology, to cell physiology, to molecular biology, to atomic physics," all of this "knowledge" being assumed to rest "on a firm bedrock of understanding the laws of quantum mechanics."[5] Morowitz remarks, however, that while psychologists and biologists were pursuing this reductionist strategy, perspectives were emerging in physics which cast a whole new light on things. Relativity theory and quantum mechanics have replaced the human observer in the center of things, have involved the observer in the very establishment of physical reality. As Morowitz says: "The mind of the observer emerged as a necessary element in the structure of the theory."[6] Nothing in the scientific study of the world is meaningful without reference to consciousness; "the human mind enters once again. . . ."[7]

We are lead in this way, Morowitz points out, to a strange kind of *epistemological circle*:

First, the human mind, including consciousness and reflective thought, can be explained by activities of the central nervous system, which, in turn, can be reduced to the biological structure and function of that physiological system. Second, biological phenomena at all levels can be totally understood in terms of atomic physics, that is, through the action and interaction of the component atoms of carbon, nitrogen, oxygen, and so forth. Third and last, atomic physics, which is now understood most fully by means of quantum mechanics, must be formulated with the mind as a primitive component of the system.[8]

The circle leads us from the mind, back to the mind. A strange, uncanny situation. What does Morowitz conclude from all this? Not much, really. He does very rightly remark on the dangers of reductionism, "since," as he says, "the way we respond to our fellow human beings is dependent on the way we conceptualize them in our theoretical formulations."[9] Very true, a most important point indeed! But what are we to make of this rediscovery, at the very heart of the scientific process, of consciousness, subjectivity? Morowitz simply concludes: "The human psyche is part of the observed data of science. We can retain it and still be good empirical biologists and psychologists."[10]

Can we? What, as scientific psychologists, are we to *do* with it? Is the mind the *ultima ratio* for everything that as scientists we have been looking for? No, it can't be quite that, since as the existence of the circle shows, it can itself be reductively explained. In his reflection on Morowitz's article, Hofstadter remarks on how an emphasis on the nonreducibility of consciousness poses problems for a "nonquantum-mechanical computational model" of the mind which, he firmly believes, is "possible in principle."[11] It poses insurmountable problems, I'm sure. Discovery of the "epistemological circle" doesn't, therefore, seem to be of much use to psychology or what today calls itself "cognitive science," nor does it get us any closer to a nonreductionist account of the human person. It just serves to give us scientific explainers a bad conscience—or else to send us off into wild metaphysical speculations. As a number of extracurricular writings by some scientists would seem to indicate, about the only way that scientific observers have yet found of coping with the circle, if indeed they attempt to, is by a desperate leap into some kind of oriental-style mysticism, aboriginal animism, or unrestrained Teilhardianism as a crowning metaphysics.

So long as we remain bound to epistemology, which is to say, to metaphysics, searching for ultimate bases or "models," sources, grounds, or origins, ultimate causal, essentialist, foundationalist explanations, we are perhaps condemned to go around in endless circles, like a dog chasing its tail in vain. Epistemologically speaking, the physical and the mental, the objective and the subjective can no more be made to inhabit one world than could Descartes's *res extensa* and *res cogitans* be made meaningfully to communicate through the arbitrating mediation of the pineal gland. Every attempted marriage between the psychic and the physical has broken down for reason of incompatibility; inevitably one of the partners has sought to repress the other. Perhaps, if we are to make better sense of the fundamentally human question, which simply will not go away, of what it means to be a subject, a human person, we need to break out of the epistemological circle, out of the metaphysical enclosure altogether.[12]

At least one thing is certain: *La subjectivité est bien indéclinable*, as Merleau-Ponty would say. Subjectivity is quite simply undeniable. One can meaningfully say, à la Foucault, "Man does not exist" or "Man no longer exists," because maybe indeed "man" dosen't exist or no longer exists—it all depends, I suppose, on what you mean by "man." (There can be little question that "man," the body-mind composite, the empirico-transcendental doublet, as Foucault would say, is very much of a metaphysical construct.) Certainly, the word *man* exists less and less in our discourse and is used, more and more, only with a twinge of sexist bad conscience. But can one, knowingly and in good conscience, say "I do not exist"? Who would believe you if you said that to them? What would they think of *you* if you said that? Subjectivity is a fact, as indubitable as the fact that I exist, *ego sum*.

But how are we to conceive of it, of the ego, the I, the self, the subject if we are not to go around in endless epistemological circles? That is the philosophical problem that confronts us in this new, postmodern era, after the collapse of the metaphysical economy. If we wish to pursue the question of selfhood nonmetaphysically, let us be clear as to what we must *not* do, as to the sort of questions that are forever forbidden us if we do not wish to fall back into the *aporias* of metaphysics, into vicious epistemological circles.

We must not ask, as in metaphysics one naturally tends to, *what* the self or the subject is. For the only kind of answer to this kind of question is a metaphysical one: The self is such-and-such a kind of *thing*. We would then be conceiving of the self as some kind of *substance* (*res*), something which somehow underlies, supports, is the basis and cause—or else the transcendental, overarching unity—of all those kinds of activities that selves are said to engage in or, again, something that somehow *emerges* out of a material body in the course of its development.[13] We would then find ourselves thrown back into the old mind-body problem: What is the relation between this fundamental, actualizing, synthesizing, substantializing something or other and those things which are observable and measurable, such as bodily movements? Since metaphysics is indeed metaphysics, it can think subjectivity only by conceiving of it as something other than objectivity, something over and beyond (*meta*) the physical, notwithstanding the relations it may entertain with the latter (but these relations themselves, are they physical or mental, material or immaterial?).

We might be tempted, in an attempt to extricate ourselves from the metaphysical predicament, to adopt a straightforward antimetaphysical stance and mode of discourse. Thus, to counteract the substantialist proclivity, we might say: The self, which most assuredly exists, is a primary datum, is nevertheless *nothing*, no-thing—as indeed it is, if substance is taken as the paradigm of being. But why should we allow ourselves to be haunted by the specter of metaphysics in this way? To speak of consciousness as nothingness (*le néant*), as Sartre, for instance, did, to say that while the essence of being is to be what it is, the "essence" of consciousness is not to be what it is and to be what it is not, is to speak a language which is simply that of an inverted metaphysics. And as the title itself of Sartre's major philosophical work, *Being and Nothingness*, indicates, this is a language which is still metaphysical, in that it is a language which works with binary, conceptual oppositions.

As Nietzsche was the first explictly to note, the "essence" of metaphysics is that it can think only in terms of opposites, as he called them. Such as: appearance-reality, sensible-intelligible, material-immaterial, becoming-being, time-eternity, *nomos-physis*, contingent-necessary, fact-essence, practice-theory and, of course, matter-spirit. Metaphysics is itself made possible only by means of the metaphysical opposition *mythos-logos*.[14] "The fundamental faith of the metaphysicians," Nietzsche said, "is *the faith in opposite values*."[15] Depending on which side of the conceptual difference one comes down on, one will evolve either a materialist or idealist (immaterialist, spiritualist) metaphysics, or some hylomorphic combination thereof. But in any event, so long as one thinks with binary opposites, one will be thinking metaphysically.

Why should we confine ourselves to opposites, however? As Nietzsche warned us: "One may doubt . . . whether there are any opposites at all."[16] To learn how to think after metaphysics would be to learn how to think without the comforting belief in the value not only of absolutes but also of opposites, by playing one off against the other (or else by evolving some kind of grandiose Hegelian-style sublating synthesis).

Setting aside the either-ors of metaphysics, let us then say that the I is *neither* an underlying, unobservable substrate, the "inner" self *nor*, as Morowitz put it, "part of the observed data of science." It is certain that I have never seen, observed my self, not even in my shaving mirror. The self is not an external visible. Nor have I ever encountered my self by, as Saint Augustine exhorted us in all his Christian-Platonic eagerness, going "inside," in search of the "inner man."[17] As Merleau-Ponty said in response to this admonition of Augustine, "there is no inner man, man is in the world, and only in the world does he know himself."[18] Inside-outside is yet another metaphysical opposition to be abandoned. Why can we not say that the self is simply a characteristic that we associate with those animate organisms referred to as humans? A characteristic of that most characteristic of human actions, pursued incessantly both in public and in private, in wakefulness and in sleep—I refer to *speech*.

Let us then, like the psychoanalyst Roy Schafer, who has made a highly noteworthy attempt to free the psychoanalytic praxis from the metaphysical ("metapsychological") interpretation Freud imposed on it, say that the self is a manifestation of human action."[19] It is itself an action, the action of speaking about itself. When we tell stories to ourselves about ourselves we are, as Schafer says, enclosing one story within another: "This is the story that there is a self to tell something to, a someone else serving as an audience who is oneself or one's self."[20] The self is not an observable datum, since it is not any kind of *thing* at all, but it nonetheless is, in Schafer's words "an experiential phenomenon, a set of more or less stable and emotionally felt ways of telling oneself about one's being and one's continuity through change."[21] In short, as he says, "the self is a kind of telling about one's individuality. It is something one learns to conceptualize in one's capacity as agent; it is not a doer of actions."[22] "The inner world of experience," he appropriately remarks, "is a kind of telling, not a place."[23] This reminds one of what Merleau-Ponty said of Descartes's *sanctum sanctorum*, the inner retreat of his supposedly wordless Cogito, that it was in fact "buzzing with words." And as he also remarked: "All inner perception is inadequate because I am not an object that can be perceived, because I make my reality and find myself only in the act." "Your abode is your act itself," he said, speaking with the words of Antoine de Saint-Exupéry. "Your act is you. . . . You give yourself in exchange"[24]

It is a basic principle of that form of postmodern, postmetaphysical discursivity called *hermeneutics* (a principle which could be labeled that of *die Sprachlichkeit der Welt*) that, as Gadamer expresses it, "Being that can be understood is language."[25] If, like Richard Rorty, we view hermeneutics as a discipline which displaces traditional epistemology, then, in regard to the question of subjectivity, we may say: *The self that can be understood is language.* However it may be with so-called physical reality, in the case of social or personal reality, the reality in question is inseparable from the language we use to express it.[26] The self requires language in order to be told what it is, and it cannot properly be said to "be" a self outside this telling.

We can find support for this hermeneutical view in the work of the famous linguist Émile Benveniste. Unlike some ultra formalist students of language, Benveniste maintains: "A language without the expression of person cannot be imagined."[27] A language without personal pronouns is inconceivable, even if in some societies, such as self-effacing Far Eastern ones, people go out of their way to avoid making overt use of them. What does *I* refer to? It refers, Benveniste says, neither to a concept nor to an individual; it refers, he says:

> To something very peculiar which is exclusively linguistic: *I* refers to the act of individual discourse in which it is pronounced, and by this it designates the speaker. . . . The reality to which it refers is the reality of the discourse. It is in the instance of discourse in which *I* designates the speaker that the speaker proclaims himself as the "subject." And so it is literally true that the basis of subjectivity is in the exercise of language. If one really thinks about it, one will see that there is no other objective testimony to the identity of the subject except that which he himself thus gives about himself.[28]

Benveniste's basic thesis in this much referred to article is, therefore, that language is responsible for subjectivity in all its parts: "It is in and through language that man constitutes himself as a *subject*, because language alone establishes the concept of "ego" in reality. . . . "[29] Who or what is "ego"? " 'Ego,' " Benveniste says, "is he who *says* 'ego.' "[30] The I exists in and by means of saying "I"; the I is not a subject, a *subiectum*, a preexistent substance, *which* speaks; it is, as subject, a speaking subject. To the degree that we can say that the subject *exists*, it exists only as a *spoken* subject. The subject is the subject of its own living discourse, posited in and by means of it. The "basis of subjectivity," to use Benveniste's expression, is not something underlying the subject's actions; it is an action, the action of speaking.

Speaking from a hermeneutical point of view, namely, one which insists on, as Gadamer would say, the essential linguisticality of all human experience, we are obliged to say that the self is the way, through the use of indicators, shifters, and appropriately self-referential linguistic functions—what linguists refer to as "person deixis"—we relate our actions, past, present, and future. The self is the way we relate, account for, speak about our actions.[31] The self is the story we tell ourselves and others, weaving together into a single fabric, as any good storyteller does, actions and events; it is the autobiography we are constantly writing and rewriting.

The problem of "personal identity," of the unity and constancy of our self-hood, is nothing other than the problem of maintaining coherence and continuity in our stories, and of following up and doing those things that we tell ourselves and others that we will do. This hermeneutical, antifoundationalist view finds welcome confirmation in the observations of an analytic philosopher, Alasdair MacIntyre, who speaks of human beings "as characters in enacted narratives" and who says: "There is no way of *founding* my identity—or lack of it—on the psychological continuity or discontinuity of the self. The self inhabits a character whose unity is given as the unity of a character. . . . personal identity is just that identity presupposed by the unity of the character which the unity of a narrative requires."[32] Thus we may say that the self is the unity of an ongoing narrative, a narrative which lasts a thousand and one nights and more—until, as Proust might say, that night arrives which is followed by no dawn.[33]

Thus the self is not something given. It is something that is acquired, achieved, by means of language, *quelque chose qui se constitue en langage, pour ainsi dire*. It is, so to speak, the significant effect of language. All the multitudinous ways in which people make sense of the world by means of their various language games are ways in which, ultimately, they make sense of themselves (all understanding, hermeneutics maintains, is a form of self-understanding), give themselves form, constitute themselves as self.[34] We must, as Rorty says, "see human beings as generators of new descriptions rather than beings one hopes to be able to describe accurately."[35]

It must not be thought that the grammatical self-referential discourse in which the self constitutes itself for itself as a self is a free-floating *monologue*, that the self is whatever it fancifully tells itself it is. In his article Benveniste emphasizes a most important feature of what he calls the instance of discourse. He says:

> Consciousness of self is only possible if it is experienced by contrast. I use *I* only when I am speaking to someone who will be a *you* in my address. It is this condition of dialogue that is constitutive of *person*, for it implies that reciprocally *I* becomes *you* in the address of the one who in his turn designates himself as *I*.[36]

This has to do with what, in traditional metaphysics, is referred to as the problem of "solipsism" and "other minds"—the whole problem of intersubjectivity. I shall return to the issue under another, less metaphysical guise. Here I shall simply say that when the self pursues a conversation with itself, this conversation is itself not a monologue but a dialogue. Who is the self the self is addressing when it "talks to itself"? It is, as Peirce (who was among the *of interpretation*

Community

R

first to stress the linguistic, semiotic nature of thought) said, "that other self that is just coming into life in the flow of time."[37] Thought or self-consciousness is an intrapersonal dialogue, and the individual self is, in the words of Josiah Royce, "a Community of Interpretation, in which the present, with an endless fecundity of invention, interprets the past to the future."[38]

At this point, though, I can anticipate the objection that the metaphysician will no doubt raise. "Your hermeneutical reconstruction of the self," he or she will say, "amounts in fact to its very deconstruction. Your position is nothing but a kind of linguistic idealism and is every bit as reductionist as those you criticize. For you the self is nothing but a matter of *words*, something purely ephemeral. You are emptying the self of all *reality*."[39] In reply I would first ask what the metaphysician means by "reality"—even though I already know what he means. "Reality" for him or her is simply another word for "substance." Thus, the metaphysician's objection is well taken. The self is in no way a "reality" in the metaphysical sense of the term (nothing, for that matter, is a reality in the metaphysical sense of the term—the metaphysician's "reality" or "substance" is simply, to paraphrase Nietzsche, the last evaporating vapors of our actual experience of things).[40] It is high time that we realized that.

In reply to the more serious charge of reductionism, I must admit that a "linguistic" account of the self *could* be such. But I do not believe that the *hermeneutical* (as opposed to a purely semiological, i.e., Saussurian-structuralist) emphasis on linguisticality lands us in any kind of reductionism—or nihilism. It is a fact, in my opinion, that certain other forms of postmodern thought do fail in this regard. While, like hermeneutics, they are essentially an attempt to deconstruct metaphysics and to overcome modern objectivism,[41] they nevertheless do not succeed in avoiding the pitfalls of relativism, using this term in Richard Bernstein's sense.[42]

Consider, for instance, the position of Roland Barthes in his famous article, "The Death of the Author." Barthes says, for instance: " . . . the whole of the enunciation is an empty process, functioning perfectly without there being any need for it to be filled with the person of the interlocutors."[43] This *is* a kind of nihilistic stance, but it can find no support in linguistic considerations such as those put forward by Benveniste. Discourse, as we have seen, cannot be understood without reference to an "I" and a "you." But Barthes does not stop there; he goes on to say, in a very revealing passage: "Linguistically, the author is never more than the instance of writing, just as *I* is nothing other than the instance saying *I*: language knows a 'subject', not a 'person', and this subject, empty outside of the very enunciation which defines it, suffices to make language 'hold together', suffices, that is to say, to exhaust it." To say that the I is *never more than* . . . , *nothing other than* . . . is reductionism of the most classic, metaphysical sort. Structuralists and poststructuralists like Barthes were able to appreciate the absolute centrality of language, but they were not able, in their treatment of the phenomenon, to free themselves from the long arm of the metaphysical law. Their contestatory, antibourgeois pronouncements remain firmly attached to a metaphysical leash.[44] One can almost hear, in much of the poststructuralist, anarchistic exuberance and fixated obsession with child-ish play and unfettered *jouissance* the continued reverberation of the *nom (ou non)* of the metaphysical *père*.

It might be noted in passing that the present postmodern situation bears some important resemblances to at least one feature of the early modern period. Just as today we see, in reaction to metaphysics and scientism, a proliferation of antimetaphysical stances, a simple substitution of relativism for objectivism, of nihilism for rationalist absolutism, so Giambattista Vico saw his times as being characterized by a divorce between "science" and rhetoric. What Vico most deplored was the antithetical choice proposed to his contemporaries be-tween, on the one hand, a Cartesianism which disparaged and knew nothing (at least on the level of its own theory) of the art of communication and, on the other, a Mannerism which played games with language and which sought to be clever, not true.[45] It is no accident, of course, that Vico's endeavors to overcome this situation met with no success and were not decisive in shaping his age and that it is really only today that we have begun to appreciate his countertraditional significance. In the spirit of Vico, hermeneutics does not simply seek to substitute "rhetoric" for "philosophy"; it seeks, rather, to em-phasize the rhetorical nature of philosophy and the philosophical status of rhet-oric.

In regard to the question of subjectivity, the phenomenological hermeneu-ticist, unlike certain other postmodernists, does not say that the I is *nothing but* a linguistic construct. Rather, he or she says that the I—which, as Kier-kegaard stressed, is essentially a process of becoming and thus never fully *is*—constructs or, to say it better, constitutes itself in and by means of language, by, as I said above, narrating itself. In a very profound remark, Husserl said: "The ego constitutes himself for himself in, so to speak, the unity of a 'Ge-schichte'."[46] In German *Geschichte* means both "history" and "story." So while there would be no subject without language, and while there most assuredly is no subject before language, the subject which does exist thanks to language is not *merely* a linguistic fabrication.[47] (This is because, as we shall see in a moment, language is not *merely* "language.")

In one of his (to all appearances) more outlandish pronouncements, or *énoncés*, Derrida said: *Il n'y a pas de hors-texte*. There is nothing outside the text, there is nothing but text and language, the implication being that language is some kind of vast prison from which we can never legitimately hope to escape.[48] No doubt the entryway into language, wherein, as a matter of fact, humans for the first time become human, bears on it the inscription: "Abandon hope, all ye who enter here." After all, don't novelists such as Sartre and others tell us that life is a living hell? But to maintain that everything is nothing but language, and, accordingly, unending *différance (avec-un-a)*, or, as Dante might say, *pénitence*, is simply to show that one has not successfully carried through with the ritual murder of the metaphysical father, that, even in one's revolt against it, one is still perhaps, like some errant, Diasporatic, disseminating son of Abraham, ever deferred from a return to the promised land of a true origin, a victim of the "metaphysics of presence."

Language does not make sense, is literally meaningless, apart from what phenomenologists call "lived experience."[49] There is "something more" than mere texts and language; there is experience. It is our lived experience that gets expressed in language and which confers on language whatever hermeneutical-existential meaning it can be said to have. However, the relation between language and experience must not be misconstrued, i.e., must not be understood metaphysically (as, unfortunately, Husserl still did so understand it). Experience is not a metaphysical "other"; it is not *something* other than language that language merely "refers" to. This means, naturally, that it is not something "outside" language (let us not fall back into the inside-outside opposition). Language is the meaning *of* experience, in the mode of the *genitivus subjectivus*; between language and experience, an emotion, for instance, there is a mutual belonging, une *appartenance*,[50] or, as Gadamer might say, an "affiliation." Language is not just the "expression" of experience; it *is* experience; it is experience which comes to know, acknowledge itself, to be this or that *specific* experience (subject, naturally, under the pressure of ongoing lived experience, to future linguistic revisions and rewritings—we will have ceased to rewrite our autobiographies only when we will have ceased to be [we don't merely add on to them as the years go by]). When we achieve a more refined way of expressing an emotion, it is our emotional life itself which becomes more refined, not just our description of it. If it is true, as Heidegger said, that language is *das Haus des Seins*, it is even truer that it is the home of meaningful experience. Expressed experience is experience which has settled down and become something "of substance." Experience is not really meaningful until it has found a home in language, and without lived experience to inhabit it, language is an empty, lifeless shell. The language that we speak is neither, as the structuralist and poststructuralist types would maintain, a formal system of pure "signs," closed in upon itself and expressing nothing other than itself, nor is it, as various analytic philosophers of language would have it, a mere means for "expressing" something completely other than itself, Thoughts (as Frege would say) or Things—language neither "refers" to "extra"-linguistic reality nor does it merely "express itself"; language is the way in which, as humans, we *experience* what we call reality, that is, the way in which *reality* exists for us.

So we come to experience as the *"raison d'être"* of expression, language, discourse. And what is the heart of experience, its "inner" *dynamis*? It is— and here I admit I am speaking in a cautiously hypothetical mode, letting in fact my heart speak itself—desire. What, you ask, is desire? As Hegel very profoundly observed, desire is the desire of the desire of another consciousness. It is, when all is said and done, because we are creatures of desire that we speak. If we speak, if we break the dark, murky silence of our formless, amorphous, polymorphous inner lives, it is not primarily with the insignificant aim of, as the cyberneticians would say, "communicating information." If we communicate, use as grist for our mill, so-called facts and figures, it is, ultimately, to captivate the attention of our interlocutors; we use these things as bait for the catch, which is, as Hegel realized, *Anerkennung*, recognition, *reconnaissance de soi*. "How can the eye see itself?" Plato asked in the *Alcibiades*. Not in a mirror, he answered, but in another eye which mirrors one's eye, the eye of another I. In order to fascinate, captivate, seduce that other regard, that other desire, to make it desire our desire, we make of our living body a speaking body. As Merleau-Ponty said: "in the patient and silent labor of desire, begins the paradox of expression."[51] Discourse, conversation is, as he would say, one piece of the flesh of the world addressing itself to another, seeking, in this chiasmic exchange, this *accouplement*, as Husserl called it, the mutual confirmation of its communal being. Perhaps, to paraphrase a line from the late Italo Calvino's recent novel, *Mr. Palomar*, the constituted I, the *de facto* ego, the *persona* is simply the window through which one desire interfaces with another.

Desire is the desire to be more and to be otherwise than one merely is; desire is not simply the desire to be, the wish for continuance or the mere instinct for survival (as Nietzsche pointed out). It is the *désire d'un plus être*, not just self-preservation but self-enhancement. The self, which desires to be itself, desires to *become* itself, to realize what it imaginatively can be, to realize its ownmost possibilities of being. And this means: The self is the desire of other selves, those selves which are other selves, to be sure, but also those other selves which are itself. It is only through that conversation that we are constantly pursuing and constantly desiring with other selves that we can become the self we desire to be and can be who we are. What then is the self? It is a function of the conversation with other similar, desiring selves, a function of the self-reinforcing narratives they pursue together in their occasional, casual conversations as well as those more serious ones which last to all hours of the night.

And so it is literally true, as Benveniste said, that the I is an *I* only when addressing itself to a *you*, that in dialogue, conversation, the *I* reciprocally becomes a *you* and the *you* an *I*, an *I* and a *you* which is what each one is only as intertwining, self-confirming halves of a conversational *we*—"an I which is a we and a we which is an I," in Hegel's words. Our own personal narratives are inextricably intermeshed with the narratives of others. As MacIntyre aptly puts it, "we are never more . . . than the co-authors of our own narrative."[52]

To deconstruct the metaphysical image of "man" is to deconstruct the very image of man as, essentially, an imager, a detached spectator of the cosmos, of so-called objective reality, a *kosmotheoros*, as Merleau-Ponty would say, engaged in the epistemological business of forming inner likenesses of things. When, to use Rorty's words, the great mirror of nature is dismantled, so also is man's glassy, specular essence.[53] From a postobjectivistic, hermeneutical point of view, understanding is not so much a reproductive activity as it is a productive one. Understanding is in fact misinterpreted when it is taken to involve, as Gadamer says, "the reproduction of an original production."[54] To understand an experience, to reconstruct the past, is not to "represent" it to ourselves; it is to *transform* it. This is why Gadamer says that to understand is to understand differently: "It is enough to say that we understand in a different way, if we understand at all."[55]

To understand is, in short, to interpret.[56] This has important implications for the understanding of self that occurs in the dialogical, conversational exchange between desiring selves.

Although the psychoanalytic situation is a special one and is atypical of interpersonal relations in general in that it is characterized by a constitutional inequality between the interlocutors, between analyst or doctor and analysand or patient—and should not, for this reason, be taken as paradigmatic of human communication[57]—it is, nonetheless—as a form of conversation *in extremis*, conversation sought after in desperation and the breakdown of self-identity— a highly instructive mode of human intercourse. For what occurs in this conversation in which transference and countertransference play such an important role is precisely a transformation of the narrating self. As Schafer says: "By means of this [psychoanalytic] strategy one also makes of psychic reality something more than, and something different from, what it has been."[58] In the psychoanalytic situation *insight* IS transformation:

> Thus, when psychoanalysts speak of insight, they necessarily imply emotionally experienced transformation of the analysand, not only as life history and present world, but as life-historian and world-maker. It is the analysand's transformation and not his or her intellectual recitation of explanations that demonstrate the attainment of useful insight. The analysand has gained a past history and present world that are more intelligible and tolerable than before, even if still not very enjoyable or tranquil. This past and present are considerably more extensive, cohesive, consistent, humane, and convincingly felt than they were before.[59]

In sum: "Increased intelligibility of persons and situations implies the transformation of agents and their situations."[60]

Lest it be thought that I am overworking the psycholanalytic model, let us consider what is uncontestably the hermeneutical situation *par excellence*, the act of reading. There is no need for us to enter into the details of that literary critical position known as Reader Reception Theory[61] in order to see what is crucial here and in this regard. Not only is it the case that the meaning of the text is what it only is in the reader's appropriation of it, but also, and more important from our present point of view, this creative appropriation of the text is at one and the same time a transformation of the very self of the reader. As a result of his or her encounter with the textual Other, the reader emerges as a renewed, different person, however minimally so. In our relation to what Ricoeur calls the "world of the text," "the subjectivity of the reader," as he says, "is displaced." He writes:

> To understand is not to project oneself into the text but to expose oneself to it; it is to receive a self enlarged by the appropriation of the proposed worlds which

interpretation unfolds. In sum, it is the matter of the text which gives the reader his dimension of subjectivity . . . : in reading I 'unrealize myself'. Reading introduces me to imaginative variations of the *ego*. The metamorphosis of the world in play [in the text] is also the playful metamorphosis of the *ego*.[62]

What can be said of the transformation of the self involved in our reading of texts can be said with all the greater force of our conversational encounters with other persons, since for someone such as Gadamer the reading of texts is itself understood on the model of interpersonal dialogue. In the conversational exchange, we ourselves are changed; in ex-changing themselves, the *I* and the *you* are reciprocally changed. The self which emerges from a fruitful dialogical exchange is one which is freed to become something more than it was. What we receive makes us different from what we were before. We thereby become truly who we are—for better or worse. Here one person becomes a genuine scoundrel; there another becomes a bit more humane. Some conversations, such as a bad marriage or family situation, hinder us from becoming ourselves and sometimes even lead to our self-destruction; others are the "that without which" we would not be the selves who fortunately we are. "Only through others," Gadamer says, "do we gain true knowledge of ourselves."[63]

Metaphysicians are constantly talking of "the truth," of "the true reality." To conclude this foray into the hermeneutics of subjectivity, we might ask ourselves what it could possibly mean in a postmetaphysical context to speak, as everyone tends to, of our stories, narratives, histories as being "true," or "not true." One thing it most obviously cannot mean is that they have truth value by conforming to, *representing* (as Foucault might say) some "objective," extralinguistic reality which simply is what it is. The aim of history, for instance, cannot possibly be simply to portray the past *wie es eigentlich gewesen ist*. That chimerical project has no meaning in a postobjectivistic situation when the Great Mirror of Nature no longer exists.[64] Nor is it the function of *la chose littéraire*, "that thing called literature," to "imitate reality." As the Mexican novelist Carlos Fuentes has said:

> We are voices in a chorus that transforms lived life into narrated life and then returns narrative to life, not in order to reflect life, but rather to add something else, not a copy but a new measure of life; to add, with each novel, something new, something more, to life.[65]

The truth about what objectivists call "the truth" is, as Nietzsche declared with uncompromising honesty, that there is no such thing. Does this mean that everything is up for grabs, that we have fallen back—O horror of horrors!— into the dreadful abyss of nihilistic relativism? Most assuredly not. For we are certainly seeking to be truthful when we say that there is no such thing as "the truth." There is no good reason why we should allow ourselves to fall prey to the Cartesian anxiety, the metaphysical either-or (either there is meaning, in which case it is objectively determinate, or everything is meaningless). (This is an either-or to which Derrida seems still to be subjugated when he says that since a text does not have a fixed, unique meaning that it would be the goal of interpretation [reading] simply to reproduce or double [a point actually insisted upon, utterly contrary to what Derrida implies, by hermeneutics], the act of reading is therefore pure, inventive play and clever parody where the very notion of a true or appropriate meaning is meaningless and everything is reduced to indecision.)[66]

Rather than speaking, nominally, of "the truth" (as if to imply that the word designates some kind of static, objective correlation obtaining between the "inner" and the "outer"), it would be better for us as hermeneuticists concerned with what people *do*, with human *action* (storytelling being the most noteworthy form of action), to speak, adverbially, of "being in the truth"—or "in the untruth." We are in the truth when we are true to ourselves. That means: when our narratives are such as to contain a significant amount of ongoing coherence (no narrative is perfectly coherent, nor ought it to be, for that, what in literary terms is called *closure*, would spell stagnation and rigidity), when in our re-writings and retellings we are able to preserve and to take up, in a more meaning-giving way, with greater subtlety of narrative, the "truth" of our past, i.e., all the "data" that we have already made use of and their interpretations. It is the same for nations as it is for persons. There is no set, universal *exemplar*, valid for all alike, by conforming to which they could be said to be authentic, true to themselves, to be what they ought to be. Rather, they are in the truth when, in their ongoing self-transformations they are able to incorporate in their even sometimes revolutionary projects their own specific traditions or personal histories.[67] They are in the untruth, are inauthentic, when they are unable to do so. Failure in this regard spells the dissolution of the body politic, the loss of national or personal identity, the fragmentation of the self. Untruth is repression, political or personal. Just as when, in the breakdown of its identity, the nation must seek it afresh in—if it is to have a healthy political life—renewed contractarian discussions (which are not to be confused with negotiations and which have a dialogical logic of their own), so also must the individual seek his or her identity afresh, in, for instance, the psychoanalytic encounter which, if successful, will enable the individual to overcome the fracturedness of his or her narratizing activity, to achieve a radical realignment or expansion of narratives.[68]

We are in the truth when we are able to overcome the distortions, systematic or otherwise, that constantly menace our conversations, the ones we pursue with our own selves as well as those we pursue with others, when we can maintain the openness of the conversation and keep it going. For what we most truly are in our ownmost inner self is a conversation.

Notes

This paper was originally composed for presentation at a symposium organized by Jeff Mitscherling at McGill University, "Contemporary Issues in Phenomenology and Hermeneutics," November 11–12, 1985. It was subsequently published in *Man and World* 21: 3–33 (1988).

1. The paper was presented to the VIII Congresso Interamericano de Filosofia, held in Brasilia, October-November, 1972, and was published in the proceedings of the congress, *Filosofia* (São Paulo: Instituto Brasileiro de Filosofia, 1974), vol. II, pp. 151–59. A somewhat revised version of this paper was subsequently published under the title "The Possibility and Limits of a Science of Man," *Philosophy Forum*, vol. 14, 1976, pp. 351–66.

2. As Scotus Erigena knew when he said that one cannot or should not ask what God is, since God is not a what.

3. This was basically the argument Augustine used to refute Academic scepticism (see, for instance, *De Civitate Dei*, XI, 26), thereby providing himself with a epistemological springboard for attaining immutable truths and "divine illumination." Since I cannot doubt that I exist, this proves that there are truths that I can attain to; it proves the existence not only of a substantial soul but also, ultimately, that of a metaphysical or ontotheological God which, as pure being, is also absolute, immutable substance.

4. Very often the metaphysical problem of subjectivity ("the metaphysical problem concerning any and all organisms capable of subjective experience") is posed, as both metaphysicians and scientists have a special proclivity for doing, in genetic terms: How does that mysterious thing called "subjectivity" come to adhere to what, initially at least, is a mere material body? The distinguished metaphysician, a philosopher of international repute, my cherished friend and esteemed colleague, Albert Shalom writes: "In terms of the problem at issue here, what this means is the necessity of finding a set of concepts which can make sense of the emergence of subjective experience, including conceptualization itself ["conceptualization," I take it, in the metaphorical, not biological, sense], in organisms which start off as embryos to which no tinge of subjective experience can possibly be attributed" ("Subjectivity," *Review of Metaphysics*, vol. XXXVIII, no. 2, December 1984, p. 229). Or, as he says a bit further on in this article, what he is in search of "are those concepts which might be able to lead us to understand how subjectivity itself emerged from the mud and slime of physical reality itself" (p. 245).

The question of origins is the supremely metaphysical question. Shalom's solution to the mind-body problem amounts to putting forward "a conception of physical reality which, while not contravening any established truths belonging to the sciences, will nevertheless account for the emergence of subjective experience" (p. 248). Taking what he calls "doggy subjectivity" as an example, Shalom, or as I shall henceforth refer to him with a suitably worthy metaphysical name, Albertus, says, in a most time-honored metaphysical way: " . . . we are in search of something which is actually present in the dog ovum, and which is potentially what will actualize itself as the dog's subjectivity, in the course of time" (p. 251). If the reader believes he detects here the reverberating echo of the old Thomistic-Aristotelian hylomorphism, he would not be mistaken. Albertus immediately goes on to say that the only "philosophically explanatory model" for dealing with the problem "is the Aristotelian model of potentiality and actuality" (p. 252). All of our conceptual problems come down to the simple fact that we have forgotten the principles of Aristotelianism (see ibid.).

Since it obviously takes time for the fertilized ovum to develop into an entity endowed with "subjectivity" (I don't know exactly how long this is supposed to take, and Albertus doesn't say, but I do know that human organisms only become rational on their seventh birthday), Albertus conveniently latches onto *time* or temporality as the metaphysical essence of personhood, viewing it as a "real or actual factor" (p. 264): " . . . temporality is to be used as the basic or key concept in a conceptual framework designed to explain the emergence of subjective manifestations from an initial cell not possessing such manifestations . . . " (p. 258). " . . . in place of Aristotle's key-terms of 'matter' and 'form', we must appeal, to begin with, to one of the essential components of physical reality itself, namely time" (p. 260). So Albertus even manages to substantialize time, no mean metaphysical feat, you must admit. Time, he says, is "a reality which is itself a constituent element of physical existence" (p. 268). What he is in search of is " . . . a locus of permanence at the root of a sentient organism," and this, he says, is "a very concrete reality" (ibid.). We seem suddenly to find ourselves right back in the company of the old presocratics and their foundational "roots," *rhizomata*, and "elements." With, let it be noted, a fair amount of solid, old-fashioned ontotheology thrown in for good measure. He says at the end of his paper that the emergence of various "loci of permanence or identity" in "the course of evolution points both to the necessity of evolution, and also to the necessity of interpreting evolution in terms of a God who appears to have created this evolutionary process as a stage on which have appeared a succession of entities endowed with increasingly greater capacities of subjective internaliztion" (p. 273). We are well on our evolutionary way, no doubt, to Teilhard de Chardin's cosmic "noosphere" and "omega point."

All in all, Albertus's paper would appear to be a good illustration of how hopeless the metaphysical quest is and how barren it is when it comes to enabling us better to understand—and cope with—the mystery of our human existence. What, when all is said and done, does it really mean to speak of moments of self-awareness being "centered on a personal identity which is *what* each of us primarily is" (p. 261; emphasis added)? How is that supposed to enlighten us about ourselves? Perhaps it does; I just don't see how. It sounds like yet another variation on the metaphysical "explanation" of why sleeping powder causes sleep—because it possesses that thing called a *vis dormativa*, which is what each individual portion of it primarily is. Albertus's paper is undoubtedly to be recommended to any serious-minded person who has a taste for pure and unadulterated metaphysics in the grand old style.

5. Harold J. Morowitz, "Rediscovering the Mind," in D. Hofstadter and D. Dennett, *The Mind's I* (New York: Basic Books, 1981), p. 36.

6. Ibid., p. 37.

7. Ibid., p. 39.

8. Ibid.

9. Ibid., p. 41.

10. Ibid., p. 42.

11. Ibid., p. 43.

12. If that form of epistemological thinking known as positivism is a hermeneutical absurdity, it is because it is hopelessly entangled in the "epistemological circle." As Jürgen Habermas has effectively pointed out, if, as positivism maintains, sensations are the elements out of which reality is constructed, it is hard to see how it could "deny the function of consciousness, in whose horizon sensations are always given" (*Knowledge and Human Interests* [Boston: Beacon Press, 1971], p. 83). And yet since positivism asserts that the real is the factual, consciousness or the knowing subject must be reduced to the factual. The ego is inconsistently given the same status as the external facts it seeks to describe. The positivist thinker does himself in as a thinker, commits epistemological hari-kari: "The only reflection admissible serves the self-abolition of reflection or the knowing subject" (ibid., p. 85).

13. As the metaphysician Albertus so conceives it.

14. A distinction which I have attempted to deconstruct genealogically in my paper "Metaphysics as Myth," presented at the Guelph-McMaster Philosophy Colloquium, "Metaphysical Thinking: Foundational or Empty?" May 7–9, 1984 (included in this volume as essay 8).

15. Friedrich Nietzsche, *Beyond Good and Evil*, trans. Walter Kaufmann (New York: Vintage Books, n.d.), § 2. For a discussion of binary opposites (philosophical "couples") from the point of view of contemporary rhetorical theory, see Chaim Perelman and L. Olbrechts-Tyteca, *Traîté de l'argumentation: La nouvelle rhétorique* (Bruxelles: Éditions de l'Institut de Sociologie, Université Libre de Bruxelles, 1970, 2d ed.), §§ 89–96.

Among other things, Perelman points out how in the appearance-reality opposition, for instance, the second term has meaning only in regard to the first and how it does not merely designate something given but is in fact a *construction* (§ 90). When Perelman remarks how, from the point of view of argumentation, the positing of the second term serves the argumentative or rhetorical tactic of *devalorizing* what thenceforth is opposed to it (appearance becomes illusion and error), one thinks immediately of Nietzsche's critique of Platonism (that it is in fact a devalorization of this world). *Rhetorical theory (the Theory of Argumentation) shows, in effect, how metaphysics cannot but result in nihilism.*

16. Ibid. Perelman notes: "La pensée contemporaine s'efforce, dans beaucoup de domaines, à abolir des couples. C'est au prix d'un grand effort . . . " (ibid., § 92, p. 569).

17. *"Noli foras ire, in te redi, in interiore homine habitat veritas"* (St. Augustine, *De vera religione*, 39, n. 72).

18. Maurice Merleau-Ponty, *Phenomenology of Perception*, trans. Colin Smith (London: Routledge and Kegan Paul, 1962), p. xi.

19. Roy Schafer, *Language and Insight* (New Haven, Conn.: Yale University Press, 1978), p. 86.

20. Schafer, "Narration in the Psychoanalytic Dialogue," in *On Narrative*, ed. W. J. T. Mitchell (Chicago: University of Chicago Press, 1981), p. 31.

21. Schafer, *Language and Insight*, p. 84.

22. Ibid., p. 86.

23. Ibid., p. 197.

24. Merleau-Ponty, *Phenomenology of Perception*, p. 456.

25. Hans-Georg Gadamer, *Truth and Method* (New York: Seabury Press, 1975), p. 432.

26. In regard to social reality, see Charles Taylor, "Interpretation and the Sciences of Man," in *Interpretive Social Science: A Reader*, ed. P. Rabinow and W. Sullivan (Berkeley: University of California Press, 1979). Taylor says, for instance: "The language is constitutive of the reality, is essential to its being the kind of reality it is" (p. 45). To insist on the relation between social reality and language is to maintain, as Taylor does in this article, that the social sciences are not primarily *explanatory* disciplines (as the natural sciences are thought to be) but *interpretive* or *hermeneutical* disciplines.

27. Émile Benveniste, "Subjectivity in Language," in *Problems in General Linguistics*, trans. M. Meck (Coral Gables, Fla.: University of Miami Press, 1971), p. 225.

28. Ibid., p. 226.

29. Ibid., p. 224.

30. Ibid.

31. It could reasonably be argued that only those entities which are capable of narrating their actions, making sense of them by telling stories about them (i.e., humans), can be said to *perform actions* and, accordingly, to be *moral agents*. Animals don't *act*, even if they do do many interesting things, none of which, of course, are either moral or immoral even though, as is the case with pets, they may sometimes be bad. To be a moral agent is to be responsible, which means to be able to respond, to discuss, and to give an account (*un récit*, a narrative) of one's doings, assuming thereby the authorship of one's deeds (for action is, as Ricoeur might say, a kind of text). A hermeneutical approach to subjectivity dispenses us, when we attempt to account for responsibility, of having to have recourse to the metaphysical concept of "free will."

32. Alasdair MacIntyre, *After Virtue* (Notre Dame, Ind.: University of Notre Dame Press, 1984), pp. 217–18.

33. See Proust, *À la recherche du temps perdu* (Paris: Gallimard, "Pléiade" ed., 1954), vol. III, p. 1035.

34. As I mentioned in a previous paper, the self which gets constituted in certain

kinds of language games is a very peculiar kind of self. It is a characteristic of scientific language games, for instance, that in them the narrating self does not show through as such, is, in fact, denied as a self (by, for example, being interpreted as the mere vehicle for genes getting about and meeting other genes). See "Husserl's Hermeneutical Contribution to the Explanation-Understanding Debate" (included in this volume as essay 3).

35. Richard Rorty, *Philosophy and the Mirror of Nature* (Princeton, N.J.: Princeton University Press, 1979), p. 378.

36. Benveniste, "Subjectivity in Language," pp. 224–25.

37. C. S. Peirce, "The Essentials of Pragmatism," in *Philosophical Writings of Peirce*, ed. J. Buchler (New York: Dover Publications, 1955), p. 258.

38. Royce to Mary W. Calkins, March 20, 1916, quoted in Milton Singer, *Man's Glassy Essence: Explorations in Semiotic Anthropology* (Bloomington: Indiana University Press, 1984), p. 94 (chs. 3 and 4 of this book present an excellent account of Peirce's views on the semiotic nature of the self).

39. Frankly, it seems to us that it is the metaphysician who loses us in mere words. Albertus's article (see note 4 above) is no doubt as good an example as any of empty metaphysical talk, ontotheological *Gerede*. (Metaphysics, we may note, is described thus: "The purpose of a metaphysical analysis in this domain is to formulate key-concepts designed to make sense of the actual existence and evolution or organisms, which the sciences can only describe in terms of their specific framework" [p. 266]). For instance, it is hard to resist asking what it *really* means to speak of subjectivity as being essentially "a locus of permanence which then explicates itself spatio-temporally as the development of 'that specific particular' " (p. 265).

Here are some more nice metaphysical insights: " . . . it is the locus of permanence which, by virtue of its fundamental role of determining a particular to be that specific particular, thereby determines those reactions which the biochemist describes as the multiple functionings of the genetic code, the brain code, and all the other elements which cooperatively combine to actualize or deploy the potentiality of the initial fertilized ovum" (p. 265); "Activity of this determining sort implies that this locus of permanence is a center of power. The power of which it is the center is the power of bringing into actualization the unitary particular or individual which is potentially implicit in the initial fertilized ovum" (pp. 265–66); "Such a conception can only make sense if we conceive the locus of permanence as an actually existing timeless potentiality indefinitely actualizable as a result of actions which refer back to it, or which stem from it" (pp. 268–69).

The self, we are told on a later page, is "the internalization within the locus of permanence of its own processes as identity" (p. 273). What in the world, you may wonder is this "locus of permanence"? Albertus tells us: " . . . this locus of permanence is not to be conceived as a separate entity, an entity apart from the physical entity as a whole, but as the permanent *locus of* that physical entity as a whole determining the entity to be and to become what it potentially is . . . " (p. 269). Albertus tells us even more: " . . . 'experiencing' is a particular mode of the reflecting, or internalizing, of specific spatio-temporal energy transactions of particular identities or loci of permanence. That is to say, from this standpoint, 'experiencing' is a derivative reality from the more fundamental principles of the constant dialectic within living and sentient organisms and actualized by means of their particular identities or loci of permanence" (p. 270). " . . . this identity," he says, "is conceived as a timeless moment [*sic*], determining and defining the specific sort of identity itself . . . ," which means: " . . . the transformation of incessant and complex physical processes into a quasi-timeless analogue of the constant repetitions of these physical processes themselves. . . . In other words, the varied mass of bodily processes, as they are internalized in the locus of permanence or identity, constitute the emergence within that identity of a sense or a feel of that identity itself. Sensations are part of that sense or feel of identity. The sense of selfness is the organism's identity reflected or internalized in the locus of permanence, through and by means of the mass of specific processes which define that locus as a 'self' or identity of a specific kind. The locus of permanence operates, so to speak, a fixating and therefore a transforming, of pure physical process. Sensation, that is to say, is physical process rendered temporarily motionless—temporarily, because it is constantly succeeded by fresh physical processes" (p. 271).

What real, existential, experiential meaning do these nice-sounding words have? It is hard to shake off the nagging suspicion that what we have here is really nothing more than an erudite word game. Metaphysics is undoubtedly one of the more fascinating of such games that humans have come up with, and it cannot be denied that it does afford some kind of vicarious understanding of ourselves, a *simulacrum* of understanding. (But then, of course, what, one might well ask, does metaphysics deal with, if it be not *simulacra*, ghostly figures flitting across the inner surface of man's glassy essence?)

Albertus's text is one which cries out for a deconstructive reading. The aim of deconstruction, as "deconstructionists" practice it, is to show how a given text undermines its own claims to truth-value and logical consistency. It is, in the words of Christopher Norris, " . . . a textual *activity*, a putting-into-question of the root metaphysical prejudice which posits self-identical concepts outside and above the disseminating play of language" (*The Deconstructive Turn* [London: Methuen, 1983], p. 6). A deconstructive reading of a metaphysical text will reveal how its key-concepts, to use Albertus's expression, are not the pure, transparent, semantically exact, homogeneous idealities the metaphysician takes them to be but are in fact disguised, unawoved metaphors and rhetorical tropes and *topoi*; it makes visible the conceptual blind spots in a text which claims to be no more than a straightforward representation of some supposedly determinate reality.

Now, Albertus's text would lend itself magnificently to this kind of reading. It would be quite instructive to see how, for instance, although he inveighs against any kind of Cartesian reification of the "mind" and Descartes's taking of extension and spatiality as paradigmatic of worldly being, he himself does much the same with his "key-concepts" of *internalization* and *loci of permanence*; temporality is here curiously spatialized. Albertus's "locus of permanence" is perhaps but a *locus communis* or commonplace, a worn-out *figura verborum* of classical metaphysical rhetoric.

40. For a nonmetaphysical account of reality, see G. B. Madison, *Understanding: A Phenomenological-Pragmatic Analysis* (Westport, Conn.: Greenwood Press, 1982).

41. Actually, deconstructionism, *as Derrida practices it*, apparently does not seek the overcoming of metaphysics, given his conviction as to the inescapable closure of metaphysical thinking. If there is any basis for charging Derrida with nihilism, it lies perhaps in the fact that for him what is beyond or exterior to metaphysics is "unnamable by philosophy" (see *Positions*, trans. Alan Bass [Chicago: University of Chicago Press, 1981], p. 6). Derrida's position would be nihilistic in that on this same page he appears to equate philosophy with metaphysics, which it is, of course, his goal to deconstruct. The inevitable question is: What does this leave us with? Here we run into the "end of philosophy" theme.

42. See Richard Bernstein, *Beyond Objectivism and Relativism* (Philadelphia: University of Pennsylvania Press, 1983).

43. Roland Barthes, "The Death of the Author," in *Image, Music, Text* (New York: Hill and Wang, 1984), p. 145.

44. Much the same point is made by Barbara Herrnstein Smith in her excellent article, "Narrative Versions, Narrative Theories," in *On Narrative*, ed. W. J. T. Mitchell. In opposition to structuralists (who, as she says, continue to operate with metaphysical dualities), she presents an alternative conception of discourse which emphasizes its act character and situatedness and says: " . . . this sort of alternative conception of discourse

and symbolic behavior generally may help clarify why traditional assumptions and latter-day affirmations of a correspondence between 'language' and 'the world' [what in hermeneutics is called *objectivism*] are untenable and thus move us beyond the mere *denial* of such a correspondence [i.e., beyond mere nihilistic *relativism*] (as in the Heideggerian and post-structuralist insistence on 'discrepancies,' 'failures,' 'ruptures,' and 'absences')—in short, beyond the whole 'problematic of language,' " (p. 222).

45. See Michael Mooney, *Vico in the Tradition of Rhetoric* (Princeton, N.J.: Princeton University Press, 1985), p. 85.

46. Edmund Husserl, *Cartesian Meditations* (The Hague: Martinus Nijhoff, 1960), § 37.

47. In a recent work (*Personal Being* [Cambridge, Mass.: Harvard University Press, 1984]), Rom Harré defends a linguistic interpretation of the self ("The primary human reality is persons in conversation" [p. 58]). Unfortunately, Harré veers toward a kind of relativistic reductionism, maintaining that the self is but a convenient fiction, a theoretical, hypothetical entity or construct as this term is understood in the philosophy of science (see, for instance, pp. 82, 100, 145, 147, 160, 162, 167, 193, 212–14, 265). People devise all kinds of theories about themselves, but the self which does this devising is hardly just a *theory*.

48. Or a padded cell. Derrida speaks of "the padded interior of the 'symbolic' " (see *Positions*, trans. Alan Bass [Chicago: University of Chicago Press, 1981], p. 86).

49. This is why a structuralist such as Claude Lévi-Strauss, who rejects the phenomenological notion of experience, maintains that language is indeed meaningless, that words refer only to themselves and that, accordingly, meaning is a mere linguistic illusion. In a famous interchange with Paul Ricoeur, he was led to say: " . . . le sens résulte toujours de la combinaison d'éléments qui ne sont pas eux-mêmes signifiants. . . . dans ma perspective, le sens n'est jamais un phénomène premier: le sens est toujours réductible. Autrement dit, derrière tout sens il y a un non-sens, et le contraire n'est pas vrai. Pour moi, la signification est toujours phénoménale" ("Réponses à quelques questions," *Esprit*, November 1983, p. 637). In opposition to this view, Ricoeur stated, twice-over: "Si le sens n'est pas un segment de la compréhension de soi, je ne sais pas ce que c'est"(ibid., pp.636, 641). He fittingly summed up his reaction to Lévi-Strauss's position by saying: "Vous êtes dans le désespoir du sens; mais vous vous sauvez par la pensée que, si les gens n'ont rien à dire, du moins ils le disent si bien qu'on peut soumettre leur discours au structuralisme. Vous sauvez le sens, mais c'est le sens du non-sens, l'admirable arrangement syntactique d'un discours qui ne dit rien" (ibid., pp. 652–53).

50. See Merleau-Ponty, *Signs* (Evanston, Ill.: Northwestern University Press, 1964), p. 18: "There is not *thought* and *language*. . . . There is an inarticulate thought . . . and an accomplished thought, which suddenly and unaware discovers itself surrounded by words. Expressive operations take place between thinking language and speaking thought; not, as we thoughtlessly say, between thought and language. It is not because they are parallel that we speak; it is because we speak that they are parallel."

51. Merleau-Ponty, *The Visible and the Invisible*, trans. Alphonso Lingis (Evanston, Ill.: Northwestern University Press, 1968), p. 144; see also G. B. Madison, *The Phenomenology of Merleau-Ponty* (Athens, Ohio: Ohio University Press, 1981), pp. 180–81.

52. A. MacIntyre, *After Virtue*, p. 213.

53. Also, we divest ourselves of the entire *metaphysical* problem of solipsism and "other minds" and leave it decisively behind when we realize the speaking (or spoken) nature of the self, for we realize then that it is only in the linguistic exchange that there *is* a self and an other. To suppose that what is initially given are two specific, well-defined subjectivities or "minds" which must then find a means of "communicating" with each other (as metaphysicians are prone to do) is the height of hermeneutical

absurdity. Benveniste makes the following very pertinent remark: "We are always inclined to that naive concept of a primordial period in which a complete man discovered
another one, equally complete, and between the two of them language was worked out
little by little. This is pure fiction. We can never get back to man separated from language
and we shall never see him inventing it. We shall never get back to man reduced to
himself and exercising his wits to conceive of the existence of another. It is a speaking
man whom we find in the world, a man speaking to another man, and language provides
the very definition of man" ("Subjectivity in Language," p. 224).

54. Gadamer, *Truth and Method*, p. 263.

55. Ibid., p. 264.

56. "All understanding is interpretation" (ibid., p. 350).

57. See, in this regard, Gadamer's remarks in *Philosophical Hermeneutics* (Berkeley:
University of California Press, 1976), pp. 41–42.

58. Schafer, *Language and Insight*, p. 15.

59. Ibid., p. 18.

60. Ibid., p. 26.

61. See, for instance, Wolfgang Iser, *The Act of Reading* (Baltimore: Johns Hopkins
University Press, 1978); and S. R. Suleiman and I. Crosman, eds., *The Reader in the
Text* (Princeton, N.J.: Princeton University Press, 1980).

62. P. Ricoeur, "Hermeneutics and the Critique of Ideology," in *Hermeneutics and
the Human Sciences*, ed. J. B. Thompson (New York: Cambridge University Press,
1981), p. 94. It should be noted that although for (phenomenological) hermeneutics the
goal of interpretation is not to reproduce or to reconstruct (as E. D. Hirsch would say)
a meaning supposed to exist objectively *in* the text (such as the authorial intention) and
although it maintains that the act of reading is *productive* of meaning, it does insist,
nevertheless, that the meaning which emerges through interpretation (and only through
interpretation) is not a matter of mere virtuosity or improvisation (as it sometimes seems
to be for the "deconstructionists") but is the meaning *of* the text itself.

63. Gadamer, "The Problem of Historical Consciousness," in *Interpretive Social Science: A Reader*, eds. P. Rabinow and W. Sullivan (Berkeley: University of California
Press, 1979), p. 107.

64. See Nietzsche, *On the Genealogy of Morals*, 3d essay, § 26: "Its [modern historiography's] noblest claim nowadays is that it is a mirror."

65. Carlos Fuentes, "The Novel Always Says: The World Is Unfinished," *New York
Times Book Review*, March 31, 1985, p. 25.

66. Derrida does say that, although "reading is transformation," "this transformation
cannot be executed however one wishes" and that it requires "protocols of reading"
(*Positions*, p. 63). He does not tell us what this is supposed to mean. If Derrida can so
totally mis"represent" the basic hermeneutical position (see his vague remarks on the
subject in *Spurs*, trans. Barbara Harlow [Chicago: University of Chicago Press, 1978],
and in "La question du style," in *Nietzsche Aujourd'hui* [Paris: Union Générale d'Éditions, 1973]; what he says here about hermeneutics does not in any way whatsoever
apply to *phenomenological* hermeneutics, which is, after all, what today people generally
have in mind when they talk about hermeneutics), one wonders what usefulness these
unspecified "protocols" might have.

67. The notion of *tradition* is absolutely fundamental to philosophical hermeneutics.
MacIntyre also makes some very pertinent remarks on the subject (see *After Virtue*,
p. 220ff.).

68. It is in fact a hermeneutical (transformational) understanding of "truth" that
Schafer expresses when he says: "Under the influence of the psychoanalytic perspective,
the analysand not only begins to live in another world but learns how to go on constructing it. It is a transformed world, a world with systematically interrelated vantage
points or rules of understanding. It is a world of greater personal authority and ac-

knowledged responsibility. It is more coherent and includes a greater range of constructed experience. It is more socialized and intelligible" (*Language and Insight*, p. 25).

For a discussion of truth, as it applies, hermeneutically, to the political realm, see G. B. Madison, *The Logic of Liberty* (Westport, Conn.: Greenwood Press, 1986).

ELEVEN

The Philosophic Centrality of the Imagination: A Postmodern Approach

In this presentation I would like to take an imaginative look at, draw a picture of, what the imagination might or should look like in the postmodern, post-metaphysical age we are now entering, an age whose primary characteristic is perhaps that it has divested or is divesting itself of the insistence that the old metaphysics of presence placed on the primacy of the image, the *imago*, the *eikon*, the picture, the primacy of referentialist-representationalism. Philosophy, in the traditional metaphysical sense, officially began when Plato defined being in the supreme sense as *eidos*, or *idea*. Being is that which shows, reveals itself in all of its self-originating, radiant splendor. It is what is immutably and forever simply there, to be simply looked at and taken in by means of a disinterested, purified gaze. This definition of being prescribed a corresponding definition of man, *anthropos*. Man is essentially *noesis*, rational intuition. To lead a truly human life, as the philosopher does, is to lead a life of contemplation, as Plato's pupil, Aristotle, tells us in the last book of his *Nicomachean Ethics*. Philosophy, in this context, is an ethical-religious undertaking, the ascetic *purification du regard*. Man's vocation is to reflect, mirror, that being whose essence is to be there and to show, reveal itself. Between being and man there is, or should be, a perfect *coincidentia* or *adequatio*, a showing-reflecting mimetic correspondence. Man, as thinkers were later to say, is the Microcosm which mirrors the Macrocosm. Present-day scientists, Plato's metaphysical heirs, are people who seek to have a highly polished, nondistorting mirror for a mind. Like their metaphysical forefathers, they are obsessed with the fear that their representations may be only *eidola*, mere *phantasm*-ic semblances, *simulacra*.

The metaphysics of presence has thus perpetuated itself up until our times, though not without notable metamorphoses. The form it assumed in modern philosophy could perhaps best be labeled *representationalism*, the metaphysics of *re-presentation*. For indeed with the advent of Cartesianism man is thrown back upon himself, the "subjective" emerges as that which stands over against and is cut off from the "objective," true being is no longer directly present to the mind's eye but needs to be re-presented to it by the senses. The immediate objects of man's knowing, of his reflective gaze, are no longer the things themselves in their true being but the "inner" contents of the closet of his consciousness, his own subjective mind, *cogitationes* or *ideas*, as they were fondly called by the English-speaking empiricists. The notion of presence continues to dominate modern man's thinking, but what is now present to him is no longer being but his own mental states, the *idea* in a purely subjectivistic sense. In accordance with this mutation in the metaphysics of presence, reason, the essence of "man," is henceforth no longer *noesis*, rational insight, but rather *method*, rational procedure. Indeed, motivated by a nostalgic desire somehow to coincide with being "as it is in itself," modern man believes that he may be able to know that reality which is not directly present to him if only he orders his own ideas in accordance with the unquestionable laws of logic. If only he can string his ideas together in the right way, the result will supposedly be that they will form a true representation or likeness of "objective" reality—though to be sure this is something, the modern philosopher will likely admit, that he can never ever really *know*, be absolutely sure of. In any event, representationalism has been the name of game from Descartes up to our twentieth-century positivists.

It is, however, a game which an increasing number of thinkers are declining the invitation to play. Thinkers as diverse as Heidegger and Wittgenstein, Foucault and Rorty have raised enough questions to make us doubt seriously whether the epistemological game is one which is worth playing at all. *Est-ce que la mèche vaut la chandelle?* I for one have come to believe that there is no worthwhile prize to be won from playing the metaphysical-representationalist-foundationalist game, and accordingly I would like to deal with my assigned topic—the imagination—in a different context altogether. I would like, in what follows, to speculate on what we might say about the imagination were we to set aside the rules of the epistemological language game as they have been worked out over the course of several centuries. Since in any event traditional philosophy has never had much of any great interest to say about the imagination (even though most of the great traditional philosophers were, like Plato or Descartes, quite adept at imagining things, such as ethereal Forms or *malin génies*, let us see what could be said about it were we to take up a nontraditional approach. I will begin with a brief outline of the traditional approach to the issue.

About ten years or so ago, when I was doing background research for my *Understanding* book, I decided to give a special graduate seminar on the imagination. It seemed to me at the time that this was likely to become a hot topic for philosophers, just as that of action had become. Obviously, however, it took much longer than I had anticipated for it to catch on, witness the fact that we here assembled are only just getting around to discussing it publicly. My graduate seminar took the form of a workshop; each student was sent out to scour a particular domain or period to see what he or she could drag up. Like the American constitutionalists when they undertook their unprecedented task, we ransacked our cultural archives to see what we could come up with. The results were, in a sense, mediocre and disappointing. What we discovered was that throughout the history of philosophy, philosophers, on the whole and by and large, have never had anything of much worth or interest to say about the imagination. This is an observation that Ed Casey makes in his book *Imagining* (one of the few good ones on the subject), which was published subsequent to our seminar. Casey notes "the tendency on the part of many Western philosophers to belittle imagination—or, still worse, to neglect it altogether." The fact is, as he says:

> the claims of imagination have been rebuffed or ignored at almost every critical juncture. Far from being the "Queen of the faculties" revered by Poe and Baudelaire, imagining has been regarded, with rare exceptions, as the impoverished chimneysweep of the mind, performing tasks (if it is given any tasks at all) that are considered beneath the dignity of other psychical powers.[1]

The reason for this curious state of affairs also readily became apparent to us. The "tradition of condemnation and neglect," as Casey puts it, is due to a considerable extent to the overwhelming but thoroughly regretable influence that Aristotle has had on our intellectual tradition. On the whole, philosophers have never properly understood the importance of imagination, for they have followed in the footsteps of Aristotle and have relegated the imagination to a chapter in their treatises on psychology. They have taken the imagination to be that lower faculty, which men share with the brutes, whose business it is to coordinate and to reproduce sense impressions. To be sure, this is consistent with the basic rationalist or metaphysical prejudice that there exists "in itself" a fully determinate reality and that the function of human understanding is to form a correct picture of this reality (the function of the imagination, *qua sensus communis*, being to fit together the fragmentary bits of information received through the different, individual senses into one unified picture).[2]

A revealing document in this regard is the entry on imagination in Dagobert D. Runes's *Dictionary of Philosophy*. It reads:

> Imagination designates a mental process consisting of: (a) The revival of sense images derived from earlier perceptions (the reproductive imagination), and (b) the combination of these elementary images into new unities (the creative or productive imagination). The creative imagination is of two kinds: (a) the fancy which is relatively spontaneous and uncontrolled, and (b) the constructive imagination, exemplified in science, invention and philosophy which is controlled by a dominant plan or purpose.[3]

Take careful note of what this implies. The creative imagination in philosophy or science consists in nothing more than combining elementary sense impressions into new patterns. What could be more absurd? How could the General Theory of Relativity ever be derived from sense data? As long as we view the imagination as having essentially to do with *images*, we will never understand what it means to speak of the creative imagination in the arts and sciences. It is not without significance, I think, that the devalorization of the imagination whereby it is reduced to a faculty for producing mere senselike images (*eidola*) goes hand in hand, in the hands of the father of metaphysics, with a devalorization of the arts, and that this double devalorization is consequent upon conceiving of the mind in general as that whose business is to form *images* (*eikones*) of things (material or ideal). It is not surprising that Plato should have likened the painter to someone who does not really produce anything, except a mirror out of his pocket which he holds up to the sun and all the things in the sky and on earth, reduplicating them in this effortless, sham way.[4] To understand properly the creative imagination, it would be necessary to transpose discussion of it from an eidetic or imagistic context to another one altogether. I shall return to this pivotal issue in a moment.

Right now let us just note that in the mainline, orthodox, traditional view of the matter—whether in Aristotle, Hobbes, or Kant—the imagination is a mere transitory stage, a mediator between sensation and knowledge. The position that Hume took in regard to the imagination is eminently typical of modern representationalism. Hume represents both a high point and a low point, the zenith and the nadir of modernism, of the tradition instituted by Descartes's foundationalist project which seeks certainty in the knowing subject. In his works we find representationalism carried to its logical, albeit absurd, conclusion. For here we see how the Cartesian, modern emphasis on the "subjective" leads to an internal undermining of the whole representationalist project. I am referring, of course, to Hume's celebrated skepticism (which has nothing whatsoever to do with classical, Pyrrhonian skepticism, which knew nothing of "subjectivity" in the modern sense). We find in Hume a copy-relation view of the imagination; imagination is a mere mode of perception or, to be more precise, a secondhand copy of perception: "all our ideas," he says, "are copy'd from our impressions."[5] This is, as Casey says, a supremely "reductive" view of the imagination. " . . . the content of imagining," Casey says, speaking of Hume, "is ineluctably a repetition or recombination of what we have already perceived; hence a complete analysis would reveal a close correspondence between any given imagined content and the content of some previous perception or set of perceptions.[6]

Kant adds nothing radically new to the representationalist, imagistic view of the imagination, although, after having been awoken from his dogmatic slumbers by reading Hume, he does add a new twist to the epistemological undertaking. This is, of course, his transcendental turn, his Second Copernican revolution, whose purpose was to circumvent the skepticism which Hume had shown to be the logical outcome of modern representationalism through the invention of a Transcendental Ego as the ultimate underwriter of the objectivity of objects. The foundationalist enterprise continued subsequently undaunted in the exuberant excesses of German Idealism and in the later, lower-keyed *Erkentnisslehre* of the Neo-Kantians, finding its purest expression in Edmund Husserl, who quite rightly viewed his transcendental phenomenology as responding to the deepest longings of traditional philosophy for apodictic certainty. As we know now, of course, in the pursuit of the Platonic-Cartesian quest for a philosophical science of reality, Husserl came up with a philosophical device—the phenomenological reduction—the use of which by Husserl and his errant disciples has resulted in the deconstruction of the entire epistemological project (and in the consequent demise of "sense-data").[7]

The modern, representationalist view of the imagination finds perhaps its fullest, but also most banal, expression in what today goes under the impressive epithet of "cognitive science," the technological understanding of human understanding. Those with a penchant for serious-minded scientific inquiry but who can no longer subscribe in good conscience to metaphysical system building of the old-fashioned, traditional sort will find in cognitive science a means of pursuing with sophisticated technicity the old metaphorics of the mirror. "Algorithmic metaphysics" might not be a bad name for present-day cognitive science, for its presuppositions are fully those of traditional metaphysics and its image-making, mirror view of the mind. KA (knowledge acquisition) theory, for instance, works with a "mental models hypothesis." In the words of two specialists in the field: "The mental models hypothesis states that an individual understands the world by forming a mental model, that a cogniting [sic!] agent understands the world by forming a model of the world in his or her head."[8] When computer people and cognitive scientists speak of language, they generally mean "representation languages," by means of which humans or machines (there is no essential, cybernetic difference between the two), "know what is 'out there in the world,' "[9] form an inner representation ("mental model," MM) of outer reality.

In the traditional, orthodox, or received view, "cognition," in which imagination plays an often necessary but nonetheless always minor role, is the means whereby the epistemological subject transcends himself, steps out from the inner sphere of his "mind" and makes—somehow—contact with what is so charmingly called "the external world." In this context, imagination is generally viewed as a merely "internal" process; it is the generator of "subjective," "private," "mental" images which may or may not subsequently pan out, i.e., be a means of enabling us to form adequate representations of "reality." The imagination finds its worse press in British empiricism, for which, as Casey aptly puts it, it is but warmed-over sensation or, as Hobbes said, "decaying sense."[10] Let us note, finally, that in the traditional view *meaning* is in one way or another generally viewed as something somehow "objective," as a certain determinate state of affairs which has to be copied, pictured, mirrored, reproduced, replicated, re-presented, reflected on the inner, glassy surface of the mind's eye.

After having himself rehearsed the history of the subject in his book, Casey writes:

> Taken together, psychological and philosophical theories of imagination teach a similar lesson: if the mind is regarded as a mere processor of perceptions or as a graduated series of successively higher functions, imagination will be denied a genuinely distinctive role of its own. In the constrictive views of mental activity

that we have considered . . . , imagining has almost invariably been relegated to a secondary or tertiary status in which it merely subtends some supposedly superior cognitive agency such as intellect or (more frequently) modifies some presumably more original source such as sensation. Either way, the uniqueness of imagination as a mental act fails to be acknowledged.[11]

Casey sought "to view imagination as nonderivative, as a phenomenon to be evaluated on its own terms." My goal here is much the same; even more, I wish, in opposition to all treatments which marginalize it, to bring the imagination forward to center stage and to argue for its philosophic centrality. The strategy I shall adopt is nevertheless not the one favored by Casey. In his attempt to do justice to the imagination, Casey follows the classical Husserlian method of eidetic insight and seeks simply to describe its (supposedly) essential traits. As a deconstructed Husserlian who does not believe in essences, who, indeed, unlike both Husserl and Casey (at least at the time of the writing of his book), believes that "essential meanings" are not something which can be *seen* in an eidetic insight (*Wesenschau*) but are, rather, *spoken* meanings, linguistic in nature through and through, I find this tactic is not one that appeals to me.[12] The strategy I shall adopt instead is dictated by the deconstructive nature of postmodern thought itself.

What, we might ask, happens to the imagination when there is no longer any "objective" nature that it would be the essential business of the "mind," in its more important functions, to mirror? How are we to view the imagination once the great mirror of nature has been deconstructed and we turn to "doing philosophy without mirrors," as Rorty would say? The answers to these questions will readily become apparent if we simply ask ourselves what the most salient characteristic of postmodernism is. It is, I think it safe to say, the emphasis that has come to be placed on language, *die Sprachlichkeit, le discours*, textuality. When the modern epistemological paradigm is deconstructed, when, that is, the natural bond that modernism assumed to exist between *les mots et les choses* is broken, language, as Foucault has noted, assumes a unique and special status. Fully representative of postmodernism is also Gadamer's famous statement: "Being that can be understood is language."[13] Adapting this to our context, we could say: *Being that can be imagined is language.*

Directly related to the emphasis that postmodernism places on language is the renewed interest that has begun to be shown in rhetoric. Postmodernism happily revives the Greek defininiton of man as *zoon logon ekon*, the speaking animal. As the greatest of the Greek rhetoricians, Isocrates, said, the distinctive trait of man is that he is the being which has the *logos*.[14] The Latin translation of the Greek—*animal rationale*—is less felicitous, because it is less polyvalent and thus says less. And yet it is not without its own semantic resources. For if there is any one thing that seems most manifestly to characterize human beings, it is that they are constantly engaged in the business of *rationalizing*, i.e., in devising *rationes*, in *coming up with reasons* for what they do, *giving accounts, récits* of their actions. "Man" (to use the classical linguistic term for the entity in question) is the narrating, storytelling animal. Language is not just another ability ("faculty") alongside others. To speak quasi-metaphysically (i.e., mythically), the advent of language in the course of human development was not just another significant development alongside others, such as the invention of tools. The advent of language represented rather a complete, "essential" transformation of the man-animal. It represented a complete transformation of man's animality in that it completely sundered him from nature. The advent of language is the advent of reflexivity. Thanks to language, man becomes a potential object for himself, and thus the subject matter of self-understanding. "Know thyself!" is a dictate of language. What as humans we are is in fact something that is constituted by means of language. We understand ourselves by narrating ourselves. Man is not a natural given but a cultural, i.e., linguistic, construct.[15] Because it is language which makes what humans call "thought" possible in the first place, language must not be viewed, as modernism viewed it, as merely the "vehicle," the "expression," of thought. Language *is* (human) thought. It is also *reality*, at least that reality which, phenomenologically-pragmatically speaking, is there for us as the object of our "thinking," since, as Rorty has pertinently observed, "there is no way to think about either the world or our purposes except by using our language."[16]

So what I want to do here is to argue for a view of the imagination, that most human of human faculties, as something essentially linguistic in nature. I don't want to deny that we humans have the ability to call up mental images of things, in some sense or other (usually, though, just a word suffices; you don't have to expend all that mental effort of actually picturing something). I suspect that we imagine, in the sense of forming mental, mere sensuous presentations of absent things, a lot less than we imagine that we do. Much more important, occupying a much more significant position in the life of understanding (I will not say our "mental" lives), than what Casey calls "imaging" is that other form of imagination which he labels "imagining-that."[17] He very pertinently observes that when we imagine *that* such and such a state of affairs obtains in its own imaginary space, this form of imagining "*does not have to assume a sensuous guise.*"[18] He remarks, of course, that it may, but, even if it does, it is something I would want to downplay, since I am inclined to believe that even in this case the sensuous imagery is mostly a function of certain semantic values, is essentially semiological.

It seems to me that Casey inadvertently concedes this point. In any event, to the trained eye of the postmodern deconstructionist, certain admissions seem to transpire through the links in his modern discourse. He says, for instance, that in the case of imagining-that:

> The term "state of affairs" . . . designate[s] the sort of imagined content *whose description in words would take the form of a complete sentence* [emphasis added]. A state of affairs is the intentional correlate of a non-simple act of intending—a correlate *whose expression in language has both a nominative and a preverbal element* [emphasis added]: (I imagine that [note the performative utterance]) 'the

Washington monument is walking'. The state of affairs imagined here involves an internal, reciprocal relationship between what is designated by the nominative component ('the Washington monument') and the verbal factor ('is walking').[19]

Could such a state of affairs be imagined without language? If not, language is, at the very least, the necessary condition for the possibility of imagining-that. Consider also the following case of imagining which Casey brings forward: imagining what it might be like to follow a certain law. Casey writes (take note of the internal quotation marks):

'How would I appear if I were to act in accordance with the third formulation of the categorical imperative?' Here I might envision myself as a righteous member of the Kingdom of Ends, performing certain altruistic acts such as ministering to the sick without recompense.[20]

Although Casey uses such terms as "appear" and "envision," these are obviously purely metaphorical. An imagining such as this is linguistic through and through. Although I am prepared to grant that my dog is capable of *imaging*, I do not imagine for a second that he, lacking as he does the *logos*, is capable of *imagining* what it would be like to be a rational being acting in accordance with the third formulation of the categorical imperative.

Again, and finally, Casey writes:

. . . imagined content is the strictly specifiable aspect of the imaginative presentation—i.e., the presentation *insofar as it can be indicated with some degree of descriptive precision* [emphasis added]. This content is normally specified by what one *says* [Casey's own emphasis] one has imagined—that is, by the actual description one gives, or would offer if asked, of a given imaginative experience.[21]

Since I cannot imagine what it would be like to "specify" something with any "degree of descriptive precision" without language, I really cannot imagine how one could have any imaginings worth talking about without language, what they would be if in fact they were not linguistic through and through.

In accordance with the Husserlian, essentialist approach that he takes in this book, Casey wants clearly and distinctly to demarcate imagination from, and to situate it properly with regard to, other kinds of "mental acts." Let us simply note what he says of the relation between imagination and perception. Speaking, as he says (as indeed he is at this point), from an "epistemological viewpoint," the imagination, he says, presupposes perception. I could not imagine if I were not first of all a being who perceives.[22] Imagining "is dependent on the prior existence and exercise of perceptual powers."[23] This may be true "epistemologically speaking," but what exactly is the situation hermeneutically speaking? Can perception itself, human perception, be divorced from language? Is not perception, as Lacan says of the unconscious, "structurée comme un langage"?

Speaking of what Husserl called the "internal horizon" of a perceptual object, Casey says that it is "determinate as to *type*. It gives itself," he says, "as the internally delimiting horizon of a particular *kind* of object: as the horizon of a house and not of a horse, of a table instead of a tree."[24] To speak of "houses," "horses," "tables," and "trees" and, *a fortiori*, of "*types*" and "*kinds*" is, it seems to me, to be engaged in a thoroughly and irremediably linguistic sort of activity. One thing we have learned in this century is that words are not mere labels that we simply stick onto things willy-nilly. Or as Heidegger has expressed the matter: " . . . words and language are not wrappings in which things are packaged for the commerce of those who write and speak. It is in words and language that things first come into being and are."[25] Things would not be *what* they are in the first place, would not be perceived the way they are perceived by us, if we did not have the kind of linguistic dealings with them that we in fact do have. To be a being who perceives is to be a being who interprets, who is engaged in the playing of particular language games. The notion of "brute data," of things which are simply what they are, waiting around "out there" for an epistemological subject to come along and mirror them (" . . . realities in themselves are just what they are regardless of subjects that refer to them . . ."),[26] is a notion which evaporates along with epistemological foundationalism. As one of the first philosophical postmoderns, William James, asked so exquisitely when he tried to imagine what it would be like to be a thing and to have a mind "come into being from out of the void inane and stand and *copy* me": What good would it do me to be copied, or what good would it do the mind to copy me?[27] The notion of brute data is one which analytic philosophy has also made a stab at deconstructing in the person of Wilfred Sellars when he attacked the "myth of the given."[28] It is, again, one which an avowed deconstructionist such as Derrida is discarding when he discards the very notion of "perception." As he says:

> Now I don't know what perception is and I don't believe that anything like perception exists. Perception is precisely a concept, a concept of an intuition or of a given originating from the thing itself, present itself in its meaning, independently from language, from the system of reference. And I believe that perception is interdependent with the concept of origin and of center and consequently whatever strikes at the metaphysics of which I have spoken strikes also at the very concept of perception. I don't believe that there is any perception.[29]

Long before Derrida, Hegel had already realized that we have to have recourse to universals even to begin to describe sensory experience. As we shall see shortly, the linguistic imagination has to do with the application of universals, with the way particulars are categorized. To see something is to see it *as* this or that (this is the "hermeneutical *as*" [as opposed to the apophantic or judgmental "*as*"]). To see something in an imaginative (here meaning creative) way is to see it otherwise than it has been seen before; it is to integrate it into a new semantic context. So rather than saying that we would not be

imaginative beings were we not first of all perceiving beings, it might be closer
to the truth to say that we would not be perceiving beings were we not first
of all imagining beings, beings who, thanks to the free play of their language,
can imagine *that* such and such is the case—and who also have a tendency to
take their interpretive constructs for reality itself.[30]

The general point I am trying to make could perhaps best be made with
the aid of an example, one which suits my purposes superbly, since it is drawn
directly from the metaphorics of textuality. It is an example which I recall
Michael Riffaterre as having made in the course of a public talk and is one
which I found useful in an aesthetics course I gave recently, since it displaces
a persistent misinterpretation of what is involved in the interpretive process,
the act of reading. Most of my students, I found, seem to think that when one
reads a novel one forms a series of mental pictures of the action described—
as if reading novels were merely a poor substitute for watching TV. The following example is an argument to the effect that this is not, or is not primarily,
the case.

In his novel *Salambō*, Flaubert, in accordance with his program of fictional
realism, sought to depict a completely lost civilization about which little is
known, that of ancient Carthage, with unerring historical accuracy. He even
traveled to the site and studied archaeology with great diligence in the attempt
to paint as accurate a picture as possible of what life was like in the ancient
city, one which has left absolutely no vestiges of itself. In a letter to the critic
Sainte-Beuve, who had charged that the archaeological detail was fictitious,
Flaubert responded vehemently that it was not and furnished chapter-and-
verse references justifying all of his material. Now, at one point in the novel,
in order to enable his readers to visualize the particular scene, Flaubert describes a camel in the process of lying down. A description is obviously called
for, since the quasi totality of his readers would never have seen a camel and
would have only the vaguest of ideas of what they're supposed to look like (does
a camel have one hump or two?), let alone the motions they go through when
they lie down. So Flaubert writes: "The camel lay down, like an ostrich" (or
words to that effect). Does that enable you to visualize the scene? Of course
not. Unless you're an avid watcher of The Wonderful World of Nature or have
hung around the African Lion Safari near Hamilton, you don't have the slightest
idea of what an *ostrich* does when it lies down. So when you "picture" the
scene to yourself ("a camel lying down, like an ostrich"), you really don't have
any determinate picture going through your mind at all! A remark of Wittgenstein's could be used perfectly in the present discursive context (if only you
use your imaginations). What he said was: "When I think in language, there
aren't 'meanings' going through my mind in addition to the verbal expression:
the language is itself the vehicle of thought."[31] Like all literary "representations," Flaubert's "description" does not provide his reader with a determinate
picture but is, as Roman Ingarden might say, schematic and indeterminate.
You do not have a factually accurate picture of an ostrich lying down (let alone
that of a camel) when you read the sentence, *and yet* it is not meaningless for

you as a reader. You read the sentence and perhaps say to yourself, *sotto voce*, "Yes, indeed, that's exactly the way it is," and you go on reading, thinking all the while how marvelously accurate and to the point Flaubert's descriptions are and how "realistic" a writer he is.

The point, then, is simply this: Meaning is not something that has to be "pictured" in order to be; it is not something that has to be mentally copied in order to be "grasped."[32] What, then, is it? The Flaubert example has the additional merit of indicating what in fact meaning is. What happens when you read the sentence is exactly what Flaubert supposedly wanted to happen: The net effect of describing camels in terms of ostriches (the foreign in terms of the even more foreign) is to create in the reader a *feeling of exoticness*, of encountering an exotic, foreign land—which is exactly what has to happen if the sentence, and the novel, is to be successful, *un texte réussi*. In other words, meaning is not some kind of state of affairs to be pictured; it is not any kind of *thing* at all but rather an *event*, a *happening*. The meaning of the text is what the text *does* to the reader, what *happens* to the reader when he or she reads it. Imagined meanings are simply ways in which, by means of language, we *relate* to, take up an *existential attitude* toward something or other (toward, in this case, what Ricoeur calls "the world of the work"). *New* meanings are simply new ways of relating to things by means of new or unusual usages of words (or their semiotic equivalent in other expressive media).

Such is the hermeneutical view of meaning, which is the necessary and inescapable consequence of the abandonment of epistemological-centered philosophy. The literary hermeneut Stanley Fish describes it appropriately when he says: "In this formulation, the reader's response is not *to* the meaning; it *is* the meaning."[33] The hermeneutical assumption, as Fish says, is "that the text is not a spatial object but the occasion for a temporal experience."[34]

By linking imagination up with language, I am, as you can see, insisting on its centrality in the "life of the mind," since, from a postmodern, hermeneutical view, language is absolutely central. Now, the center of language itself is *metaphor*. As one writer has remarked: "Metaphor is as ultimate as speech itself, and speech as ultimate as thought."[35] The nature of imaginative thinking can therefore be further illuminated by analyzing it in terms of metaphor. Indeed, the best definition of the linguistic imagination is perhaps that it is the "faculty" for producing metaphors.

In my *Understanding* book I argued that "the 'meaning' of metaphorical discourse is nothing other than the practical transformation it brings about in the listening and speaking subject, the orientation it communicates to understanding."[36] Metaphor, as I also said, performs an "existential function in that it provokes a change in the way we view things, it brings about a transformation in our thinking. Its meaning lies entirely in its 'perlocutionary force,' in the effect the words have on us."[37] One thing this does *not* mean is that metaphors have no meaning in any proper sense of the term—that they are, strictly speaking meaningless, as Don Stewart, in his critical piece on the Madisonian theory of metaphor that he published in *Dialogue*, nevertheless claims I mean to say.[38]

Metaphors, under my definition, would be meaningless only if one believed in the "proper" (as Derrida would say), only if one sought to make sense of them while laboring under the epistemological paradigm.

The meaning of a metaphor is what it does. And what is that it does? Let us take as an example what I suppose is the favorite metaphor of philosophers (trite and hackneyed though it naturally be): "Man is a wolf." When we say this we most definitely do not visualize man as having the physical appearance of a wolf, with pointed ears, long teeth, and a furry coat. It is not even correct to say that we "view" man as a wolf, unless the word "view" is used in a thoroughly metaphorical sense. To *picture* man as a wolf would have absolutely no meaning whatsoever (or would not have the meaning that the metaphor does have). When we say that man is a wolf we *mean* that he is vicious and inhuman, i.e., that he "preys" on his fellow creatures and is a "wolf" to man. The meaning "wolf" is here something definitely bad. But I can easily imagine cultures in which wolves do not conjure up something bad, in which they even conjure up something good, or don't conjure up anything in particular at all. If to a member of such a culture we were to say, "Man is a wolf," our hearer would either visualize man in the form of a wolf, in which case his or her response would likely be, "So what? I can just as well picture him as a pumpkin. Why should I visualize him one way or the other?" or else the *metaphorical* (linguistic) meaning that he or she understood would not at all be the one we intended (he or she would perhaps take this as a complimentary way of referring to man since in the hearer's culture wolves are considered to be caring, family-oriented creatures).

Thus the metaphor means what it does only because we *think* of wolves in certain ways, and when we say of man that he is a wolf we are transferring to man some of the semantic values that we normally and—in the case of wolves— quite arbitrarily associate with wolves. This is, of course, the interaction theory of metaphor defended by I. A. Richards, Philip Wheelwright, Max Black, Nelson Goodman, Paul Ricoeur, and others. Taking metaphor as our model, we could therefore say that the essential business of the linguistic or semiological imagination (imagination as it functions in all creative endeavors) is to bring together disparate semantic or semiological fields, the net effect of this bisociative act (as Arthur Koestler would call it) being to alter the way we think of, categorize, interpret things. As Max Black has expressed the matter: "A memorable metaphor has the power to bring two separate domains into cognitive and emotional relation by using language directly appropriate to the one as a lens for seeing the other; the implications, suggestions, and supporting values entwined with the literal use of the metaphorical expression enable us to see a new subject matter in a new way." And as he goes on to note: "Metaphorical thought is a distinctive mode of achieving insight, not to be construed as an ornamental substitute for plain thought."[39]

It is by means of the metaphorizing imagination that facts are categorized the way they are, that ideas and theories are woven together to make new theories, and that theory and experience are linked together in such a way as to produce what we call "knowledge." Imagination is absolutely central, since it is the primary means whereby we form an understanding of what goes under the heading of "reality." Imagination is what is responsible for the texture of our actual experience, thus also for the text-like character of our lives. "Man," as Wallace Stevens says, "is the imagination or rather the imagination is man."[40]

One of the most important consequences of postmodernism, from a philosophical point of view, is the way it has undermined various traditional metaphysical oppositions, such as appearance-reality, belief-knowledge (science), mind-body, material-spiritual, subjective-objective, inside-outside, fact-fiction. Only when oppositions such as these are deconstructed can the imagination, like language, assume its rightful importance. Only then can it be understood how the imagination is the very heart of understanding, which is not merely a matter, as the traditional metaphor has it, of "facing the facts." The theory of knowledge put forward by "objective, data-respecting modernism," the postmodern economist, Donald McCloskey, says in his recent book, *The Rhetoric of Economics*,

> is that the privileged form of knowing is knowing by the lone person himself *solus ipse*. That is, real knowing is said to be individual and solipsistic, not social. No one needs to *say* anything to you, the Cartesian says, to persuade you of the ancient proof of the irrationality of the square root of 2. One turns towards it (the Cartesian professor now turns and talks in the direction of an imagined object), and there it is. We face "observations" for "the real tests." No need to talk.[41]

The crux of modernism, McCloskey says, is its solipsistic, monological theory of truth. Indeed, in the traditional, Platonic-Cartesian view, knowledge is an essentially private affair, a matter of the individual's communing through his gaze with "objective" reality. If only the lone individual can manage to place himself in the right relation with reality, the truth will be his.[42] On this view the imagination is necessarily solipsistic and idiosyncratic, a matter of calling up purely *within* oneself various quasi- or pseudorealities which have no "objective" counterparts out there in the "real world." It is quite understandable how in this view the imagination should be relegated to the limits of the "cognitional." Everything changes, however, when we attempt to conceive of the imagination not in a representational but in a linguistic, hermeneutical context and when, moreover, we abandon the traditional metaphysical oppositions.

For those of us who, in the turbulent wake of Nietzsche's devastating deconstruction not only of modernism but also of the entire metaphysical tradition, no longer believe in, have indeed lost the naive confidence we formerly placed in the myths of the metaphysicians and, in particular, the greatest herd-consoling myth of all, the myth that, as Bertrand Russell put it in his charmingly naive way, "the essential business of language is to assert or deny facts,"[43] or, as the metaphysicians of presence would say with more sophistication, to reveal, "express" "reality," a world that lies, unchanging and impeccably pure beyond it—for us the imagination becomes, once we make the postmodern turn, the prime means for understanding reality, i.e., for forming interpretations of it, or, to be more precise still, for interpreting our lived experience in such a way as to construct semantic objects to which the epithet "real" can conveniently be attached. Being a *linguistic* affair, understanding is perforce a cultural, public, intersubjective sort of thing. Solipsism is not an issue here, precisely because there are no "unconditioned facts" to which the isolated "cognizer" could have privileged, representational access. Purely private meanings exist only for a theory which maintains that the essential business of words is to refer to ideas existing in the "mind," i.e., for epistemological representationalism. Is this to say that there are no facts at all, that everything is mere imaginative fiction? Of course not. Just because, as Nietzsche said, all being is interpreted being doesn't mean that there aren't any "facts." "Facts" there always are for any speaking community, but they do not descend on it like some kind of empiricistic manna. "Facts" are precisely what a cultural, conversational community agree they are. The "facts," as Stanley Fish says, are what "the conventions of serious discourse stipulate them to be."[44] In any event, as he aptly says, "like it or not, interpretation is the only game in town."[45] The linguistic imagination is indeed the very life of the mind, thus also of reality (assuming, of course, that we have gotten rid of the metaphysical opposition appearance-reality).

In conclusion, I might remark that if you are like me and believe that the essence of "man," that essenceless being, is freedom, *la liberté*,[46] then you will believe also in the philosophic centrality of the imagination. For it is through the imagination, the realm of pure possibility, that we freely make ourselves to be who or what we are, that we creatively and imaginatively become who we are, while in the process preserving the freedom and possibility to be yet otherwise than what we have become and merely are. But I shall stop here, yielding the last word, *cédant la parole* (as certain deconstructionist minoritarians might like to say), to the poet, that master craftsman of pure possibilities. As Wallace Stevens (who else?) has said: "The imagination is the liberty of the mind and hence the liberty of reality."[47]

Notes

This essay was composed in response to an invitation from the Ontario Philosophical Society and was presented at the annual meeting of the Society, held at Glendon College in Toronto, October 18–19, 1986.

1. Edward S. Casey, *Imagining: A Phenomenological Study* (Bloomington: Indiana University Press, 1976), pp. ix, x.
2. The remarks made in this paragraph are reproduced from my book, *Understanding: A Phenomenological-Pragmatic Analysis* (Westport, Conn.: Greenwood Press, 1982), p. 257.
3. "Imagination," in *Dictionary of Philosophy*, ed. Dagobert D. Runes (New York: Philosophical Library, 1942).
4. See Plato, *The Republic*, 596e.

5. David Hume, *A Treatise of Human Nature*, ed. L. A. Selby-Bigge (Oxford: Clarendon Press, 1967), p. 10.

6. Casey, *Imagining*, p. 133.

7. In addition to the mainline, orthodox approach to the imagination, there is a secondary, heterodox line, coming prominently to the fore in the Renaissance and in Romanticism (but which, like the mainline view itself, has its origins in Plato—see *Timaeus*, 70–72, and *Phaedrus*, 250) which views the imagination not as a mere mediator between sensation and intellection but as a separate and distinct faculty providing us with its own distinctive access to "reality." Characteristic of this secondary tradition is its emphasis on inspiration, divine madness, direct intuitive accesss to the inner resorts of Nature itself, the World Soul; the imagination is here a mystical faculty enabling the Knower to bypass what Coleridge called the "cold inanimate world which is accessible to the mere senses and rational intelect." The heterodox tradition still views the imagination in a representationalist way, nevertheless, as a means of making contact not with the "external world" but with the inside of Nature itself.

8. Stephen Regoczei and Edwin P. O. Plantinga, "Ontology and Inventory: A Foundation for a Knowledge Acquisition Methodology," unpublished paper, p. 4.

9. Ibid., p. 8.

10. Casey, *Imagining*, p. 5.

11. Ibid., p. 19.

12. Casey takes over the Husserlian view of the relation between meaning and expression, according to which meaning precedes and can exist independently of expression (see ibid., pp. 24–25).

13. Hans-Georg Gadamer, *Truth and Method* (New York: Seabury Press, 1975), p. xxii.

14. See Isocrates *Panegyricus*, 48; and *Nicocles*, 5–7.

15. See, in this regard, my paper, "The Hermeneutics of [Inter]Subjectivity, Or: The Mind/Body Problem Deconstructed," in *Man and World* 21: 3–33 (1988) (reprinted in this volume as essay 10).

16. Richard Rorty, *Consequences of Pragmatism* (Minneapolis: University of Minnesota Press, 1982), p. xix.

17. See Casey, *Imagining*, p. 41ff.

18. Ibid., p. 43.

19. Ibid., p. 42, n. 6.

20. Ibid., p. 180, n. 6.

21. Ibid., p. 50.

22. See ibid, p. 172.

23. Ibid., p. 192.

24. Ibid. p. 160.

25. Martin Heidegger, *An Introduction to Metaphysics*, trans. Ralph Manheim (New Haven, Conn.: Yale University Press, 1959), p. 13.

26. Edmund Husserl, *Phänomenologische Psychologie*, Gesammelte Werke, IX (Martinus Nijhoff, 1968), p. 118.

27. William James, "Pragmatism's Conception of Truth," penultimate paragraph. James did not fully follow through with his deconstruction of epistemology, for he does say: "Copying is one genuine mode of knowing." Pioneers, like Moses, do not always make it to the Promised Land.

28. See Wilfred Sellars, "Empiricism and the Philosophy of Mind" in *Science, Perception and Reality* (New York: Humanities Press, 1963).

29. Jacques Derrida, "Structure, Sign, and Play in the Human Discourses," in *The Structuralist Controversy*, ed. R. Macksey and E. Donato, (Baltimore: Johns Hopkins University Press, 1972). Merleau-Ponty had already written: "In the natural attitude, I do not have *perceptions*" (*Phenomenology of Perception* p. 281).

30. Alluding to Merleau-Ponty's thesis regarding the primacy of perception, Casey writes: "Perception is certainly a condition of imagination because imaginers are necessarily also perceivers. Indeed, as human, we *must* be perceivers, whatever else we are capable of. Human imaginers all have bodies; and the body is, in Merleau-Ponty's words, 'the subject qua perceiver.' To be human is to be incarnate, and to be incarnate is to perceive, to be in various forms of sense contact with the immediate environment by means of our own body. If imagining is also one of our capacities, then it, like every other capacity, is dependent on the prior existence and exercise of perceptual powers. These powers accordingly represent a condition of possibility for imagination" (*Imagining*, pp. 192–93).

One is tempted to say of Casey's treatment of the imagination, which takes the sensuous imagination as paradigmatic, as a kind of *proton analogon*, what Paul Ricoeur said of Merleau-Ponty, that "the project of a phenomenology of perception, in which the moment of saying is postponed and the reciprocity of saying and seeing destroyed, is, in the last analysis, a hopeless venture" (Ricoeur, *History and Truth*, trans. Ch. A. Kelbley [Evanston, Ill.: Northwestern University Press, 1965), p. 309.

31. Ludwig Wittgenstein, *Philosophical Investigations*, trans G. E. M. Anscombe (Oxford: Basil Blackwell, 1963), par. 329.

32. Although Wolfgang Iser maintains in a very traditional fashion that the imagination in reading is a matter of image building, what he actually says about these "images" leads one to doubt that there are any such things at all. Speaking of the case where one sees the film version of a novel one has read, he remarks on how the reaction is often that of disappointment, and he asks himself why this is so. It is, he says, because "the characters somehow fail to live up to the image we had created of them while reading." Listen carefully to what he goes on to say: "The difference between the two types of picture is that the film is optical and presents a given object, whereas the imagination remains unfettered. Objects, unlike imaginings, are highly determinate and it is this determinacy which makes us feel disappointed. If for instance I see the film of *Tom Jones*, and try to summon up my past images of the character, they will seem strangely diffuse, but this impression will not necessarily make me prefer the optical picture. If I ask whether my imaginary Tom Jones was big or small, blue-eyed or dark-haired, the optical poverty of my image will become all too evident, but it is precisely this openness that will make me resent the determinacy of the film version. Our mental images do not serve to make the character physically visible; their optical poverty is an indication of the fact that *they illuminate the character, not as an object but as a bearer of meaning* [emphasis added]. Even if we are given a detailed description of a character's appearance, we tend not to regard it as pure description, but try and conceive what is actually to be communicated throught it" (*The Act of Reading: A Theory of Aesthetic Response* [Baltimore: Johns Hopkins University Press, 1978], p. 138.

If our "mental images do not serve to make the character physically visible," one wonders what point there is to speaking of "mental images" in the first place. In Iser's own example we have to do not with an *object* which is *pictured* but a *meaning* which is *communicated* (by means precisely of the pseudo-description). It is interesting that in this discussion of image building, Iser, like us, alludes to Wittgenstein. The Wittgenstein he quotes is not, however, the later Wittgenstein, who did much to clear out the cluttered attic of the empiricist mind, but the early Wittgenstein of the *Tractatus* defending a referentialist-representationalist theory of meaning (see ibid., p. 141).

To Iser's credit, however, it must be said that—even though he continues to use the unfortunate term "mental image"—he nevertheless does, later in his study, criticize Ingarden for suggesting that the way we fill in spots of indeterminacy in a text is by *visualizing* the missing element (as when we deliberately picture a character described as an "old man" as having gray hair). Iser writes: "He [Ingarden] seems to assume that in concretizing we really visualize the omitted color of the old man's hair—in another example, it is the unspecified eyes of Consul Buddenbrock—so that the picture of the old man actually achieves the degree of determinacy normally applicable only to optical perception. The implication is that a concretization must produce the object in such a way that it gives at least the illusion of perception. This illusion, however, is just one paradigmatic instance of image-building and is no way identifiable with the whole process of ideation. The mental image of the old man can be just as concrete without our giving him grey hair" (ibid., pp. 176–77).

33. Stanley Fish, *Is There a Text in This Class? The Authority of Interpretive Communities* (Cambridge, Mass.: Harvard University Press, 1980), p. 3.

34. Ibid., p. 345. Iser writes: "We do not grasp it [the text] like an empirical object; nor do we comprehend it like a predicative fact; it owes its presence in our minds to our own reactions, and it is these that make us animate the meaning of the text as a reality" (*The Act of Reading*, p. 129).

35. J. M. Murry, cited by Philip Wheelwright, *Metaphor and Reality* (Bloomington: Indiana University Press, 1973), p. 69.

36. *Understanding*, p. 212.

37. Ibid., p. 308.

38. Donald Stewart, "Madison on Metaphor," *Dialogue*, vol. XXIV, no. 4, 1985, pp. 707–12 (included in this volume as essay 9).

39. Max Black, *Models and Metaphors* (Ithaca, N.Y.: Cornell University Press, 1962), pp. 236–37. As Ricoeur has noted, we cannot properly understand the "transfer of sense" involved in metaphorical predication if, as in traditional rhetoric, we restrict our analysis to the level of the *word* and, like Aristotle, define metaphor as the transfer of the everyday name of one thing to another in virtue of their resemblance. See his remarks in "On Interpretation," in *Philosophy in France Today*, ed. Alan Montefiore, (Cambridge, Eng.: Cambridge University Press, 1983), pp. 182–83. As I argued in *Understanding*, it is altogether misleading to say that the "transfer" of the word from one thing to another is done "in virtue of their resemblance." "Resemblances" are precisely what first get created by means of metaphor, of semantic innovation. Ricoeur also makes much the same point when he writes: "The imagination can justly be termed productive because, by an extension of polysemy, it makes terms, previously heterogeneous, *resemble* one another, and thus homogeneous. The imagination, consequently, is this competence, this capacity for producing new logical kinds by means of predicative assimilation and for producing them in spite of . . . and thanks to . . . the initial difference between the terms which resist assimilation" ("On Interpretation," p. 184). Ricoeur interestingly remarks on how from this point of view the act of understanding "consists in grasping the semantic dynamism by virtue of which, in a metaphorical statement, a new semantic relevance emerges from the ruins of the semantic non-relevance as this appears in a literal reading of the sentence. To understand is thus to perform or to repeat the discursive operation by which the semantic innovation is conveyed" (ibid.).

40. Wallace Stevens, "Adagia," *Opus Posthumous* (New York: Alfred A. Knopf, 1957), p. 177.

41. Donald N. McCloskey, *The Rhetoric of Economics* (Madison: University of Wisconsin Press, 1985), p. 99.

42. In classical metaphysics this was a moral matter; in modern metaphysics it is a matter of method.

43. Bertrand Russell, introduction to L. Wittgenstein, *Tractatus Logico-Philosophicus* (London: Routledge and Kegan Paul, 1961), p. ix.

44. Fish, *Is There a Text in This Class?* p. 237; on pp. 239–40 Fish writes: "Of course the conventions of "serious" discourse include a *claim* to be in touch with the real (that is what being the standard story means), and therefore it comes equipped with evidentiary procedures (routines for checking things out) to which members of its class must

be ready to submit. But these procedures (which fictional discourse lacks, making it different, not less "true") inhere in the genre and therefore they cannot be brought forward to prove its fidelity to some supraconventional reality. The point may be obscured by the fact (I do not shrink from the word) that the fiction of this genre's status as something natural (not made) is one to which we 'normally' subscribe; but this only means that of the realities constituted by a variety of discourse conventions it is the most popular. That is why we give it the names we do—'real workaday world,' 'normal circumstances,' 'ordinary usage,' etc. . . . But these names are attempts to fix (or reify) something, not proof that it *is* fixed, and indeed the notion of normal or ordinary circumstances is continually being challenged by anyone (Freud, Marx, Lévi-Strauss) who says to us, 'Now the real facts of the matter are. . . .' Even in the real-workaday (as opposed to the philosopher's) world, where the operative assumption is that the facts are stable and once-and-for-all specifiable, we very often subscribe to different versions of what those facts are."

Nietzsche was saying much the same thing, albeit in his customarily blunter manner, when he wrote: "to be truthful means using the customary metaphors—in moral terms: the obligation to lie according to fixed convention, to lie herd-like in a style obligatory for all" ("On Truth and Lie in an Extra-Moral Sense," in *The Portable Nietzsche*, trans. and ed. Walter Kaufmann [New York: Viking Press, 1968], p. 47).

45. Fish, *Is There a Text in This Class?* p. 355.

46. "There is," Gadamer says, "no higher principle of reason than that of freedom" (*Reason in the Age of Science*, trans. F. G. Lawrence [Cambridge, Mass.: MIT Press, 1981], p. 9.

47. Wallace Stevens, "Adagia," p. 179. After I had completed this paper, my attention was drawn to the following text by Paul Ricoeur, of which I had been unaware: "Allow me to conclude [the preceding discussion of metaphor] in a way which would be consistent with a theory of interpretation which places the emphasis on 'opening up a world'. Our conclusion should also 'open up' some new perspectives, but on what? Perhaps on the old problem of the imagination which I have carefully put aside. Are we not ready to recognise in the power of imagination, no longer the faculty of deriving 'images' from our sensory experience, but the capacity for letting new worlds shape our understanding of ourselves? This power would not be conveyed by images, but by the emergent meanings in our language. Imagination would thus be treated as a dimension of language. In this way, a new link would appear between imagination and metaphor. We shall, for the time being refrain from entering this half-open door" ("Metaphor and the Central Problem of Hermeneutics," in Ricoeur, *Hermeneutics and the Human Sciences*, ed. and trans. J. B. Thompson [Cambridge, Eng.: Cambridge University Press, 1981], p. 181). Without realizing it, what I therefore in fact did in this paper was to pass through a door which Ricoeur had already unlocked for me. Which is an apt metaphor for much of our relationship in general.

Index

Abnormality: as variant of normality, 62
Absolute, 13–14, 19, 70–71, 76
Absurd, philosophy of the, 102
Act: of consciousness, 7–8; relationship to the object, 8–10
Action, 22, 101, 113, 169, 183; as manifestation of self, 160, 172 n.31; relationship to language, 96–98; Ricoeur on, 91; teleological structure of, 100, 102
Adventures of the Dialectic, The (Merleau-Ponty), 72–73
Agreement, 30, 31–32
À la recherche du temps perdu (Proust), 116
Albertus. *See* Shalom, Albert
Alienation, 58, 69, 73
Alston, W., 144, 147
Analogy, 87, 145, 147; role in creativity, 133–34, 135, 142 n.26
Analysand: in psychoanalytic situation, 168, 176–77 n.68
Analytic philosophy, 165, 186
Anarchy: as postmodern belief, 61, 72
Anaxagoras: on reason, 127
Animality of man: and language, 184
Animal rationale: as definition of man, 183
Anthropology (Ethnography), 50, 56 n.45, 66, 156
Anti-institutionalism, 61, 72
Antinomianism, 61, 72
Anxiety: allayed by myth and metaphysics, 125–26
Apel, K.-O., 40
Appearance, 127, 139; realm of, 129, 135, 138
Appearance-reality opposition, 136, 172 n.15, 190
Application: Gadamerian notion of, 109, 113–14, 116
Appropriateness, 29–30, 150–51
Appropriation, 49, 115
Archaeology, 58–60
Arendt, Hannah, 22, 97, 102
Argumentation, 31–32, 33, 35, 39 n.11
Aristotelianism, 129, 170 n.4
Aristotle, 130, 131, 134, 178, 180; on ethics, 34, 39 n.14; on metaphor, 144, 147, 194 n.39; on numbers, 128–29; quoted, 25
Arithmetic, 127
Arts: and imagination, 180–81
Astronomy, 127
Aubenque, Pierre, 52
Augustine, Saint, 17, 32, 57, 160, 170 n.3
Austrian economics, 101
Author's meaning, 5–6, 13

Bachelard, G., 150
Barthes, Roland, 163

Baudelaire, Charles, 64
Begrifflichkeit (Conceptual framework), 17–18
Behaviorism, psychological, 18
Being, 74, 101, 136, 139, 155, 166, 178; in ancient Greek thought, 127–28; for Gadamer, 117, 118; Heidegger on, 37–38 n.6, 86; as interpreted being, 45, 137–38; as language, 150, 161, 183; for Merleau-Ponty, 66, 68; ontological primacy of, 27, 38 n.6; possibilities of revealed in text, 95–96; as referent, 86, 87; as subject of metaphysics, 130, 132; substance as paradigm of, 159; and thinking, 152. *See also* Ontology
Being, undivided (*l'Être d'indivision*), 64, 66, 68
Being and Nothingness (Sartre), 159
Belief, 87, 113; fixation of, 31; and knowledge, 135–36, 137, 190
Benveniste, Émile, 100; on language, 161, 162, 163, 166, 176 n.53
Berger, Gaston, 8
Berkeley, George, 146
Bernstein, Richard, 46, 51, 108, 116, 118 n.2, 152; on Winch, 53 n.5
Betti, Emile, 3, 36 nn.2, 3, 4, 55 n.32, 109
Beyond Good and Evil (Nietzsche), 55 n.26
Beyond Objectivism and Relativism (Bernstein), 108, 152
Biology: as basis of human behavior, 157–58
Bisociation: and creative act, 142 n.23
Black, Max, 144, 147, 189
Bloom, Harold, 112
Body, 91, 140 n.12, 156, 170–71 n.4; flesh as not, 64, 67. *See also* Mind-body problem
Boehm, G., 36 n.3
Braithwaite, R. B.: definition of science, 47
Bricolage: creative work as, 133, 142 nn. 23, 26
Bronowski, Jakob, 134
Brown, Norman O., 60–61, 62, 79–80 n.21

Calvino, Italo: *Mr. Palomar*, 166; quoted, 155
Camus, Albert, 72, 102, 126
Canons, 32, 33
Carnal knowledge: as knowledge, 80 n.21
Carr, David, 44, 54–55 n.22, 59
Cartesianism, 40, 53–54 n.10, 95, 164, 178, 190; demise of, 46; and Dilthey-Winch solution, 42, 53–54 n.10; influence on Husserl, 43; and mind-body problem, 57–58
Cartesian Meditations (Husserl), 43
Casey, Ed: on imagination, 180–81, 182–83, 184–86, 193 n.30
Castoriadis, Cornelius, 76
Categories, 40, 84, 87, 88
Causal explanation: and empathetic understanding, 41